NAVIGATING THE STORM

Maria,

Thank you for all of your support!

I really appreciate your help throughout this process.

SJP

For my Mother

CONTENTS

CONTENTS

No one gave me a ladder; if there was one, no one told me about it. I had to climb the walls instead, and some days I truly felt like I was clawing at them just to stay in the same place. I couldn't look up or down for fear of falling, and I felt all alone, hanging on for dear life.

ROBIN ROTENBERG

INTRODUCTION

My Fairytale - How this Project Began

My decision to write this book collided with the TimesUp and MeToo Movements. I was planning my exit strategy from the corporate world where I'd notionally punched in over 30 years ago and had never punched out. It was time for me to move on, but every day the news was worse. Trusted men - actors, authors, broadcasters and others who were in my living room every day and in my favorite films were accused of heinous, abusive workplace crimes. I was shocked, disappointed and beyond betrayed. How could someone like Bill Cosby - America's model husband and father - be accused of drugging and assaulting women? How could someone like Harvey Weinstein assault and intimidate women in exchange for movie roles? More poignantly, how could they get away with it for so long? Why didn't anyone speak up? It made no sense to me, and rocked my world.

Instead of looking for answers where they would be impossible to comprehend, I decided to respond. Women, especially early in career women, need some positive stories about ordinary women in attainable careers as we chase our dreams. Not all men are monsters, yet not all career paths are smooth sailing either. They are, however, still very much worth pursuing. I had never before felt the need to talk about my experiences, or to showcase those of my other Alphas, but the time had definitely come.

This book is a pathfinder - a series of positive stories and guideposts to showcase Alpha Women who have overcome obstacles to chase our dreams. Our dreams are all different, but we each traded the fairytale of the glass slipper to chase some form of the glass ceiling. In the process, we pounded on that glass ceiling to try to break through and grab the brass ring.

I know all the Alpha Women in this book. Some I have known for decades, and others for a shorter time, but each one has taught me a lot and offered me a helping hand along my journey. Like the women themselves, their stories are motivating, inspiring, warm and funny. They are offered as a source of strength and hope for us all. My story is included here too.

Enjoy and learn. Let me know what you think at:

www.alphawomenrock.com.

A TIMELINE OF WOMEN'S RIGHTS

I am fascinated, and sometimes appalled, with women's treatment and rights in the United States and Canada. I am including a timeline of women's rights for both the United States and Canada as an overview of how far we have come, and how we got here. While we have a long way to go on our search for true equality, these milestones, achieved by courageous Alpha Women, give us hope that we are on the right track.

MILESTONES IN U.S. WOMEN'S HISTORY

1760

Men and women are one at law. [1]

The colonies adopt the English system of laws decreeing that women cannot own property in their name or keep their earnings. 1 and [2]

1777

All states pass laws taking away women's right to vote. [3]

1839

Married Women's Property Acts are passed by the States beginning in 1839. [4]

1848

Elizabeth Cady Stanton and four friends call a Women's Rights Convention and draft a "Declaration of Sentiments" at Seneca Falls, NY. [5]

1868

Congress passes the 14th Amendment to the Constitution, with "citizens" and "voters" defined as males in the Constitution. [6]

1869

Arabella Mansfield is granted admission to practice law in Iowa and becomes the first woman admitted to the legal profession in the United States. [7]

Wyoming, the Territory, grants women the right to vote in all elections. [8]

1870

Ratification of the 15th Amendment; African Americans can vote, but women, while not explicitly prohibited from voting, are not expressly guaranteed the right to vote either. [9]

Women start serving on juries in Wyoming. [10]

1873

Conviction of Susan B. Anthony, for "unlawful voting." [11]

The Supreme Court of the United States rules that a state can exclude a married woman (Myra Colby Bradwell) from practicing law. [12]

1874

The Supreme Court of the United States rules that women are "non-voting" citizens in Minor v. Happersett and that states remain free to grant or deny women the right to vote. [13]

1887

Susanna Madora Salter is the first woman elected Mayor of a town in Argonia, Kansas. [14]

1890

Wyoming is the first state to grant women the right to vote in state elections. [15] [16]

1900

By now, every state has legislation granting married women the right to keep their wages and to own property in their names. [17]

1916

Jeannette Rankin is the first woman elected to the House of Representatives (Montana). [18]

1918

Margaret Sanger wins her lawsuit in New York, thereby allowing doctors to advise married patients about birth control for health purposes. Her clinics later became Planned Parenthood. Sanger opened her first clinic in 1916. 18 and [19]

1920

The 19th Amendment, passed by Congress on June 4, 1919, is ratified on August 18, 1920, granting women the right to vote. [20]

1923

Alice Paul, suffrage leader, and attorney, initiates the campaign for the Equal Rights Amendment. [21]

1932

Hattie Wyatt Caraway of Arkansas becomes the first woman elected to the U.S. Senate. [22]

Frances Perkins, Labor Secretary, is the first woman to serve as a U.S. Presidential Cabinet Member. She was appointed Secretary of Labor under Franklin Delano Roosevelt. [23]

1934

Lettie Pate Whitehead Evans becomes one of the first female Directors of any major corporation when she is appointed to the Board of the Coca Cola Company. [24]

1936

Birth control is legal under medical direction under federal law and in all but a few states. [25]

1960

The Food and Drug Administration approves Enovid for contraceptive purposes for no more than two years at a time. [26]

1963

Betty Friedan publishes "the Feminine Mystique." [27]

The Equal Pay Act passes, prohibiting sex-based wage discrimination between men and women performing substantially similar jobs in the same establishment. [28]

1964

The Civil Rights Act passes, [29] which in Title VII bars discrimination in employment on the basis of race and sex. [30]

The Equal Employment Opportunity Commission (EEOC) is established to investigate complaints and impose penalties. [31]

1965

The United States Supreme Court overturns a Connecticut law prohibiting the use of contraceptives by married couples. [32]

1968

The EEOC rules that sex-segregated help wanted ads in newspapers are illegal. [33]

1969

California adopts the nation's first "no-fault" divorce law, allowing divorce by mutual consent. [34]

Shirley Chisholm of New York becomes the first African American woman in Congress. (She was elected in 1968, and was inaugurated in 1969). [35]

1971

The Supreme Court of the United States rules that Marietta Corporation cannot refuse to hire women with preschool-aged children while hiring men with preschool-aged children.

The Civil Rights Act 1964 requires uniform minimal qualifications for males and females unless there is a reason to differentiate based on business necessity. [36]

1972

The Equal Rights Amendment is passed by Congress and sent to the states for ratification, but dies in 1982 since it is not ratified by the 38 state minimum. [37]

Title IX of the Education Act prohibits sex discrimination in education programs that receive federal support. [38]

The Supreme Court of the United States upholds the right of married couples to use birth control. [39]

Juanita Kreps becomes the first woman director of the New York Stock Exchange. [40]

1973

The United States Supreme Court decides in Roe v. Wade that women have autonomy over their pregnancy during the first trimester. [41]

1974

Congress outlaws housing discrimination based on sex. [42][43]

Cleveland Board of Education v. LaFleur declares it illegal to force pregnant women to take maternity leave. [44]

U.S. TIMELINE CONTINUED

POUND ON!!

1976

Nebraska enacts the first marital rape law. [45]

1978

Title VII of the Civil Rights Act of 1964 passes, prohibiting sex discrimination on the basis of pregnancy. [46]

1980

Paula Hawkins becomes the first woman elected to the U.S. Senate without following her father or husband into the job. [47][48]

1981

Sandra Day O'Connor is appointed as the first female United States Supreme Court Justice. [49]

1983

Dr. Sally K. Ride becomes the first American woman to be sent into space. [50]

1984

Geraldine Ferraro becomes the first woman nominated Vice President on a major party ticket. [51]

1986

The Supreme Court of the United States holds that a work environment can be declared hostile or abusive as a result of sexual harassment. [52]

1992

1992 is declared Year of the Woman after the 1991 Anita Hill/Clarence Thomas hearings. [53][54]

1994

The Violence Against Women Act passes, tightening federal penalties for sex offenders, and providing for specialized training of police officers. [55]

1996

Ruth Bader Ginsburg writes her landmark decision in U.S. v. Virginia stating that the Virginia Military Institute could not refuse to admit women.[56]

1997

Madeleine Albright becomes the first woman Secretary of State. [57]

2005

Condoleezza Rice becomes the first African American female Secretary of State. [58]

2007

Nancy Pelosi becomes the first woman Speaker of the House. [59]

2008

Sarah Palin becomes the first woman to run for Vice President on the Republican ticket. [60]

2013

The ban against women in military combat positions is removed. [61]

2016

Hillary Rodham Clinton is the first woman to lead (as a Presidential candidate) the ticket of a major political party. [62]

As of January 2, 2016, women can serve in any job in the armed forces that meets gender-neutral performance standards. [63][64]

2017

Congress has a record number of women. 105 women hold Congressional seats - 21 in the Senate and 84 in the House of Representatives. [65]

The Women's March is organized to advocate for women's rights. Upwards of 3 million people turn out, marking one of the most massive and peaceful protests in U.S. history. [66]

MILESTONES IN CANADIAN WOMEN'S HISTORY

1756 - 1866

With few exceptions to the colonies that would later form Canada, the vote is a privilege reserved for limited segments of the population, mainly men. [1]

1849

Harriet Tubman, born a slave in Maryland, escapes. She leads many other slaves to freedom by helping them escape to Canada through the Underground Railroad network. Tubman remained a suffragette until her death in 1913. [2]

1851

Mary Ann Shadd Cary, born in 1823 as a free American black woman, emigrated to Canada in 1851, where she opened a school for the children of fugitives. [3]

1853

Mary Ann Shadd Cary becomes the first black woman in North America to found a weekly newspaper - The Provincial Freedom. She later returned to the U.S., where she became one of only two black women ever to have cast a vote in a U.S. Federal Election. [4]

1859

Upper Canada allows married women to own property, but not to sell it without the agreement of their husbands. [5]

1875

Grace Annie Lockhart graduates Mount Allison University with the first university degree awarded to a woman. [6]

Dr. Jennie Trout returns from an American medical school with a degree. She is the first woman licensed to practice medicine in Canada. [7]

1885

In Alberta, unmarried women property owners are granted the right to vote and can hold office in school matters. [8]

POUND ON!!

1892

The Law Society of Upper Canada gains discretionary power to admit women as solicitors. [9]

1897

Clara Brett Martin becomes the first woman lawyer in the British Empire after having challenged the Law Society of Upper Canada. [9], [10]

1903

Emma Sophia Baker is one of the first two women to earn a Ph.D. from the University of Toronto. [11]

1909

The Criminal Code of Canada is amended to criminalize the abduction of women. Similar penalties had already existed for stealing cattle. [12][13][14]

1916

Manitoba, Saskatchewan, and Alberta give women the right to vote and hold office. Manitoba is first. [15][16][17]

Emily Murphy is appointed Canada's first female magistrate (judge) and is the first female police magistrate in the British Empire.[18]

1917

Roberta Macadams and Louse McKinney become the first women members of a Legislative Assembly (Alberta). [19]

1918

With some exceptions, the Canada Elections Act gives all women over 21 the federal vote. (Some provinces followed later). [20]

1919

Women in New Brunswick get the right to vote in provincial elections. [21]

Helen Armstrong, as the President of the Winnipeg Women's Labour League, is a leader of the Winnipeg General Strike in which 30,000 striking workers shut the city down.[22] [23]

1921

British Columbia passes maternity leave legislation, becoming the first province to provide maternity leave for working women. [25]

Agnes MacPhail becomes the first elected woman member of the Federal Parliament (the House of Commons) by campaigning for prison reform, old-age pensions, and gender equity, among other things. [26] [27]

1922

Some women in Prince Edward Island win the right to vote in provincial elections. [28]

1925

Federal Divorce Law changes allow a woman to divorce her husband on similar grounds to those under which a man could divorce his wife. [29]

Mary Irene Parlby becomes the first female Cabinet Minister in Alberta. [30]

1921 - 1926

Nellie McClung becomes the Liberal member of the Alberta Legislature for Edmonton. [24]

1928

Anna Dexter becomes the first woman radio broadcaster and is known as the "Queen of the Airwaves." [31]

Canada's Olympic Team includes women for the first time. [31]

1929

The Judicial Committee of the Privy Council (JCPC) overturns a Supreme Court of Canada case to the contrary, and declares women to be "persons" and therefore eligible to hold the office of Senate in Canada. [31.][32]

1940

Women gain the right to vote and run for office in Quebec elections. [33]

1942

Eileen Tallman Sufrin organized the first Canadian bank strike in Montreal. [34]

1948 - 1949

Asian women gain the right to vote in Federal Elections. [35]

1951

Ontario is the first province to put equal pay legislation into effect. [36]

1957

Ellen Louks Fairclough becomes the first woman Cabinet Minister, as Secretary of State under Prime Minister John Diefenbaker. [37]

1960

Aboriginal women (and men) are granted the right to vote in Federal Elections. [38]

1964

Bill 16 passes in Quebec, giving married women the same rights as their husbands. [39]

1969

The Federal Government decriminalizes contraception and allows abortion under certain circumstances. [40][41]

1971

Amendments to the Canada Labour Code establish a 15-week maternity leave. [42]

1972

Rosemary Brown is the first black woman in Canada elected to a Legislature. [43]

1974

Pauline Jewett becomes the first woman president of a co-ed University (Simon Fraser). [44]

The first female RCMP recruits for regular police duties begin training in Regina, Saskatchewan. [45][46]

CANADIAN TIMELINE CONTINUED

1980

Alexa McDonough becomes the first woman to be elected leader of a provincial party (the Federal New Democratic Party) while holding a seat in the Legislature. [47]

Jeanne-Mathilde Sauvé becomes the first woman Speaker of the House of Commons.[48]

1982

The Canadian Charter of Rights and Freedoms is enacted, including s.15, the Equality Clause. [49]

Bertha Wilson is the first woman justice to serve on the Supreme Court of Canada. [50][51]

1983

The Criminal Code of Canada is amended to allow spouses to charge each other with sexual assault. [52]

The Canadian Human Rights Act prohibits sexual harassment in workplaces that fall under Federal jurisdiction. [53]

1984

The Right Honourable Jeanne Sauvé becomes the first woman Governor-General of Canada. [54]

1985

Indigenous women are permitted to retain their Indian status even if they marry non-status men. [55]

1988

The Supreme Court of Canada strikes down Canada's abortion law as unconstitutional. [56]

1989

Audrey McLaughlin becomes the first woman to lead a national political party.[57]

The Canadian Human Rights Tribunal rules that obstacles to military jobs must be removed for women (with a few exceptions). [58]

1993

Kim Campbell becomes Canada's first female Prime Minister. [59]

2000

Beverly McLachlin is appointed Chief Justice of the Supreme Court of Canada. [60]

2004

Louise Charron is the first native-born Franco-Ontarian to serve as a Supreme Court of Canada judge. [61]

Rosalie Abella is the first Jewish woman to sit on the Supreme Court of Canada. [62][63]

2005

Michaelle Jean is the first Afro-Caribbean Governor-General.[64][65]

2006

Bev Busson is the first woman commander of the Royal Canadian Mounted Police. [66]

2009

Andrea Horwath is the first woman leader of the Ontario New Democratic Party. [67]

2010

Kathy Dunderdale is sworn in as the first female premier of Newfoundland and Labrador.[68]

2013

Kathleen Wynne becomes the first female Premier of Ontario and is the first openly gay premier in Canada.[69][70]

2015

The Federal Election saw 88 women winning seats in the 338 member House of Commons, a gain of 12 seats over the previous record of 76 women elected in the previous Parliament.[71]

The Government of Canada announces a fully gender-balanced Cabinet consisting of 15 women and 15 men, the first gender-equal Cabinet in Canadian history.[72]

2017

Saskatchewan passes legislation providing protected leave for victims of domestic violence. [73]

2017

Millions globally participate in women's marches and rallies to call for a more inclusive, equitable, and just society for all. [74]

WHAT IS AN ALPHA WOMAN?

Becoming Alpha

The concept of an Alpha Woman is somewhat revolutionary and evolutionary at the same time. In today's world, Alphas are trailblazers, leaders of the pack who drive change and make our own rules. The term "Alpha" was not initially used to describe a woman, as it was intended to connote a leader rather than a follower, a dominant and determined being who would fight undeterred toward the goal of survival i.e. an Alpha Male or other animal. Referring to women as Alphas is a revolutionary concept. With original roles of support (Beta or Omegas), we were gatherers rather than hunters; submissive followers. The characteristics of Alphas in common parlance referred to Alpha males, or Alpha dogs or other "top" animals. Times, however, have changed, as have archetypes, role models and stereotypes. Here is what an Alpha woman may look like today, as divided into 5 Categories or Phases on the Rotenberg Axis (Figure 1).

First and foremost, it is important to remember that Alpha Women evolve. We are not born in the end state of a super charged Alpha Woman, knowing the ropes & sharing war stories. We start out more starry-eyed and naïve than that, not knowing what awaits us as we commence our climb toward the glass ceiling. Once we abandon the glass slipper dream and chase a different fairytale, we start out with certain qualities and characteristics which evolve through various phases and stages.

While there may be some overlap along the climb, I would fit the Alpha characteristics into 4 main stages of development or phases, with a 5th Stage of "Absolutely Alpha" where the Alpha has truly arrived, with some traits being more dominant than others at any given phase. They are: Attempting Alpha (Phase 1), Learning Alpha (Phase 2), the Professional Alpha (Phase 3), the Hard Driving Alpha (Phase 4), and the Absolutely Alpha (who rocks!) (Phase 5).

Not all Alphas will have every characteristic, and any of these qualities may ebb and flow throughout our careers. It is very likely that women along our career paths will possess qualities from each

Phase at any given time. What is important is the desire to succeed and improve, to learn and grow continuously along the way, and to help one another both celebrate success and learn from opportunities as we go.

Just as a side note - the first initials of all of our Phases spell the word "ALPHA"...Attempting, Learning, Professional, Hard Driving, and Absolutely Alpha.

ATTEMPTING ALPHA

Phase 1 of our Evolution

The Attempting Alpha is our colleague, sister, aunt, mother, daughter or friend who is beginning her journey. In this first phase she will be very AMBITIOUS with HIGH ASPIRATIONS and a very strong desire to succeed. She's hungry for success and DREAMS BIG. The Attempting Alpha must be AGILE, able to switch gears quickly, and to grasp concepts or understand situations with relative ease. There are different kinds of agility, and the Attempting Alpha must show signs of them all in some way - intellectual, people and change agility, for example, so she can navigate all the obstacles being thrown in her path. Similarly, her DETERMINATION must be unflinching and resolute. Otherwise the Attempting Alpha will be thrown off course easily and may stray from her dreams and goals. It is difficult to be determined and stay that way, but stay that way she must.

CURIOSITY may have "killed the cat", but it is a necessity of life for the Attempting Alpha woman. A strong desire to learn and inquire is essential to Alpha growth, especially now. This spirit of INQUISITIVENESS will evolve over time, but will stay with her and fuel her drive forever. Moral PRINCIPLES and STRONG ETHICS are essential for the Attempting Alpha who will encounter many people along the way who do not share this quality. She must use her unimpeachable ETHICAL grounding to evaluate her path right from the start. Straying and short cuts are the easy way out; having ethics and INTEGRITY are a strong and critical differentiator for any Alpha.

LEARNING ALPHA
Phase 2 of our Evolution

As the Alpha evolves, her CREATIVE ideas begin to shine through. Her IMAGINATION and ORIGINAL IDEAS are essential to her recognition and ascent. Being INNOVATIVE and having ORIGINALITY separate the Learning Alpha from the rest of the pack. Feelings of CONFIDENCE and SELF-ASSURANCE are similarly indispensable for a Learning Alpha. She must learn to appear POISED and COOLHEADED in the face of any challenge. She can never let them see her sweat!

The INTELLIGENCE of a Phase 2 Alpha begins to shine brightly through the maze of early obstacles and challenges. ASTUTE, INTUITIVE thinking starts to show and differentiate her from others. This DISCERNING NATURE will serve her well, especially when combined with an ELOQUENT and ARTICULATE speaking style. Being articulate helps Learning Alphas persuade others and state her goals and aspirations clearly and definitively. She will have to learn it if it is not innate. The ability to ASSERT herself is an important differentiator as well. She must always say what she wants. No one will ADVOCATE for you as well as you can advocate for yourself!

PROFESSIONAL ALPHA

Phase 3 of our Continuous Evolution

Alphas must remain UNDETERRED along the way, and keep her LION-HEARTED DAREDEVIL nature alive. COURAGE is a daily requirement for a Professional Alpha who by now has several years of TENACITY under her belt. To others she may appear BOLD and DARING, to her this is her mantra coupled with her firm and constant LOYALTY. Our Professional Alpha remains FAITHFUL and true to those who have helped her get this far. She needs her community and strong SOCIAL ties since the collective is of penultimate importance to her. She must still put herself in others' shoes (Manolo's or Louboutin's, of course!), able to understand and share the feelings of those around her. This high EMPATHY will be needed to feed her success and drive her brand. It also compels others to follow her example, and to respect her as she is RESPECTFUL of others.

HARD-DRIVING ALPHA
Phase 4

The Hard-Driving Alpha is a powerhouse AUTHENTIC woman whom others lean on and APPROACH for advice and good counsel. She is the real deal with nothing fake or spurious about her (except maybe a few eyelashes), with a GENUINENESS which is palpable and TRUSTED. Unlike others in so many ways, her trademark WELCOMING disposition draws others to follow her like the Pied Piper. While DEVOTED to her career and those important to her, she demonstrates an admirable DEDICATION to causes, people and places to which and whom she is inseparably CONNECTED. She is RESOLUTE in her staunch INTEGRITY and can be relied upon in that regard. While not afraid to show her VULNERABLE side, her weaknesses do not hold her back. Her incredible GIVING NATURE can compensate for challenges and showcase GENEROSITY and KINDNESS. Never perfect, but always striving to do better, the Hard-Driving Alpha is universally sought after and admired.

ABSOLUTELY ALPHA

SHE ROCKS !! - Phase 5

The Absolutely Alpha woman is a fabulous mix of all characteristics of the other earlier categories. Through continuous improvement and self-awareness she has demonstrated HIGH PERFORMANCE and HIGH EMPATHY. She recognizes and is recognized for her strength and determination, and is a sought after mentor, speaker, teacher and advocate. The Absolutely Alpha has learned to balance all aspects of her life of greatest meaning to her, giving 100% of her presence to family, friends and colleagues when called upon to do so.

She understands that just showing up matters, and that what you say to others has impact. Above all else she is a mature contributor who has endured many challenges to achieve her success. On any given day she will exhibit many Alpha qualities, giving back to her community and those around her. She is fastidious when choosing confidantes, and while always striving for more, she is grateful for what she has achieved. Her positive stories of her attainable career serve to inspire and motivate others. She rocks!

THE ROTENBERG AXIS AND HOW TO USE IT

Figures 1 and 2 are an assessment tool for determining where we are in our Alpha journey. Alphas are asked to choose up to 10 characteristics which describe herself at the time she is using the Axis.

The x axis represents IQ, and the y axis represents EQ, or emotional quotient characteristics. Each of the Alpha quadrants sets out characteristics of that Alpha Phase. For each of the Phases, the characteristics are assigned points.

The characteristics in Quadrant 1, or the lower left quadrant represent the earliest characteristics displayed by a developing Alpha Woman. She is agile, ambitious, determined, curious and ethical. These traits are visible early and are essential to Alpha development. So far, she has lower confidence and is building her skills. Each of the traits in Quadrant 1 is assigned 1 point.

In Quadrant 2, the Alpha has progressed along the more intellectual traits, showing herself to be creative, confident, intelligent, articulate and assertive. She is starting to have career success, but is not as developed on the empathy side. If any of these traits are chosen, they are each assigned 2 points.

Quadrants 3 and 4 represent higher Alpha characteristics which emerge when the EQ and the IQ are more evident in the climb. Quadrant 3, or the top left quadrant, showcases more ruling characteristics. The Alpha Woman is becoming move involved with those around her, and is courageous, loyal, social, empathetic and respectful. Each of these traits is assigned 5 points.

Quadrant 4 represents both extremely high intellect and high emotional intelligence. This Alpha Woman is authentic, approachable, dedicated, vulnerable and generous. Each trait is awarded 10 points.

To use the Rotenberg Axis, the Alpha chooses up to 10 characteristics which best describe her at the time. She then tallies the points assigned to each trait to find her Alpha Score. The Scores are as follows:

0 - 10 Points - Attempting Alpha

11-25 Points - Learning Alpha

26-40 Points - Professional Alpha

41-50 Points - Hard-Driving Alpha

51 Points or more - Absolutely Alpha

Once she has determined her Alpha category, the participant can purchase our Tip Sheets for each Alpha Score if desired. See alphawomenrock.com for details.

Alpha levels can vary greatly depending on your then current circumstances, and will change and evolve over your career and life. It would not be unusual for an Alpha to toggle between the various Alpha Phases as she ascends, given career and life changes. The important thing is to continue the climb, and always attempt to ascend to the Absolutely Alpha Phase where you have learned much and have great positive lessons to share. POUND ON!!

FIGURE 1

Rotenberg Axis
BECOMING ALPHA

FIND YOUR ALPHA SCORE

- A — 0-10 Points *Attempting Alpha*
- L — 11-25 Points *Learning Alpha*
- P — 26-40 Points *Professional Alpha*
- H — 41-50 Points *Hard-Driving Alpha*
- A — 51 Points or More *Absolutely Alpha*

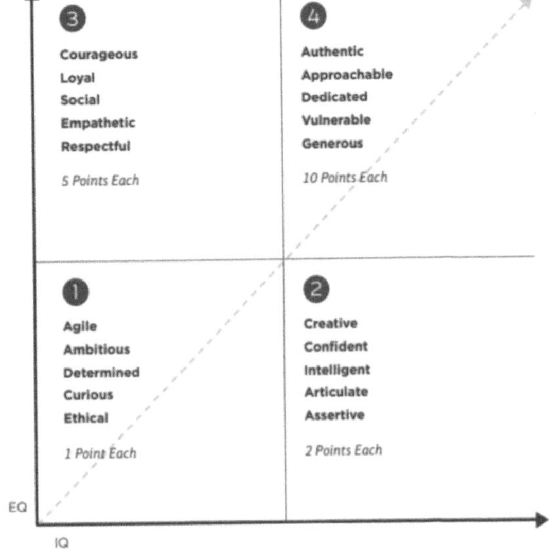

FIGURE 2

WHAT DOES YOUR ALPHA SCORE MEAN?

0-10 Points
Attempting Alpha

11-25 Points
Learning Alpha

26-40 Points
Professional Alpha

41-50 Points
Hard-Driving Alpha

51 Points or More
Absolutely Alpha
SHE ROCKS!

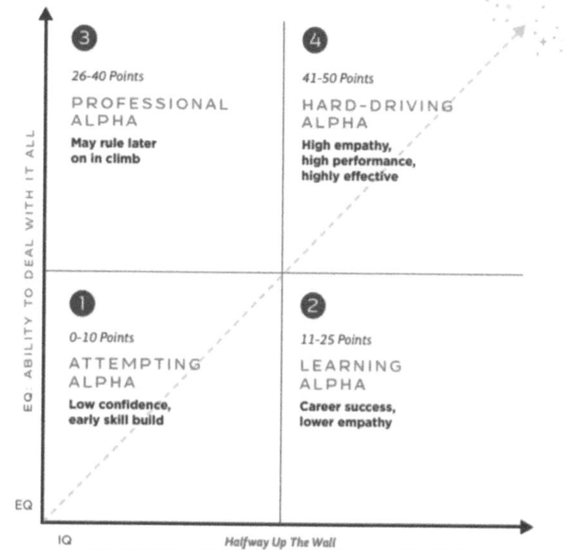

INTERVIEW QUESTIONS FOR ALPHAS

To provide a preview of what you can expect in the pages ahead, I'm sharing the interview questions sent to each of the Alphas in the early phases of developing this book.

BACKGROUND QUESTIONS

- Describe your early life. Where did you grow up, and with whom? Who were your friends? What sorts of activities and sports did you participate in? Where did you vacation with your family? Etc.
- With whom did you spend most of your time with growing up? How do you believe they might have influenced you?
- What was your favorite subject in school? In which subjects did you excel? In which subjects were you challenged?
- Where did you receive your education and what was your focus? What was the most important thing you learned during your education?
- Were there women you admired growing up? If so, who were they, and why?

CAREER BACKGROUND

- Did you choose your career, or did it choose you? Tell us about your career progression and what you learned from each step.
- How did you develop your most utilized skills? Are there skills you wish you had developed further?
- Did you have mentors? If so, who were they, and what did you learn from them?
- Did you receive any memorable feedback? If so, what did you gain from it?
- What challenges did you face as a woman leader? How did you rise to meet them?
- What is the biggest compliment you ever have received regarding your leadership? Your career?

CURRENT LIFE

- Describe your life now. Where do you live? With whom do you live? Who in your circle of family, friends, and professionals, do you spend the most time with? Do you have any pets?
- What do you like to do to relax?

POUND ON

- What is your current job and what do you love most about it?
- Describe your typical workday.
- How would you describe yourself as a leader? How might others describe you?
- How has your career affected your relationships, both past and present?
- Describe your typical weekend.
- What is it you might like to do next in both your personal life and career?
- Are you working toward a legacy? If so, what does that look like for you?

INTROSPECTIVE:

- Who do you think has had the most influence on you overall?
- Who or what inspires you today? In particular, which women leaders inspire you today?
- What accomplishments are you most proud of, in both your personal life and in your career?
- What do you believe have been the keys to your success? What does success look like to you?

- Where do you believe you have failed? What did you learn from your biggest mistake?
- What do you think makes a good leader?
- What does balance mean to you and how do you pursue it?
- What do you know now that you wish you had known when you started out?

IDEALS:

- How might leadership be different for women than it is for men?
- Name three things a woman leader must do to succeed. Would these same three things be required of a man? Why or why not?
- Do you believe it is easier for working women today than it is when you first started? Why or why not?
- What three pieces of advice would you give to young working women today?
- What three pieces of advice would you give to young women in middle school, high school, and/or college today?
- What is one thing younger women still need to remember (or learn) about the gender gap today?
- What are some steps we need to take today in order to continue narrowing the gender and pay gaps?

POUND ON

- Do you feel women unfairly bear the "mental load," and if so, do you have any ideas of how to adjust the scale?
- What do you think women's leadership will look like in ten years? What do you hope it looks like?
- Do you think women can "have it all?" Why or why not?
- What traits, in your opinion, define an "alpha woman?"

YOUR FAVORITES:

Please list your "favorites" and give brief reasons as to why:

- Vacation Destinations (both visited and wanting to visit)
- Foods (dessert counts)
- Artists (of all mediums)
- Music (singers, bands, Broadway, composers)
- Books (or authors)
- Sports/Exercise (which you play, watch, or support)
- Hobbies
- Movies
- Television Shows
- Mobile apps (what has made your life simpler?)

ROBIN ROTENBERG

Glass Slippers and Steel Stilettos

POUND ON!!

ROBIN ROTENBERG

My Story - Glass Slippers and Steel Stilettos

At this point in my life and career, I often have young women and men seeking my advice and counsel. This always surprises me; I feel like I have very little to offer them. I always thought I'd come in every day and work hard, and that that would be enough. I couldn't have been more wrong. I never thought myself worthy of recognition or greater opportunity. It shocked me when I was selected for executive C-suite jobs. Any recognition by peers or other women was a surprise to me too. In hindsight, I see that I was different, that I had a different drive and ambition, different work standards, as well as different ideas about success and what it looked like to me.

I never intended to be a trailblazer. I simply went into work every day working hard at everything I was handed to do. While this may not be the story of every woman who puts her head down and perseveres, I believe that this very work ethic led me to greater opportunities and aspirations, including researching and writing my own book.

In crafting the introduction to this book and reflecting on my past, I thought back on what a tremendous influence my family had on me. One lesson in particular stands out: Be proud of how you behave. The strong women who came before me taught me that lesson, and with this book and with every day of my life, I continue to honor their memory by making every day count.

I grew up in a peaceful, safe and over-protected suburb of Toronto Canada. I am the eldest of two daughters, born to a housewife and an economist. My father wanted a boy but claimed repeatedly that he was just as happy when he learned I was a girl. I have always doubted that.

Both of my parents and three out of my four grandparents were college educated. My father was a brilliant student, finishing high school at 16 and earning a Masters Degree in Economics before he was 21 years old. My mother had a degree in General Arts, with a focus on Art History, and loved the arts. Like the rest of my family they had gone to the University of Toronto. My paternal grandmother, my Grandma Tessie, was a very strong influence on me, and had also excelled academically. Unlike most women of her time, she had attended university. She not only attended, she had earned a Masters in Applied Math. While she was permitted to excel academically, her mother didn't like it if she played sports, considering it unladylike. My Grandma Tessie used to tell me that she had to lie to her mother when she came home with red cheeks after playing basketball after school. Rather than tell her mother she was playing a sport, she told her instead that the wind had reddened her cheeks. This had a profound effect on her; she always encouraged me to pursue whatever activities I wished and to be proud of it. In terms of her life, she married a wealthy Toronto businessman who owned properties and had an insurance company. I never knew my paternal grandfather Charles; I am named in his memory (my middle name is Charlotte). They gave my father, their eldest child, what looked to me like a charmed, privileged life. He and his siblings, a brother Harvey and a sister Leila, grew up in a wealthy Toronto area. Their families had been in Canada for several generations, were university educated, and extremely successful.

I saw my Grandma Tessie once a month for dinner at a fancy restaurant. As a child I thought she was strong and powerful, capable of anything. I still do. She must have thought so too. She even ran the insurance business and their apartment buildings after my grandfather died. I have always felt that she was way ahead of her time. Her strength and liberal ideas were truly remarkable for a woman born in the early 1900's. In spite of her toughness, my Grandmother had a good heart. She told me that she didn't raise the rents of her tenant families who couldn't afford to pay because she didn't think it was right. She also advocated for me to my parents who were very overprotective. I once wanted to go to a school dance when I was 12 or 13 and my parents wouldn't let me go saying that I was too young, and that I would be out too late. I called my Grandmother who asked a few questions about what the activity was, and declared that I should be allowed to attend. It was my first successful negotiation. I learned early to figure out who was on my side, and to use it to my full advantage.

My mother Bonnie was the middle of three siblings, and had an older sister Evelyn and a younger brother (also) Harvey. She grew up in a nice area, much less affluent than that of my father's family. My maternal grandparents were Russian immigrants who came to Canada at the turn of the 20th century to avoid religious persecution. They came to the country as small children and lived in an immigrant "ghetto" area. My maternal grandfather (also Charles), known to us as Grandaddy, was very entrepreneurial, and had worked in danger climbing the city trains to earn money for his university tuition. He graduated as a dentist in the 1920's, after having been expelled with 11 of the 12 Jewish students and thereafter reinstated with the help of the organization B'Nai Brith. He recounted this story to me several times during my childhood, as it had had a strong effect on his identity and security. Grandaddy was always suspicious of people, and worried that they were somehow going to harm him if they could. He really struggled as a young dentist. The economy in the 1920's was tough, and he had a lot of trouble getting paid by his patients. Grandaddy told me that a patient once paid him in chickens. I have vivid childhood memories of him making collection calls to try to get paid. This left its mark on me as well. I wanted to make sure I worked for people or companies who could pay me. It just didn't seem right that Grandaddy would work so hard, do a good job, and not get paid for the work. I've always carried a bit of that insecurity as well, never being sure that I can count on anyone or anything to take care of my needs.

Grandaddy was also an inventor. He worried a lot about the radiation from x-rays. In his early days as a dentist there was a lot of radiation exposure from the equipment. After suffering with skin cancer on his hands from taking dental x-rays, Grandaddy developed several radiation-blocking devices like lead aprons which he sold to large companies. I don't think he made much money from all his inventions, but he wrote papers and kept developing protective devices. I was the model for his promotional brochures and I remember posing for pictures wearing weird headgear or aprons from the time that I was 4 or 5 years old.

My maternal grandmother, Jeannette (known to us as Grandma Jeannie) always claimed that she was born in Toronto rather than Russia and that her passport was incorrect. She also said her age was wrong, and that she was much younger than her documents said. Grandma Jeannie was eccentric in other ways as well, and while a style icon she only wore the color purple. She said other colors washed her out. In fact, her whole house was decorated in purple, as was Grandaddy's dental office including his dental chair. Grandma Jeannie was the only one of my grandparents who was not formally educated, since she had to go to work to support herself when she was only a teenager. Grandaddy, however, trained her to be his dental hygienist and surgical nurse. Grandma Jeannie insisted on being paid for her work and opened her own bank accounts to save her money, a lot of which she spent on me and my sister. As a young woman, Jeannie was a milliner and had owned a store with her sisters selling hats, gloves and makeup before her siblings moved to California. Her siblings had a store in Watts, California which had been burned down in the riots of the 60's. We talked about that a lot in my household; how unfair it was that they lost their livelihood to violence. I could not understand that kind of hatred. I still don't.

While profoundly deaf, Grandma Jeannie never let on, reading lips and carrying on conversations that didn't reveal her challenges. In her 80's she taught herself to type so she could contact us through the newly created hearing-impaired phone operator.

Grandma Jeannie also collected antiques which I thought were junk. She said she wanted her children to have nice things, so she shopped and stored a lot of silver, china and home goods in their home and basement. It was all junk to me, but treasures to her. That junk now represents my treasured memories of my Grandma Jeannie, along with her teachings about makeup, hair, nails, fashion and independence.

My childhood summers were spent at summer camps in a Northern Ontario, Canada provincial park where I made lifelong friends, learned to sail, canoe, horseback ride, smoke, kiss boys and many other things not fit for print. Mostly, I learned independence and how to fend for myself. After my initial feelings of abandonment for having been sent away, I felt free. Freer than I have ever felt before or since, which is odd since I was actually trapped at camp in the middle of a forest with no way out. I learned how to take care of myself, portage a canoe, build a campfire and safely put it out, and how to avoid conflicts with the mean girls, of which there were many.

My first experiences with the mean girls were at camp as a ten-year-old, which created in me bewildering feelings of exclusion and failure. It was the first time that social experiences were negative for me. I'd always had lots of friends in my neighborhood, and gotten along with all of them. The mean girls I encountered at summer camp were very different than the other children I had known, and formed groups or clicks of girls who were "in" or "out". Being the nerdy smart girl coupled with being very shy did not earn me a spot in the clicks of the "in" crowd. In fact, I was excluded from all the cool social happenings, and left to feel isolated. I found other friends who were more similar to me, experiencing the same exclusion. I also learned strength of character and to choose friends wisely; a lifelong hard-taught lesson.

Camp was my first job. I became a Camp Counselor as a teenager, and spent my summers working at camp until I was in University. I returned summer after summer to the comfort and safety of old friends and familiar wild surroundings. Lying out on a dock at night staring at the summer stars to the rhythm of lapping lake water brought me a peace and calm I had never known. I still feel that way about stars and water. Not about the camping – now I only camp in 5-star hotels!

During the school year, I was always over-programmed with dance and music lessons, swimming, skiing (I was horrible at it) shows and concerts. I was always very busy as a child, and didn't have much time outside my various activities. I believe that it was my mother's goal for me to be competent at many sports and activities, many of which I still pursue to this day. Her love of the arts was also passed to me. She started taking us to children's concerts and ballets as small children which instilled in me a true appreciation for those with talent. The Nutcracker and Toronto Symphony Orchestra childrens' concerts are very happy memories for me.

Of course, there was family and food – not necessarily in that order. I spent Friday nights and Sundays with my maternal grandparents. Grandma Jeannie would cook all week for us and send home food with my mother every Friday night. My mother, while beautiful, was a lousy cook. My father said he had to buy a rotisserie for the oven when they were first married so that he wouldn't starve. There were holiday parties with cousins and friends, a Yacht club where we went on weekends when I wasn't shipped off somewhere, and lots and lots of schoolwork. I knew early on that school was very important and that I too was expected to go to University. Even though I wasn't a boy.

Life continued into my teenage years, and seemed pretty good, at least from the outside. My mother had a deep adoration for prescription drugs, especially valium, and my father suffered with bouts of depression. I was quite oblivious to these problems at the time, and was more concerned with my activities, school work and the few close friends that I'd developed.

My life changed radically when I was 15. During that year both my mother and my Grandma Tessie died. Their deaths tore our family apart and sent me into a tailspin. I learned grief and sadness far too early. I also learned about perseverance, inspiration and honor. I vowed to live my dreams, inspired by the women who had gone before me, and to appreciate every day. During this unimaginably tough time, I sought ways to honor the role models I had lost, hoping that I would never feel worse than I did during that time. I learned perspective, and to view career and other setbacks in their proper place. I think that these early losses taught me to look at life with gratitude and perspective. I still try to keep a good balance and not take things too seriously. As long as my feet hit the floor and I can brush my own teeth, I know it's a good day.

After my mother and my Grandma Tessie died, I plastered a smile on my face and carried on, aware that I was different than the other teenagers, and eventually throwing myself into school. I understood that other children had the support of their families, and was painfully aware that this would be pretty much lacking in my life going forward. Certain family members who were not fond of my father started excluding us from the celebrations we had always attended. While I don't have high inclusion needs, being ignored after a lifetime of inclusion in family celebrations really hurt. Like dealing with the mean girls, I started forging my own path and developing my own relationships. I also knew that an education was my ticket out, and a means to finding recognition and value. I was good at it, at least on the languages and arts side, and I had teachers who took an interest and encouraged me. School became both my validation and salvation. I didn't realize it at the time, but a good education would also provide economic freedom; with a good education I could get good jobs and not have to rely on anyone who might abandon me.

When the time came for me to apply to Universities, I applied to a few – none of them where my family wanted me to go. I was expected to go to the University of Toronto like all my family members before me. I didn't apply there, and I got accepted into every other school where I applied. My father initially refused to pay my tuition, so I got a job and off I went, leaving my family members shocked at my steadfast independence and my determination to think for myself. My father eventually relented and helped me out, proudly telling me that I could become anything I wanted to be, and that he would help me. I think he just didn't know what else to do, but I am grateful for the support he offered.

Leaving home was the best thing I ever did and was the first of many decisions I made in defiance of or in contradiction to the advice of others. These decisions were mine, and mine alone, and I had no intention of letting anyone else make them for me. I never quite trusted that anyone else had my best interests at heart. While listening carefully and considering the consequences, I made the very important decision of where to go to school based on what I thought was right for me, not the wishes or desires of other people, even my father. I never looked back, and I have carried the motto of making my own decisions with me throughout my life. I make decisions based on what I think is right at the time, not on what other people think is right for me. Even if my decisions are wrong, at least I will have made them myself.

In the end, I earned three University degrees from two different universities, neither of them the University of Toronto. I did take a summer school course there one year, which made me even more sure that I'd made the right decision to go somewhere else.

My degrees were in studies of my choice, again in defiance of and in contradiction to the advice or desires of others. I had no real advisors or counselors, so I made my decisions on my own with a little help from my friends. My high school and Universities offered no meaningful counsel either, so I was really left on my own to decide what to study. I earned degrees in Political Science, Education with an emphasis on special needs children, and a law degree. A good basic foundation for a girl from the Toronto suburbs to find a job and support herself.

I taught special education for a year, which surprised no one, but wasn't enough for me. It was also fraught with bureaucracy and government administration. Many of the families didn't have the means to get the help their children needed, and I had to help them apply for government funding in order to provide appropriate educational tools for the students. I found this very frustrating, but it led me to advocate for the children and their parents, which was one of the reasons I decided to return to school.

Although I loved my students and stayed in touch with many of them for years after I taught them, I thought I could do more. I'd always secretly dreamt of being a lawyer – it was impressive and sounded so glamorous. I could also do more for children and their families than I could in the bureaucratic maze of the education system, so I applied to law school. There are no lawyers in my family. There are lots of architects, designers, artists and medical professionals. I had no one to rely on to ask about the practice of law, but I applied and went anyway despite the opposition of family and friends. My ongoing independence continued to lead me to forge my own path.

University was the first place where I figured out that I'd had a nice upbringing, and that I'd had lots of options that other girls didn't have. Some girls I met had to pay their own way through school, even though their brothers didn't. I felt that this was really unfair and I didn't understand it at all. Didn't women have a right to an education and to earn a living? How could we achieve equality and have independence without a good education? It was one thing for my father to refuse to pay initially because I wouldn't go where he wanted me to, but I was learning that other girls were disadvantaged in their families simply because of their gender. The reality horrified me.

In law school I started realizing that men and women did not have the same career options. Less than 1/3rd of the class was women, which surprised me. I didn't understand why it wasn't at least 50%. We women students seemed to win a lot of the awards and were just as dedicated to the law as the men. My eyes were starting to open wide to the issues of gender and career opportunities. At least the female professors were activists, who inspired me to learn about women's rights and how the court system treated women. Some areas of law regarding women's rights were so antiquated that I had a hard time believing it. Systemic discrimination continued to open my eyes as I saw how important it is to find our voices and use them. I learned the importance of speaking up, not just for myself but for others. Most importantly I learned to speak up for injustice and for what I believed in. I loved the study of law and worked hard to be recognized and to achieve.

My first legal job was with a big Bay Street law firm. I learned a lot from the senior lawyers who gave good advice about ethics and taught me practical skills. In other ways, working for a big Bay Street law firm tested my naïveté. The few women lawyers didn't help each other, were highly competitive and worked incessantly. I questioned why they hired overachievers with lots of outside interests, and then took away all of our free time. At the time there were no real mentoring programs, so we young lawyers had to figure it out on our own. In addition to the legal advice from skilled advocates, I got a lot of unsolicited advice from the secretaries who were the gatekeepers to the senior partners. For example, the secretaries told me to cut my long hair and take off my red nail polish, neither of which I did. They also didn't like my earrings (I wore 5), which I continued to wear. I didn't see how changing those things would make me a better lawyer. Clients with little filter on how they behaved repeatedly asked me if was old enough to do the job, and wanted to take me out to dinner. Although I loved the work, I started to question whether I was strong enough to withstand the pressure to perform and conform, the bureaucracy, and the unwieldy clients. I was looking for a guidepost and for encouragement, or at least a good role model. Not finding it, I instead honed my people skills, grew an even tougher skin, and soldiered on.

I admired many women during those early days, but they were all in virtually unattainable careers. Heads of state, performers, movie stars, journalists, singers and dancers. I looked for their common traits and tried to figure out how I could be like them even without their talent and fame. I saw that they thought for themselves, made their own decisions, took on meaningful work, and most particularly they earned their own money. My father always told me to learn to type so that I wouldn't starve. For his time, he was right. I had no intention of starving, but I intended to do a lot more than type for my career.

I started to figure out that women had to behave much differently than men to succeed, which seemed patently unfair, but was the grim reality. I was spending a lot of time proving that I had a brain, and an equal, if not greater amount of time, hiding it from the people who couldn't handle it. I'm smart, but no rocket scientist; I just work really hard with what I have. Another lesson from my

Grandaddy. I couldn't figure out why my being smart was scary to others, but that's what I was repeatedly told. How could an early in career lawyer be so smart she scared the clients and partners? I think it was more that people underestimated me and were surprised that I could think. It made no sense to me but made me feel like an excluded outsider; somewhat like how I felt with the mean girls at camp, although now the stakes were higher. I had rent to pay, and I'd spent years of effort to get there.

I felt like I had to conform to succeed, which for me was somewhat counterintuitive. I had fought hard to get where I was, defying the views and opinions of others, and refusing to conform. I didn't think I should have to conform and be like everyone else for my contribution to be valued. For women to succeed we need to find our voice, use it without apology, and speak up when we have a point of view. This does not mean that we have to think like everyone else, or hide our views or intelligence from others who can't handle it, both men and women alike.

Over the years I have developed many self-taught rules around finding my voice and using it. While difficult at first, I have learned that using my voice is a strong differentiator and provides a role model to others. If we just sit back and take it, we can be seen to acquiesce. If we acquiesce we are accepting how others treat us, which will only perpetuate existing systemic problems. No matter how much opposition is in the room, my hard fought rule is to speak up within the first ten minutes of a meeting if at all possible. That way I can find my voice early on, making it easier to continue to do so. It also shows attendees that I intend to participate not just watch, and that I expect to be heard and my contribution to be respected, even if it is rejected.

I went from a large law firm to a smaller one, hoping to get more interesting work and have a better life balance. The work was fundamentally better; if the senior partners were unavailable for court attendances I got to go in their place. For me, this was incredibly rewarding; to have an audience in front of the Ontario Court of Appeal as a young lawyer was truly a dream come true. Back at the office I found similar issues around proving myself, being heard and having a voice. This seems to be a constant theme for women in professional positions which I have continued to hear over the years. The issue of women not helping each other has also continued. It would be a long time before I saw any change in that, watching it happen with the advent of women's organizations which I was initially reluctant to join for fear of being singled out rather than accepted.

The fact that women didn't help one another left an indelible mark on me. I vowed to change that in my career wherever I could, and to always help promising young women coming up behind me. I continue to do that by making time, no matter how little, to spend with earlier in career women who want to have coffee or are seeking a little advice. It doesn't take much to make a big and memorable difference to others.

I was learning that in order to succeed I needed to keep my confidence high and develop a high and healthy self-awareness and self-evaluation system. Not getting much validation from others, nor feedback whether it be positive or negative, I developed my own performance rating system which I still use to this day. I evaluate my performance at the end of every day and after every meeting. What could I have done better? What did I learn? I have always kept a running list of improvement opportunities to make sure that I continuously do better.

Time marched on, as did my career. I had gotten married (for the first time) soon after university, and my daughter Taryn was born while I was practicing law at the smaller firm. As a mother, my career became even harder to pursue, as did proving my capability and credibility. I took nearly a year off when Taryn was born, which was unheard of in those days, being told that I would sacrifice my career. I did it anyway. When Taryn was almost a year old I rejoined the workforce with a company, rather than staying at the law firm. I moved to a part-time in-house legal job, so that I could supposedly have better life balance. New computer technology allowed me to take the work home, which turned out to be both a blessing and a curse. I was still working all the time. While grateful for the opportunity and truly loving the work, I still found myself struggling for recognition and acceptance, never confident that my contributions were valued. I worried every day whether I'd have a job the next. I think some of that insecurity was borne from watching Grandaddy's struggle to get paid. I felt I had no one to help me if I was in need, which also creates different concerns than if you have a strong family behind you. Necessity is the mother of invention.

The Corporate world was a whole new experience for me, offering different kinds of opportunities and challenges alike. Having worked in a law firm surrounded by other lawyers, I was suddenly thrust into a world full of engineers, scientists, sales people and marketing professionals. It was a different world, and one which I found perplexing and mesmerizing at the same time. In a law firm you hang up the phone or shut your office door and your clients are gone; you don't live with them and confront them all day long. In a corporation it is much different; you have only one client and they are in your face constantly. While the closeness allowed me to give better advice, it also meant that I was much more vulnerable to not having a job if my client became displeased. This placed many different pressures on me as an in-house lawyer.

I have always enjoyed the creativity of being in a Company. This creativity allowed me to try to prove myself in different ways. As a result, I found myself in a position of being the first woman in many situations – the first General Counsel, first to be on the Management Team, first to Chair the Pension Committee, the first woman President, and later the first woman Chief Communications Officer. Like being the firstborn, I felt a tremendous responsibility to live up to the expectations of my bosses, as well as the weight of responsibility to other women. I felt like any failure on my part would be seen as theirs as well, and that I would be letting everyone down if I couldn't do my job to a high level of excellence. I once had a boss say to me as I took on a new assignment "Failure is not an option". No pressure there.

In the early days, I worked part-time in the office, but until all hours of the night at home. I wanted to keep my part-time status, perform to a very high standard, and still have time with my daughter. My feelings of responsibility to other women weighed on me as well, and compelled me to work judiciously remotely so no one complained that I wasn't physically present. Teleworking was virtually unknown at that time, and it was unusual to be out of the office unless you were traveling on business. Hence, I felt like an experiment that had to succeed.

Being the first at anything puts you under a microscope, and I was told that repeatedly. I knew that I was closely watched, and that I carried a big burden. If I failed, it would be a very long time before other women were offered the same opportunities and I knew it. I had never intended to trailblaze. I just went in to work every day and worked hard at everything I did. The fact that it led me into great opportunities was just a coincidence, I felt. These feelings of responsibility have never left me. I just try to use them to energize myself to aim higher and do better.

I have tried to ignore the burden of trailblazing and enjoy the ascent and the view, knowing that I would have to continue to climb the walls and hang on tight. Forget about a corporate ladder – I was too busy trying not to slip and fall or land on a mine-field to look for one. I always try to be proud of how I behave – a lesson from my Grandma Jeannie – and another one of my rules. "You have to look in the mirror and face yourself every day", she would say. "If it doesn't feel right, don't do it", I was told by an admirable senior partner at my first law firm. Good guiding principles as I was starting to figure out that not all people behaved like I did. I have always wished I'd learned that sooner.

I recall a management meeting discussing a new dress code proposal where I was not only the sole woman at the table, but a different generation than the men. The discussion degenerated, and I received a few insults which I didn't appreciate. I later marched into the offender's office and demanded a public apology. He apologized privately, but I told him that wasn't enough; he couldn't insult me publicly and try to apologize within the safe closed-door confines of his office. Today I would have spoken up right away in order to be true to myself and follow my "speaking up" rule. In any event, I got my public apology at the next management meeting.

It is also important to be true to oneself. Whatever your values, wishes and dreams, they are yours alone and should not be compromised for anyone else. Otherwise, it will be impossible to look at ourselves in the mirror. I had a key chain that had the Shakespearean quote "To thine own self be true" which I'd picked up along the way. I carried it around for years until it broke, but still carry that message in my head every day. There are lots of opportunities to compromise our principles. Don't do it.

My first leadership roles involved administrative assistants, and it wasn't until later that I supervised managers. Supervising administrative assistants can be challenging if they don't have the skills or they have a lousy work ethic, but they are expecting you to direct them which in some ways makes it easier. I learned the hard way to set the expectation that my assistants keep my private information private, and not talk about me to the rest of my department. I was unpleasantly surprised early on by some assistants who spent more time chatting around the office than working, and needed to be reminded that they were there to get work done and not create a soap opera environment where there are layers of social acceptance. There are no mean girls in my department, at least not for long.

Expectations for women bosses are different; there is a level of friendship expected that does not seem to be expected from men. It is a tricky balance between being their boss and keeping a bit of distance, and being friendly enough to have a pleasant working relationship. The best assistants don't want or need your friendship, but others are resentful when they don't get it.

Leading managers is harder still, and setting expectations early on is invaluable. Managers are an entirely different type of worker and pose many challenges for their leader. While this appears the same for men, for women it can be even harder, especially if the male workers resent having a woman boss. In one role I had to supervise managers who had been promised my job. It was very difficult to try to win them over, and some never came around. I had to make difficult decisions and move people around, including exiting a few. It was tough, but I couldn't risk having unmotivated disloyal employees.

That would not have been fair to me, to the other employees, or to the company that was paying our salaries. I was amazed at the daring entitlement that some of the employees had; why did they think they were owed something by the company? It is an employment relationship; you have to do your job in order to keep it and get paid. While new in the role, I drew on my fierce tenacity to lead, but it was no easy task.

Women's leadership is different than a man's. Women walk a fine line between directing and mandating, and we have to be careful how we deliver advice. If we appear too pushy we are admonished for being nasty and too direct. If we are too polite we are seen as soft and easily intimidated. It's important to remain true to our own personalities, and not change how we act simply because others are trying to get us to be different than our true selves. On the other hand, we have to appear professional, tough and capable, which can look different to different people. We also need to establish our own brands; mine is to always be extremely well-groomed, the best dressed and the best prepared, no matter what the work occasion. Confidence is built from the inside out; we have to feel it in order to convey it. Even though our employees want autonomy, when the going gets rough they look to their bosses for direction and advice. I once confronted a situation where a very sick employee had to be wheeled out of a rest room by ambulance attendants. She had just returned after a lengthy illness, which she'd obviously not conquered. I was very upset, having been the one who assisted her when she fell ill, and afterward I showed it. I was surprised how much that had affected my staff; they must have always expected me to be strong but emotionless. When I showed emotion they were even more upset about their sick colleague, and talked about my reaction for days. It was a big lesson to me about showing my humanity more often. My colleagues shouldn't have been so surprised by my reaction when a sick colleague was wheeled out of the office on a stretcher.

I'd had my credibility questioned for so long as a young professional that it took some coaching to push me along as a strong, authentic and connected leader. It took a while for me to understand that people needed to trust me to follow my lead and to deliver beyond the bare minimum. I made the mistake of seeming too aloof at the beginning; my shyness from the mean girl experience made me hang back. I didn't have the awareness at the time to realize that this was preventing my larger team from performing to their highest potential. Around that time, 360 feedback was coming into vogue, as were leadership retreats which were focused on team building. As part of the feedback I solicited responses from my direct reports. I was shocked to learn that I was seen as cold and aloof. My direct reports wanted to know me better, and I was told that this lack of knowledge of "who I was" prevented them from fully trusting me and delivering at their highest levels. I have since worked hard to show my genuine warmth and empathy without seeming soft. In particular, I talk to people more and share some personal information. A delicate balance, but one that's attainable.

My initial foray into leadership had a hard and turbulent landing. Aside from the issues with my direct reports, I found that people didn't work like I did, and they didn't have the same goals and ambitions. That was a very tough lesson for me. When the clock struck 4, it was like a fire alarm for some workers. Out they ran, with no intention of doing anything work related until the following day. It took me a long time to adjust to that, and to find consistently hard workers to work with me. I also learned to accept that not everyone wanted or needed a career like mine, and that was ok. I was very surprised the first time I offered a promotion to someone and they turned it down. They liked their job, their lifestyle, and had no ambition or desire to do anything different or tasks which were more challenging. It has taken me a long time to accept that, but I now do.

Leadership is a lot like being a mother. You have to know and understand the capabilities of your children, strive to bring out the best in everyone, and never (or almost never) give up. I learned that the defeats or shortcomings of others were neither mine nor mine to fix, but this took time. While warming up and becoming more approachable, these were still work relationships and I had to keep up a certain barrier. Leaders at work are not meant to solve everyone's problems or even talk about them. While I need to be aware of team members' capabilities, I am not their mother, partner, sister, aunt or friend. To this day, I remain circumspect about what I ask and what I share. I just don't think that my co-workers need to know the most intimate details of my life, and frankly, I don't want to know theirs. We all need to leave things at the door and come in to work and work hard every day. This can actually be very helpful when things are tough personally. Work can be a safe place to hide from personal problems at times; I've used it that way throughout my career when I have had the need to throw myself into my work to find validation or salvation. Kind of like how I threw myself into school after my mother and Grandma Tessie died when I was a teenager.

I think the most important thing about being a good leader is being consistent. Your employees, colleagues and bosses should know that you have the maturity to come in every day and behave appropriately. Even if things go wrong you have to show a demonstrated capability to find your way to a good solution. As a leader, your employees should know they can always come to you when things go wrong; that you are approachable and won't blow their heads off. I once had a boss in a law firm who threw the furniture around his office when he got mad. We could hear it from the adjoining offices. It certainly didn't make us want to go ask him for help or deliver bad news. We all have our bad days, but we still have to show up as strong leaders who can cope. As I often say to my leadership team, "Be careful how you behave today. The first thing your employees will talk about around the dinner table tonight will be about you – their boss. What do you want them to say?".

It is equally important not to talk about people behind their backs, especially your boss. I have a rule that I don't say anything behind someone's back that I wouldn't say to their face. I might say it differently, but the message would be the same. Also, I rarely forward my boss's emails. I need to trust my bosses and have them trust me, and private conversations should remain that way, even in writing. It's important to treat people with dignity and respect, and that includes what you say about them when they're not there, or what you do with their information and correspondence. Be careful what you say about others. They will invariably find out, so you might as well find a way to say it to their face in the first place.

Emails travel easily and can get you into a lot of trouble if you're not careful. We can be far too lax with our written correspondence, and let it become too casual. It is dangerous to forget that emails at work are company property, and could land in a court case if an issue is contentious. Pretend your boss is looking over your shoulder before you hit the "send" button, or imagine that your notes might end up in front of a judge. That way, you will pause to reflect before you send something that can be potentially problematic. On the topic of gossip, be careful what you say about others.

I hope people would say that I am an honest, consistent and fair leader. I certainly try to be that way. I give a lot of thought to how I treat people, and carefully consider all options before making a decision that will affect someone's career or life. Fairness and justice are very important to me and are big reasons why I went to law school. I just think there isn't enough justice in the world; maybe I can add my little bit to make the world better. At the same time, I also want people to see me as a tough leader and negotiator. One of the greatest compliments I received early on was from a schoolmate on the other side of a difficult case. The case was very contentious, and involved disputed facts and a lot of money. Neither client wanted to go to court, so we reached what I thought was a good compromise. My colleague on the other side later said that he'd settled the matter because I was such a tough negotiator that he took what he could get and closed the file. His comments were early confirmation to me that I could be seen as an equal - tough, fair, yet feminine - and still win.

I have found that negotiating, like leadership, is different for men than women. It is easy to be underestimated, which makes others think they can take advantage. Social norms and mores teach young girls to be nice and get along; that's what we all heard from our mothers. It was not, however, what I heard from my Grandmothers who taught me to fight hard and not worry so much about being "nice". We have to move away from the social expectations of being "good", test our mettle and bargain for all we're worth. We must repeatedly prove ourselves for others to trust our strength and tenacity.

Through my own experiences I've seen that women also have to fight harder to be taken seriously. I always found it aggravating to be underestimated or treated like I'm an idiot. Underestimate me at your peril, I would think to myself, but it's a disadvantage all the same. If we're underestimated, it's hard for people to take chances on us for jobs and other opportunities. Letting others believe I'm a fool might be advantageous during a negotiation, but it still makes me mad. I don't want to set that as the norm for women coming up behind me and have them think that they have to look weak to succeed.

When I first started working there were no formal mentoring programs like there are now. In fact, there was very little informal mentoring happening either, especially among women. Most women made it their business not to mentor other women, and said so quite openly. I've never had a mentor per se, but I've had some bosses who have taken chances on me and sponsored me. Since I've largely kept my head down and worked hard, I've been surprised at being identified for bigger opportunities. The fact that I've been considered always flattered me, since I know I wouldn't have been on a candidate slate unless others had confidence in my ability. My bosses also knew I didn't shy away from change, and that I embraced a new challenge even if it scared me to death. Good practices, albeit somewhat frightening. I always expressed gratitude for the new opportunities, and I hope I never let them see that I took on the new challenges with a bit of fear.

As a leader, I have often seen people fail because they get the question wrong. It is very important to get the question right in any task we are tackling. Over the years I've seen people expend a lot of time and effort answering the wrong questions, which is a total waste of energy. It only takes a few minutes at the outset to ask a few questions to define the task. We don't do it because we are afraid of looking stupid or incompetent. I think it's better to clarify the question at the beginning than wasting a lot of time and looking incompetent later on.

I always ask my team about the atmosphere in a meeting – what will/did the room feel like? It's important to feel the room and adjust your tone and material to fit it. It's like walking in to a courtroom. You need to listen to the judge before you start talking. If they got up on the wrong side of the bed that morning you'd better get straight to the point, get what you want, and get out fast. Similarly, if the atmosphere is warm and inviting you should embrace it, enjoy the conversation and savor the moment. Successful dialogue is a very enjoyable part of our careers and we should appreciate it.

Leadership is also about demanding respect, both for and from your team. Another one of my rules is not to take any crap from anyone, and I've learned that others are more than willing to try giving out a lot of it to mask their insecurities. Along with fairness and justice we need respect, otherwise workplaces degenerate into playgrounds with untempered mean bullies. You won't keep your good people very long in situations like that.

I feel very grateful for my life, my family and my career. I have found and seized a lot of opportunities thanks to a great start and an emphasis on education, hard work, justice and fairness. I hope that is my legacy. Whenever an early in career woman thanks me for something I have done for them, I ask them to remember it so that they can someday do the same for someone else.

It is important to "pay it forward" and treat others with the kindness and respect we have benefited from ourselves. That way we can achieve lasting, enduring change for women in our families, workplaces and societies. I have seen a lot of change in women and women's leadership over the years, and I hope we continue to grow and evolve. There are many attainable careers that women can have if we educate ourselves, pursue our dreams and aim high. Hard work and perseverance really do pay off. We must continue to Pound On!! the glass ceiling so we can bust through and grab the brass ring!

POUND ON!!

Pictured: Grandma Jeannie and Granddaddy on vacation in the 1960's.

Pictured: My mother on her wedding day, May 14, 1953.

Pictured: My parents and my Grandma Tessie, on the couch in my Aunt Leila's house, circa 1953.

Pictured: My parents, my sister Wendy and I, on the same couch in my Aunt Leila's house, circa 1966.

Pictured: Taryn at age 3, circa 1996.

Pictured: My daughter Taryn walking me down the "aisle" on my wedding day, August 3, 2008.

Mitch and I on our wedding day, August 3, 2008

Pictured: My husband Mitch and I at my daughter's Bat Mitzvah, November

Pictured: Taryn and Carter dressed up for Halloween 2017.

Pictured: Carter's School Picture 2019.

IRENE CHANG BRITT

Born in Taiwan and raised in the suburbs of Toronto, Irene Chang Britt's Alpha traits were visible early when she started a business with her brother while she was still a student. Warm and welcoming, Irene's keen business acumen led her to great corporate success where she ran a Fortune 500 Company as CEO. Now a member of several Boards of Directors, Irene continues to use her fine skills to drive top flight business results for the companies she serves.

Irene earned a Bachelor of Arts in Social Anthropology from the University of Toronto, and an MBA from the University of Western Ontario.

POUND ON!!

IRENE CHANG BRITT

An Incredible Alpha Success Story

From my first corporate assignment in 1986 to the portfolio of brands I currently serve as Board Director and Chairperson, I am known for leading turnarounds, fixing what is broken, and transforming businesses. I love solving problems, even if I'm told they can't be solved, but this takes personal resilience and a lot of tenacity. Let me tell you how I got here...

My wonderful childhood began in Taiwan, where I was born the youngest of 4 siblings - I have sisters who are older than me (10 years and 7 years respectively), and a brother who is 4 years older than me. My parents moved to Taiwan in 1948, just before the Communists took over China. Living in a democratic society was very important to them; I think they were truly remarkable for how strongly they held these values, and for the life they wanted to give us. They were really brilliant people, and I admired their great work ethic and success.

My mother was an only child, and was thrust into war and poverty in China with my grandmother after my grandfather passed away suddenly. My grandmother worked hard at menial jobs to send my mother to school, and years later, she became a successful administrator. My dad was one of 10 children, and was a very successful economist. They both spoke many languages fluently. Their hard work and educations allowed them to enjoy success in Taiwan and to have a good life there.

In 1964, when I was just 18 months old, my parents decided to move us to North America, once again seeking out a more democratic society, sacrificing their own comfort for the sake of their children's future. The six of us, and my maternal grandmother, left Taiwan and moved to North America. We moved to San Francisco first, and eventually settled in a lovely suburb of Toronto. I think a lot about the sacrifices my parents made for us; moving to Canada in their 40s with 4 young children, leaving everything behind to have a better life.

We were always a very close family. We talked about politics, history and democracy around the dinner table a lot when I was growing up, and we lived by that example. We vote in every election, and are very grateful for our rights and freedoms. We never take them for granted, and always try to give back. We have always stuck together as well, knowing that we needed each other's support and guidance as immigrants to the country.

Our experiences as a family led me to study social cultural anthropology at the University of Toronto, but even before that I had a lot of entrepreneurial spirit. While I was still in high school, my brother and I opened two stores and a mail-order business for high-end European style bicycles. We were both competitive cyclists at the time, and we decided to go into business together, starting up the company with a lot of elbow grease, plus money I'd earned teaching English to new immigrants. We learned a lot through trial and (lots of) error, and this led me to go for an MBA at Western's Business School. My business experience, and some gentle prodding from my mother to get a "practical" education had encouraged me to apply.

The hard-learned lessons from our cycling business followed me into business school, where I continued to learn about business, but also about fitting in. As an Anthropology Major and bike shop owner, I showed up to our MBA orientation in bike shorts, which was my uniform at the time. I was the only student not wearing a suit, which was not a great feeling. I felt really out of place, and went home crying, worrying that I'd never succeed in that academic environment. I did manage to work my way through the first semester, but I technically failed the semester and was told to consider dropping out. I was so disheartened that I considered it. Fortunately for me, when one of my professors learned I wanted to quit he challenged me to continue, calling me a "chicken". This only inspired me to fight back and set my sights on doing well. I didn't know it at the time, but he told me later that I reminded him of his wife who was a real fighter, and was then fighting breast cancer. He knew that I would fight back if he challenged me. He was proud, but not surprised, when I made the Dean's List 2 years later. That professor had a really strong influence on me, and was one of the first people who saw that I had potential.

I met my husband Tony in business school. In class one day, I asked the woman sitting in front of me to explain something related to accounting because I had no idea what they were talking about.

She said she didn't know either, and suggested I ask the student sitting beside her. It was Tony. He turned around, and I knew right away that this was the guy I was going to marry. When he proposed 2 weeks later I asked him what had taken him so long! He told me that he knew right away as well. We are still an incredible match that started as love at first sight.

Tony has always had a profound influence on me, largely because he sees things in me that I don't see myself. I was very intimidated in business school until Tony reminded me that I was a successful business person already, not just a successful student like many of the others in class. This was really an epiphany for me, and really helped me see myself differently. Tony has always given me tips on how to succeed, especially about not being so deferential. He is basically charming and irreverent, but has a great sense of self which helps him follow his own views and form his own opinions. His influence has helped me immensely to overcome my inherently introverted nature, and has allowed me to swim against the tide in business as well. I have really learned a great deal from Tony and how he approaches the world, and I am very grateful to him for his support.

When I was in my first year of business school and looking for internships, I had the chance to meet the Vice President of Sales and Marketing in Canada for Kimberly Clark (KC), the paper goods manufacturer of brands such as Huggies and Kleenex. When he learned that I'd owned my own bike stores and knew the sports retail industry, he mentioned that they'd just bought a running insole company and that they needed someone to start the business in Canada. What serendipity! Was I "interested", he asked? Of course I was, even though he just made the job up on the spot! I later accepted a job in sales and marketing at KC because I liked the people, even though I'd been offered "shinier" jobs. Accepting the job with KC was one of the best decisions I've ever made - I ended up staying with Kimberly Clark for 13 years. Taking the job at KC in its industrial unit rather than in consumer brand management of Oreo at Nabisco, taught me that it's not always best to grab the shiniest object. The most interesting things tend to be "dull" on the surface , as they are puzzles that need solving and can generate great opportunities.

I've learned a lot of lessons along the way, and one of them is about balance. I've learned that you are never truly balanced on any given day. You have to look at the big picture and ask whether you are happy with the choices that you've made. I count on that. For example, when Tony and I were home with our kids, we were always present, both in body and in mind. Nothing distracted us. When we found that two careers in sales and marketing were too much and we couldn't juggle it, Tony decided to stay home to run our household. This was truly amazing. He did a lot of volunteer work and fundraising, and looked after everything else. With my husband at home, I had other lessons to learn. One was that I needed to let go a little bit. I had to stop worrying about the small stuff, i.e. whether there were socks on the floor. I had to learn not to be a perfectionist and hurt myself with my own standards.

As my son and daughter grew up I continued to take on different business challenges, including working my way up to SVP and President, North America Foodservice at Campbell Soup Company. Never wanting to let "a good crisis go to waste" in 2008, at the beginning of the Great Recession, my team and I devised a breakthrough strategy to totally disrupt the industry, and we doubled the profitability of the unit in short order. This required a lot of tenacity and resilience, and I am happy that it worked. I have learned to take these kinds of chances, take risks, and drive change.

Another key learning is that you have to push back when someone is hurting you. At one point earlier in my career, I was running a $1b business in a company. My male colleague was running a $300 million business in the same entity. Although he was running a smaller business, he was always trying to use his male collegial relationships to freeze me out. One time, he succeeded in disinviting me to a business discussion by relocating it to a strip club. That was quite the effort, just to try to gain the advantage! When I suggested that the venue was inappropriate, another male colleague suggested I was being too sensitive. This was very disappointing to me, but I refused to let them diminish my voice and demanded that we meet an hour earlier the following morning to start our meetings. This was an early lesson in how people (notably a man in this case) were trying to exclude me from the business discussions by capitalizing on relationships with male peers. Women need to learn from this sort of bravado too, but it really speaks to inclusion. It's crucial to bring your whole self to work, and for colleagues and bosses to respect your voice and viewpoint. Otherwise the workplace is hard to tolerate.

If I were giving advice to a woman earlier in her career, I would tell her that networking IS working. It's very important to carve out time for networking and to build relationships. You learn so much by just talking to other people. Women need to build relationships in business, and to understand how important these relationships are to our careers. I often observed men walking around the office with their coffee cups at 5:00 p.m. chatting with others and networking. We women remained at our desks and kept working, which we thought would help us get ahead. We were wrong. We thought we could get just as far by working hard, but it's not true. We have to take the time to build relationships which will accelerate our careers. We also need to tout our accomplishments and those of our teams. We have to be our own advocates, and talk about our great work. Otherwise, others will not know or understand what we achieve.

Similarly, don't stay with a company that doesn't understand your worth. I once told a boss that "I love this company, and I respect you. But never, ever confuse that with me needing you all." I truly believe that we have to know our worth and not feel beholden to anyone. We have to take charge of our own careers, compensation and futures.

I learned early on in my expertise of turnarounds and transformations that "who is on the bus" is the most important factor, and that trimming your team of people who actively work against a strategy is critical and urgent. While difficult, it's best to find these things out early on, deal with them, and form a team that believes in the new direction. I have also learned that women need to help each other. I try to give back, and still mentor and coach many women to help advance their careers. My husband and I have the goal of establishing scholarships for students of color who might not be able to afford college.

I wish I'd known earlier on that mistakes are ok. You have to make them and learn from them too. I feel like I was always fighting for respect; something that followed me into the business world from our childhood dinner table being the youngest of 4 siblings. Being overshadowed sitting at that dinner table with brilliant siblings and parents is a feeling that I've carried with me. I never wanted to be told that I didn't know what I was doing in business, even though my thinking is not linear and my desired future state results might seem far-fetched. I've learned that it's important to listen, and would emphasize this skill to earlier in career women as well. It's a very important skill to share. Share your skills, best practices and learn from others too. Brush off the things that "hurt". If something hurts you or you argue with others, try to move past it and keep on pushing. We are taught as young girls to care and to be nice. That's fine, but that's only half of the formula. We also need to have the arguments "on the field" or in the boardroom and then go out for lunch or a drink and let them go. My daughter, who was a field hockey goalie, is really good at that. Playing team sports has helped her know to fight on the field and then drop it. It's a good lesson. Similarly, little things, like connecting, matter. When I was retiring from my CEO position I received hundreds of emails from well-wishers. The one that resonated with me most was from a man on the production line in one of the bakeries who wrote to tell me that he appreciated how I always remembered to ask how his daughter was doing. She was not in good health, and it meant a lot to him that I remembered to ask him about it when I saw him at the site. His note moved me to tears.

Over the past 15 years I have really made a strong effort to help others; to reach down and pull up. I feel so fortunate to have had such tremendous success through good luck and hard work.

I feel that it is my obligation to help other women and people of color, and I try very hard to do that. I invest in women's issues and issues for people of color. I know that some women climb the ladder and then pull it up behind them so no one else can climb up. I think that is wrong. I once had a CEO from a large oil and gas company offer me a position on her Board even though I was from a different industry. This was a very powerful lesson for me - she wanted to help me rise, and the opportunity truly helped secure my career. It helped catapult my career, both in the C-Suite and in the boardroom.

Today I serve as Board Director and/or Chairperson for 5 boards. I'm proud that I've become a "growth-oriented catalyst" having turned around businesses that have been bleeding cash, and made them successful. I've ripped apart stagnating businesses to make them thrive again. I love to solve those kinds of problems, even in my own life! I love to constantly be in motion. When I'm not helping businesses grow, I'm either deep into Tai Chi or Qigong, or taking a long walk after cooking in our kitchen, or traveling. Standing still is not my style.

Pictured: Irene and her husband Tony

LYNDA COVELLO

Photo by Peggy Lampotang

A talented musician, artist, author and lawyer, Lynda blazed her trail in the big city of Toronto, far from her remote childhood home of Thunder Bay.

Lynda's entrepreneurial Alpha Woman risk-taking led her to big Bay Street law firms, her own Intellectual Property practice, and in-house to corporations where she has negotiated complex international agreements to fully leverage her clients' rights and earning potential.

Incredibly talented, Lynda performs in jazz clubs, paints, writes novels and other works, and trains with her horse. The first university graduate in her family, Lynda earned a B.A. (Specialist International Relations) from the University of Toronto, and an LL.B and LL.M (Jurisprudence) from Osgoode Hall Law School at York University.

POUND ON!!

LYNDA COVELLO

Dreams of Space, Deep Sea, and Freedom

When I was younger, I gravitated toward men's conversations at large family gatherings because I often found them more interesting. Though I never was invited to participate, I discovered that if I made myself small and kept quiet, eventually, I was ignored and could eavesdrop on the conversation. Men talked about the world and what was happening in it. I loved to listen in. A woman's world seemed so small and confined to me, filled with nothing but recipes, housekeeping tips and children.

It wasn't until many years later that I realized that these women actually were the backbone of our family. Some of them were college educated, a rarity in that time and place, and many were even teachers. They believed in themselves when others did not, worked harder than they thought they ever could, and shattered societal expectations.

I exist because many women in my family and their feminist male partners dared to break the "rules," to cross cultural, religious, familial and geographical barriers to be together on the north shore of Lake Superior, where I was born. They were uprooted, displaced, abandoned and disinherited, yet they persisted and even prospered. They fought for the right to be accepted, educated and to love who they loved – rights people are still fighting for today – and, while none of them are written about in history books, when I think about their lives and stories, I am inspired.

My paternal grandmother, for example, was a teacher educated by the church and on her way to becoming a nun. My grandfather changed all that, after emigrating from southern Italy to Port Arthur, Ontario at the age of 13 to work with his father at the rail yards. When he and my grandmother met, she defied the Roman Catholic church to pursue a life with him, and together, they became a cultural force in their town. Though they faced prejudice and opposition, as Italians still were considered second-class citizens in those days, they were undeterred in building a family and a community around music, education and community service.

My maternal grandparents also emigrated to Canada. Though my grandmother was born in 1903 in Indiana, when her father died when she was three years old my great-grandmother remarried and relocated the family to Canada. Oddly enough, though she never lived in the U.S. again, my grandmother still always identified herself as American. She worked as a secretary and office manager before marrying (and when I got married, was the only one in my family to support me in my decision to keep my maiden name) and also survived a number of near drownings in her life, in both Indiana due to floodwaters and in Ontario due to a boating accident. She was determined to survive and was a real fighter.

Sometime in the 1920s, my maternal grandmother met my grandfather, who had come to Canada from the Scottish Highlands to search for his older brother, despite being disinherited by his traditional farming family for doing so (we later learned his brother had also been in a boating accident and drowned). My grandfather found work as a prospector, staking mining claims in northwestern Ontario, before meeting my grandmother at a community dance.

After they were married, my grandmother would move herself and their five children from camp to camp, giving birth in rough surroundings without medical facilities and keeping everyone alive despite a myriad of dangers from the vast stretches of boreal forest. My grandfather was often gone for months at a time, with my grandmother rarely having any idea of where he was. Eventually, she put her foot down and insisted they move to Port Arthur, where she believed their children would get a better education. My grandmother taught me that you must endure whatever life throws at you until you figure out how to survive. She also taught me the only person that you truly can rely on in life is yourself.

My mother was raised as a Scottish Presbyterian, and my father as an Italian Roman Catholic. When they met in high school, they belonged to worlds that were not supposed to "mix." Still, they fell for each other and never looked back. Nothing was going to keep them apart and, after more than sixty years, they are still together.

My mother insisted on completing her nursing degree before marrying my father, even though he made it clear he intended to support her financially. She continued to work as a nurse until the birth of her third child and held jobs as a retail business owner and tribunal adjudicator afterward. Intelligent, practical and creative, she taught me self-discipline and crisis management skills that continue to serve me well to this day.

My father worked full-time in the family business, a recreation center, from the time he graduated high school. When the city expropriated the center's property for urban renewal in the early 1970s, he was 36 years old, had little formal education and had four children to support. He and my mother looked at various options, including moving our family to Hawaii, where the demand for Canadian nurses was high thanks to their good training. However, around the same time, my father became friends with a man who ran the Canadian division of a multinational corporation in England (and whose son I would eventually marry). He offered my dad a job at the Thunder Bay branch of his company. This was an industry my father knew nothing about, so when he accepted the job offer, he insisted on starting from the bottom as a warehouseman rather than in sales. Eventually, he moved up the ranks to become a manager of the northwestern Ontario district and exponentially increased sales.

I grew up in Thunder Bay, Ontario with my three siblings, as well as my large extended family of 49 first cousins and 18 aunts and uncles, often attending multi-generational social events and spending weekends at Lake Superior. I spent most of my time with my family, even though growing up in such a large group of close-knit people felt like a double-edged sword. I always felt loved and supported, but I also felt restricted by their collective traditional outlook. For example, I used to get into trouble for sitting in a corner with a book during family events and special occasions. But that's who I was – I was the geeky, bespectacled, shy, skinny girl who, outside of her own family, struggled to socialize.

In school, I gravitated toward smaller groups of kids when I could find them, and was often more comfortable in the company of boys than girls. Boys seemed more straightforward and transparent, whereas I could never figure out what girls were really up to; boys were friendly to me while girls were mean; and when boys invited me over to their house to play Risk or to listen to a new album, they were there when I arrived and that's what we did. When girls invited me over, they were cruel and unpredictable, if they were even there at all.

Girls' mind games made me feel ugly, stupid and excluded, but with boys, I could build things and play strategic games without feeling that way. So, throughout my childhood and into high school,

I found a group of male friends with whom I shared many interests and am still friends with today.

I also spent a lot of time alone growing up, in my head and in books that provided me with the space to dream and imagine. I was involved in a lot of activities, including swimming, tennis, skiing, sailing, piano lessons, dance and choir, but most of all, I loved to read. The library was a weekly destination of mine and, in school, I would read Arthur C. Clarke and Frank Herbert paperbacks under cover of my math textbook. I even enjoyed reading the encyclopedia.

When I wasn't reading, I would lose myself in the active night sky, especially while laying on my back on the dock in the summertime. I wanted to become an astronaut and voyage to the stars, despite the fact that I got car sick and hated roller coasters. I figured with the way things were going in the late 1960s and early 1970s, that by the time I grew up we would have perfected warp drive and interstellar travel.

That dream ended when I fell into a coma and was diagnosed with Type 1 diabetes at the age of 14. In 1973, when I was given 20 or so years to live a limited life, there were no doctors in our town who knew much about the autoimmune disease. So, my mother became my chief medical expert.

When I fell into the coma, I lost consciousness for an entire day and effectively ceased to exist. I was faced with the reality of my own mortality in two very stark ways: one, I could simply cease to exist without warning, and two, my life expectancy was now very short. Since there was no guarantee I would be alive the next day, I made the decision then that my life had to matter. I knew I wanted to experience as much as I could, and my mother agreed. She said, "This has happened to you. This is your life now. All that matters is how you deal with it. There is no feeling sorry for yourself, no self-indulgence. This is your responsibility and you simply need to accept it."

I decided not long after that I needed to leave my small hometown and get out into the world – and I needed to be able to support myself if I was going to be able to do and see all the things I intended to. So, at 19 years old, I attended the University of Toronto to earn my degree in international relations; a cross-disciplinary study of history, economics and political science. I thought I might be a diplomat. It sounded exciting, all that travel and intrigue, but I also still loved the idea of trying to understand what happened in the world on a global scale and why.

I did well in school, but when I wasn't offered a role in government immediately after graduation, I decided to go to York University Law School. I had thought about becoming a lawyer for some time, but back home, I faced a lot of opposition. In the 1970s and 1980s in Canada, many people still thought being a lawyer was an inappropriate career for a young woman. However, I no longer cared what other people thought I should or shouldn't do with my life – I was following my plan to make my life matter and law seemed like a good match.

In law school, I was interested in how law evolves in the places where creativity and technological advances outpaced the current legal and social infrastructure and pushes up against the thresholds of culture. I thought about becoming an international lawyer, but I was also very interested in intellectual property law.

I learned that there are many aspects of the practice of law that they do not teach you in law school, such as office and gender politics. While articling, men had a huge advantage. The people making the decisions about who got to work on which files were men, and so were their clients. They were not used to women being in law firms other than as secretaries and paralegals, so in general, we were treated as though we had less education and skill than our male colleagues. I started to think that maybe this wasn't the right career for me after all.

After passing my bar exams, I was given an opportunity to clerk for a year in what was then the Supreme Court of Ontario. I was assigned to a panel of four judges to do research, read all of the briefs submitted by counsel, and take notes in court so we could discuss them afterwards and prepare draft judgments for their review.

Even though not all of the judges agreed that women should be lawyers, by the end of the year, I was on great terms with all of them. I was grateful for what they had taught me and felt I had earned their respect. One of the male judges told me I had an "amazing ability to cut through noise and get to the heart of an issue." (Years later, on a decision that had been appealed, he also said, "The Supreme Court of Canada agrees with you and disagrees with me. I'm only going to say this once: you were right.")

Clerking made me want to be a lawyer again. People aren't perfect, and judges are simply that – people with an enormous responsibility over other people's lives. The truth is - most of them take that very seriously and try very hard to get it right. I then decided to become a junior lawyer at a big Bay Street law firm, where I learned a lot about practicing law and approaching and working through complex problems.

Looking up the ladder, though, I couldn't see myself at the top. There were very few senior women and even fewer who were approachable or helpful. Two female partners in particular told me I was "too soft and feminine to make it in this profession" and that I would "eventually need to find a nanny for both day and night so that I could concentrate on my career" – that I just needed to "come home and put money on the table while someone else raised my kids."

I didn't want to be like them, so I went back to York University to obtain my master's degree in law, focusing on the unstated and unacknowledged beliefs that influence decision-makers and how judicial decisions are made. While earning my advanced degree, I worked as a research coordinator for a constitutional law project at the Institute for Public Law and Policy. I love the world of ideas, researching, analyzing and drawing conclusions, but if my work wasn't to have actual life-changing impact or the ability to help people solve their problems, then I didn't feel like what I was doing was enough. I love academia, but it always has to lead back to action in the real world.

Once the report was finished, I went back to my legal practice with a smaller, more specialized firm before becoming a junior lawyer in a mid-sized firm. Most of the time, my male colleagues were nothing but complimentary, telling me I had "a way of finding a deal and leading parties to it" and that I was "great at building teams, systems, businesses, relationships and solutions." I also found that the combination of intellectual property, international relations and business knowledge gave me a very powerful skill set to approach issues facing many companies. The world was beginning to realize the value of intellectual property assets as drivers of wealth and innovation.

I was still not a fan of the gender discrimination and sexual harassment that came with working in a firm. My next step was to co-found my own experimental boutique firm to have control over my practice and to be able to choose which clients I wanted to work with. That so many clients followed me to my new, unproven firm was very satisfying, and within our firm, a modular "practice-in-association" model worked best. "Eat what you kill" may not work for everyone, but we were happy with the fact that while we shared general expenses, our practices were financially separate.

I next took a professional risk in becoming Vice President and General Counsel for a small pharmaceutical company, because having just one client doesn't mean less work. It means you are on duty 24/7, especially when it comes to international business. I also took personal risks with high-risk pregnancies and miscarriages throughout my career until I gave birth to two healthy sons, for whom I subsequently took time out of my career. I successfully resisted the message I got at the time from the profession, which was, "You will never work again at a high level."

Today, I am an international legal and business consultant on intellectual property strategy and commercial transactions. Though I now value independence more than I value money, prestige or recognition, I still love solving puzzles, bringing innovative new technologies to market and working with innovative business leaders to achieve their goals around the world.

As a woman leader, I was often underestimated, undermined and excluded from both business deals and social events, but I had the determination, courage and confidence to do things on my own terms without changing my essential nature to be like anyone else or meet anyone else's idea of who I should be. I challenged myself to take risks and join organizations, serve on committees, give seminars and workshops, and go to conferences year after year until I was known, trusted and included.

If you work for me, I expect you to give your very best, too, and to continuously strive to improve. I am supportive but certainly not a micro-manager. I like people to try to solve problems themselves and come to me with suggested solutions when they have taken things as far as they can. I like to unleash potential in people by helping them believe in themselves and their ability to learn and handle new challenges. I am interested in developing the next generation of leaders, so I push people to exceed their own expectations of themselves.

Others might think I am tough to work for because my standards are very high, but I apply the same standards to others as I apply to myself: work hard, be smart and take your job seriously.

If you are clear about what is important to you and the priorities that you want to achieve, I strongly believe that you can plan and execute accordingly.

Women still face issues in the workplace that men do not. While the barriers to entry for many traditional male careers are much lower than they were when I first started, the fine balance between career and family is still far more difficult for women to navigate than for men, as the expectation is still that a woman will make herself available for child and elder care no matter what her career responsibilities might be. Then there is the common catch-22 that a woman will be criticized for putting family ahead of work but also for putting her career ahead of family.

I think we need to find ways of supporting women so that they can offload some of this mental burden. For instance, I never liked the idea of having to do all my work at the office. I found that I could be just as productive, or even more so, if I could work remotely part of the time. This allowed me to attend to family responsibilities, which often times were time-rigid and out of my control, and also complete work responsibilities.

Regardless, women leaders still need to be able to clearly define their priorities in ways that men often do not. A woman, for example, must establish herself as a credible and dominant leader without also appearing tyrannical or inflexible. She must somehow strike a balance between being emotionally available and likable but also must be cool-headed in a crisis. At the end of the day, a man is still judged more on the results of his leadership than his leadership style while a woman is judged on both, as well as her physical appearance.

I have five key pieces of advice by which to navigate one's career in this type of high-powered environment:

1. Learn to think like the person on the other side of the conversation and you will be a better communicator and negotiator.
2. Look beyond what is being said and done on the public stage to better understand the context, importance and impact of events.
3. Be careful who you go into business with – due diligence with prospective partners, colleagues and clients is critical – and don't believe any promises. Always get it in writing.

4. You don't need to say "yes" to every request for your time and input. If you say "no" sometimes, it will be okay. I, too, tend to oversubscribe myself, because I can usually see what needs to be done and how to do it. But you don't owe anyone anything!
5. You can't control what other people think, and a confident, successful woman is always going to be the subject of speculation and rumors. Just keep your head up, be true to yourself, and keep showing them how good you are at what you do. Over and over again.

If nothing else, remember this: a good leader has vision, intelligence, drive and ambition; she knows how to inspire people and help people achieve their best; when to push forward in spite of resistance and when to change course; and she is capable of making decisions with the information available to her at the time and not waiting until things are perfect, as things will never be perfect.

We can and must, however, continue to strive for balance. This means that all aspects of our selves are valued, cared for and allocated adequate time and resources to thrive. Physical, emotional, professional, artistic and intellectual health are all given equal importance in my life, though I have rarely, if ever, achieved equilibrium, since these shift constantly. One thing I am absolutely committed to, however, is proper diet, sleep and exercise – if I don't take care of these things, nothing else is possible.

My alarm clock goes off these days at 7:15 a.m. and if I don't get out of bed, my dog comes and gets me so we can take our daily one-hour morning walk through the woods behind our house in Toronto, where I live with my husband. I then like to deal with complex problems without interruption. Though I read email throughout the day, I've disabled notifications so that I am not interrupted. I also try to schedule calls and meetings for after 11 a.m. when I am most productive.

In the afternoon, I follow up on administrative tasks and emails before taking my dog for another hour-long walk around 6 p.m. Dinner is typically around 7 p.m. and often I'm back to work in the evening to tie up loose ends and plan for the next day.

Prior to going to sleep at 11 p.m., I unwind with music, a book or a television show, unless I'm out listening to live music, attending a play or having dinner with friends – then it can be quite late.

I also try not to work on the weekends, but rather devote my time to personal interests and my social life, as well as fitness, sleep and health. I run errands and try to get organized for the next week by planning meals and resupplying our household. I also like to paint, sing jazz, write creatively, ski, hike, and volunteer in both the arts and healthcare. And, my husband and I like to cook on the weekends, when we actually have time to spend in the kitchen.

I also go to the barn and visit with my horse, sometimes saddling him up to go for a ride. I decided at forty years old that I wanted to learn how to ride horses and I did so, despite the risks and dangers of the sport. I am proud that I never gave up on myself and that, despite my supposed limitations, I pushed through many barriers to achieve the life and career I wanted.

My idea of success has evolved over the years. It used to mean being the successful lawyer making tons of money and gaining professional recognition. Now, while those things are still important, they are no longer sufficient. Now, success is more about being at peace with myself and with who I am and being able to choose how I spend my time without worrying about what other people think. Now is the time for me.

Pictured: Vacations are critical to recharge for the challenges we face. Lynda with her husband, Jim Fabro.

Pictured: Listening is just as important as singing. Music is a collaboration.

Pictured: In balance with one of my greatest teachers.

SALLY GLICK

The best and most generous networker you'll ever meet, Sally Glick is a partner in a successful accounting firm. While not even an accountant herself, her remarkable talent at marketing and forging client connections has made her an indispensable asset to the firm.

Sally started her career in her father's accounting firm, learning marketing through experience and tenacity, and later earning an MBA. A passionate mentor and educator, Sally raised 3 children as a single parent while building her impressive career. A loving grandmother, Sally's selfless devotion to family and friends is unequaled, and appreciated by all.

POUND ON!!

SALLY GLICK

The Consummate Marketer and Mentor

Those who know me well know my work has had a very positive impact on my life, connecting me with amazing women and men whom I never would have known if not for my career trajectory. But what people don't always recognize is that building meaningful relationships by being a connector and helping others is the most fun work one could ever dream of.

As a leader who leads by example, I rarely ask others to do something I cannot or have not done. I do my best to explain the big picture to our team so that they know exactly why they are performing key tasks and how their results impact the firm. I assume responsibility, take ownership and bring energy and passion to the table to help achieve exciting results. Mostly I think I am Alpha material because I choose to pave the way for others, especially women. While men have plenty of great mentors and opportunities for advancement, I believe it is women who need more.

Having begun my career working with my father, a career which lasted more than 20 years, I do not believe I faced as many traditional challenges as other women had. My father helped carve a path to success for me without ever treating me as if I were simply a "kid." Instead, from the beginning, he demonstrated how strongly he respected my abilities and my commitment to my work, giving me the latitude and credibility expected for a more seasoned professional. In return, I did everything I could to deserve his confidence, a lesson I carried with me from my childhood years.

I grew up in an incredibly warm and culturally diverse environment on the famous South Side of Chicago. As was common in the 1950s, most of my extended family, from my cousins to my great-great-grandfather, all lived nearby and I had the privilege of knowing them throughout my childhood. This included my adoring maternal grandmother, who was a very strong influence on me. When my grandfather died suddenly in his early 50s, my grandmother, having never worked outside the home, rose to the challenge to make my grandfather's dry-cleaning business more profitable than ever. It turned out that my grandmother, who resembled a beautiful Loretta Young, had a mind for business and loved people. I thought she was fearless and I loved spending time with her. My grandmother learned to love traveling and vacationing alone, especially to winter in warmer climates, and she was very adventurous without once needing to ever enter another relationship. She used to say she married once for love but never again wanted to find some "old man's slippers under her bed," which was very independent thinking for a woman who would be 111 years old today.

My mother, on the other hand, drove infrequently and did not like to venture too far outside of her own neighborhood. She was not much of a risk taker given that my father would take care of whatever she needed, so she would not often have to leave her comfort zone. My mother had finished high school and then followed my father in the Navy awhile before taking on the responsibilities of home and childcare at the age of twenty-two.

My father finished school, passed the bar and become a practicing attorney before realizing he hated it for being too unethical. When he returned to school, he discovered he loved accounting and therefore became a solo certified public accountant with a growing practice, despite never having a staff of more than seven. I learned later in life that in my early years, this resulted in not much time or money for dining out or vacations, but I always felt my life was luxuriously happy.

My mother's fear, however, would only intensify the year I turned 11. My sister, three years younger than I, often would play make-believe games like "house" and "school" with me as we shared a bedroom. But when I was ten years old, my sister died of childhood Leukemia at the age of 8. It changed everything for me, in that I went from having a sister to being a lonely only child – and it also certainly changed my parents. Though they grew stronger as a couple, united in their commitment to raise me to be as normal and independent as possible, I knew then that I shouldered a special responsibility as their only remaining child to refrain from misbehaving in any significant way. After all, my mother's greatest desire was to keep me safe, which sometimes prevented me from doing the things I wanted. For example she did not like me going near swimming pools or roller skating rinks, and I remained good about toeing the line all while attending Chicago public high school. I still had a wide circle of wonderful friends, most of whom I remain in close contact with today. My friendships helped me maintain a strong, moral attitude as a down-to-earth South Sider, reinforcing the lessons I had learned throughout my life so that I would continue to be a good person and help others.

I would go on to work with my father every summer in high school at his firm before attending Washington University in 1967 to study speech therapy. I then transferred to Northwestern University in 1968 and took on psychology as a minor, as I loved the concept of understanding how people make choices. When I married in 1969, however, I left school to work with my father full-time. I needed a job to help continue to put my now ex-husband through school, and my dad needed help in the office identifying new business opportunities. He said he was looking for a marketing director who could work and speak with people, be articulate and figure out a way to set up seminars, partnerships and events. Looking back, I am dumbfounded that he trusted me to take on this critical role, but I accepted the challenge and together we ultimately grew his firm to nearly $1 million. At the time, this was a huge accomplishment and represented great success.

The plan had been for me to go back to school and eventually move on, but it was such an amazing experience that it impacted my entire life. My father recognized skills in me that I didn't even know I had, and I realize now that it was my father who pushed me to become the kind of professional I am today. He simply assumed I could do the jobs he gave me and reassured me that I didn't have to be an accountant to be his marketing director – I just needed to understand how to make money and deal with people.

Still, it was certainly trial by fire to start. There were never any classes to learn how to best accomplish professional services marketing. I simply learned from my father how to be energetic, passionate and committed in my career, as he loved connecting with and promoting other people as much as he did being a great dad and husband. I saw then how hard my father worked to bring in business and what a good provider he was, so I never once felt burdened by all the responsibility he entrusted in me. I frequently went out into the community, attending events, talking to bankers and attorneys, joining chambers of commerce and giving seminars. I also completed small business tasks like bank reconciliations, sales tax returns, payroll processing and basic bookkeeping on top of branding and business development. I even had to learn to work a giant bookkeeping machine as there were no automated programs like there are today. As frustrating as it was for me, it was phenomenal to watch my dad in his element. I would be working on a bank reconciliation for thirty minutes, to the point that you could see all the eraser marks, and I'd say, "Dad, I'm still off by $1.50." And he'd say, "It's in there somewhere. You cannot turn this bank reconciliation around until this is the same number as this." Then he'd peer over my shoulder and say, "Check this number." I'd check again and it was almost always a transposition error or a missing service charge – one he could easily find in a heartbeat.

I believed my dad to be the smartest person I would ever meet. While we interacted at the office every day, it was our out-of-office conversations over dinner or at family events where I truly benefited from his wisdom and amazing leadership skills. More than once, my mother unsuccessfully tried to enforce a rule prohibiting us from "talking business" at dinner, but my dad and I just couldn't help ourselves.

It is no surprise, then, that the most interesting facet of marketing to me was getting involved in the community, spending time cultivating future clients and nurturing existing relationships to promote high retention and loyalty – just like my father. I realize now how critical self-awareness is when it comes to emotional intelligence in the workplace, but in my earlier years I was more focused on my technical skills and competencies. Now, however, I believe these are second to those soft skills that will help lead others to success in the workplace.

My dad taught me to always look at things through different lenses and perspectives. For example, when I first meet someone at an event today, I try to think about how I can help them, even if there's no immediate need or reward. Should I reach out to them? How can I get to know them better? Is there an opportunity for them to shine? Why not nominate them for an award? Maybe there will be a work benefit, maybe not, but if I find things in common with someone, I try to connect. This may not be traditional marketing, but it works. It creates relationships that are long-lasting and even friendships when you are not expecting them. I've been told that this kind of activity is selfless, generous and uncommon. But frankly, I enjoy seeing others succeed and I know it means a lot to other people because we don't always stop to help or recognize others enough.

My father taught me that we need to treat clients differently than anyone else in order to gain their trust and grow business. "Wear your psychiatrist hat," he would tell me, and "find out what the most important thing is to the client to create a special bond." Working with him was like going to a mini-MBA program every day, and I am very grateful for what I learned from him.

I only left my father's firm in 1973 to have my first child; my second in 1975; and my last in 1978. I learned from motherhood the patience it requires to put someone ahead of yourself, though I loved them with a fierceness I never knew I had. It was and still is the kind of love that had me exhaustingly typing papers for them at 10pm while doing laundry after coming home from a traveling baseball tournament so my son would have a clean uniform for his next game.

Mothers tend to be nurturers, and I was no exception. But sometimes, this stops us from pursuing all of our career goals at various times. Today, for example, I don't see many women at 7:00 a.m. meetings, as they are getting their kids off to school while their husbands network over breakfast. That is why I still believe we need women-specific events - I'd rather see us together than separate, but we are not there yet. At least now we are aware. We know what is going on and we are no longer invisible. We can be more successful if we fight for ourselves and are courageous, even though the responsibilities of raising children may still provide obstacles. I am hopeful for change.

When I left the workforce for motherhood, my father found a replacement to continue basic bookkeeping for the firm. However, the woman he hired simply could not keep up. In fact, the day after I had my first baby my father arrived at the hospital with a bag full of invoices, asking if I would place them in alphabetical order for the accounting system. I did, to the horror and amazement of my hospital roommate, but I did not think anything of it. I was 25 years old and had just had my first baby, but I knew my dad needed my help.

Working for a family business has both its benefits and its downsides. You have a sense of pride and ownership, but with that comes great responsibility. You also have very little independence because you can never truly get away from your family. They control you with money even though you have security. I know other women did not have the kind of support I had, but even that can bind you in ways that can be exhausting.

My mother did offer to babysit while I spent one evening a week organizing my father's office. However, her fear for me returned when I got divorced at the age of 31. She believed my marriage would help keep me safe, but instead, I would now be alone. For me, however, this was my evolution from being a young adult into a real one. I had never lived on my own and this probably was the only way I ever would. I needed a job that would allow me to create a workday around my kids' schedules. So, I returned to work full-time with my father's firm in 1980.

I would leave for work once the kids boarded the school bus and I would leave the downtown area at 3:30 p.m. so I was home by 4:00 p.m. each day to greet them. I don't know when the phrase "flexible work hours" came into the lexicon but it wasn't ever that it wasn't an issue or that it wasn't addressed – it simply was that no one ever said, "I want to come to work and be flexible." You went to work and that was your only thought. When I went back to work with my father, it was very convenient and safe. I was never going to lose my job. If I needed my check early, I could get it. I never had to act like a single parent with three kids, juggling work and home, because for better or for worse, they were one.

I am still pretty autonomous in my career today, but nothing beats working for my father and the partnership and trust we shared. My dad knew what I was capable of, what I was accomplishing and my commitment. If I worked remotely or was out of the office, he knew I was being productive. Too often I speak with business owners or partners at professional services firms who believe out of sight means loafing, but great leaders choose their staff wisely knowing trust is imperative. In fact, I did most of my networking while at Little League games, being the class mom, carpooling and organizing school fairs. As the neighborhood changed and other mothers did not know what was required or needed for activities, I took on the task of teaching them so that they and their children would have good experiences, too. I never thought it was hard; I thought it was fun. We had to go above and beyond in our own community, you see, as a small firm who often could not compete. For example, I often would make it a priority to stop in at Palatine, Illinois on my way home to Buffalo Grove.

Why? Midas Mufflers.

My dad had a client who owned one Midas Mufflers franchise and ultimately ended up owning four, but he never outgrew our firm.

When he told us that all of their franchisees were trained in Palatine, I made it a point to meet with their office manager. I explained that my father had done a great job of training his client on how to run a business – things like how to open bank accounts, how to negotiate better interest rates with credit cards and how to successfully read financial statements. I told her our firm would be willing to continue that sort of training for all of their franchisees for free. The office manager said she would think about it and the put the proposal in a drawer.

I kept returning for well over two years with Bulls tickets and other incentives to keep us at the top of their mind. When that office manager retired and a new person came in, I got a phone call. I said this would give us a chance to share business information that everyone would be smarter for. The new office manager agreed but thought it would be more appropriate to bring in Merrill Lynch. I told her I understood the size and prestige of Merrill Lynch, but asked if she would give us a try also with a couple of training sessions over the next few months. That resulted in an easy win. My dad was passionate about this work whereas Merrill Lynch's employees were simply there to do a job. From the ground up, my father, with his experience as a sole practitioner, walked those franchisees through everything they needed for about ten years. He also was exposed to business owners across the country, some of whom changed their accounting over to our firm over time.

With our nonprofit group at SobelCo, the objective is the same – to be immersed in the community, to know all the key players, to provide training and to always be in front of the decision makers. That's what my father and I did in 1982, and it continues to work today, no matter how big or small your company is.

It takes a lot of hard work, but if one is able to prioritize what matters most and create one's own sense of balance, women, too, can manage to have it all. Holding fast to one's core values and focusing on what is most important, women can engage in targeted pursuits of what is most critical for them and their ambitions. For me, sometimes that meant asking the exterminator who came twice a year to stay with my youngest son while I ran the older two kids to the early bus for band practice. Sometimes that meant asking my mother to come to work with us when my son had strep throat for the thousandth time. We would take my son, bundled up in his pajamas, to my father's office in the high rise we worked at in Chicago. My mother would sit with him on the couch, read and color with him, feed him soup and watch him while he napped before we all got in the car and went home.

I never missed a minute of work because those things can happen when you work with family, but other women often have the additional stress of such responsibilities to juggle along with their career. When their male partners are encouraged to accept more personal responsibilities and the salaries for women increase, the situation will equalize. I believe future generations are moving swiftly toward this much more equitable approach. In fact, when my eldest son's wife declared that being a mom was difficult, my son made a gratifying comment that he didn't know how I had done it all by myself. I don't know either. I just knew I didn't have a choice. I loved being a mother and raising my children. I'd like to think my children learned to be contributing, content and kind people from me.

In 1994, with my mother's health declining before she passed from Alzheimer's in her late 60s, my father merged his practice with a larger firm of 40 people, in contrast with our five. They had never heard of a marketing director but my job with my dad was always to form great relationships, so I continued to become friendly with their clients. One in particular was a manufacturer of fasteners who I often would clip industry articles for and have her son spend time with mine. However, one day one of the partners complained to me that if his client had a question, she would call me first. They were offended at how deeply my relationships went but it was the only way I knew how. That is what my dad taught me.

I moved on to Pencor Mazur, a company that provided marketing tools for accounting firms nationwide. Yet, even though I stopped working for my father, I would do marketing webinars that he would surreptitiously watch. He would even ask questions to make sure I knew he was there. I also returned to school and finally graduated in 1998 before earning an executive MBA from Lake Forest Graduate School of Business Management in 2000. I never even viewed my job as a career until then, when I realized employees from other companies were attending the program at their company's expense. I was paying my own way, which made me feel different. I also felt like a stranger to the business learnings when I didn't even speak the same language. What was a KPI? A benchmark? EBITDA? My dad had never educated me in such things. I only did marketing and administrative work, even though I also was growing the business and marketing our brand.

I later moved to Atlanta, Georgia to work with an international accounting association, Alluvial Global, before one of its member firms, Videre Group, hired and relocated me to New Jersey in 2002. I met Alan Sobel at a local event and got to know him, so when my firm merged with J.H. Cohn in 2005, I left for SobelCo.

My father, my greatest mentor, passed at the age of 80. But I learned how to develop the power of connections from him while understanding that it is more important to give than to get. That philosophy is still at the core of everything I do here. I love my role at SobelCo as the firm's ambassador. It is my joy to represent the firm in the business and nonprofit communities and to interact with business owners and nonprofit leaders, nurturing and cultivating sustainable relationships. My day includes a mix of traditional marketing activities, such as crafting proposals and presentations, scheduling events, researching and writing articles for our firm's website, newsletter and social media, and guiding and mentoring our professionals in their own marketing initiatives. It's nice to be able to add value, especially when someone is in transition or trying to figure out their next journey. What also really matters to me is the faith and willingness my firm had to name me as their first woman partner, keeping in mind that I am not a certified public accountant. That was quite a leap of faith, and the impact of that message resonates with me every day.

Everyone should be advanced based on their competency and capabilities. Even if a woman cannot take on the most complex case load involving weeks of travel, if she is bright, articulate, and an excellent employee, she should advance even if she isn't commuting to California weekly. Today, I would tell women to be kind and bold. I would tell them to ask for what they think is fair. I would have them set goals for themselves so they can track their own success and celebrate their progress. I would tell them not to get discouraged but instead to take 100 percent control over their own careers. I would urge them to be smart, passionate and exude energy and confidence.

Still, as great as it would be to point to the many accomplishments and milestones of women in the workplace, change is so slow that it is difficult to remain positive. In the current professional climate, women still need to work harder to demonstrate greater competencies. They need to focus on being strong without being aggressive; flexible without seeming weak; seeking feedback without seeming unsure; relevant without being too serious. In short, they still need to be more careful regarding the ramifications of their behavior.

In my experience, women tend to lead better when building camaraderie and consensus. Men are traditionally seen as more authoritative leaders but given the attitudes of collaborative millennials who like to work on teams, it would seem the leadership style more commonly adopted by women will be much more successful in the decades ahead.

I'm risk averse but I raised children who are not afraid of a thing, with my son currently living in Bangkok after relocating his family to Guam, my worldly daughter recently moving from Boston to Chicago, and my other son currently taking two years away from his work in Chicago to live with his family in Turin, Italy. It's pretty cool that they were never held back by their mother. I love that adventurous spirit about them.

With my three adult children now living around the world, the people I spend the most time with include a wide range of business professionals and friends in New Jersey whom I have met over the years after networking unfettered. I am the luckiest person I know given who my friends are and how much fun we have together, as well as how much we support each other at all times. I am involved and engaged in so many different events, programs and groups that I just cannot get home as early or consistently as my two cats and my new rescue dog Rocco would like.

I also like to read great books and try different wines to relax. I visit with friends, see movies, run errands and devote a few hours each weekend to writing for the firm. Still, best of all is traveling to visit and vacation with my family. I do often get on planes alone and brave overnight stays at airport hotels to go and visit them. How else would I get to see them? I simply have to figure it out.

For me, success is a life well-lived with family and friends while keeping in perspective what truly matters most. I would not say that I have ever truly worked toward a professional legacy of my own, but I have always been committed to helping others achieve theirs, especially if I have the connections and resources to help them accomplish their goals. I would rather have a reputation for being nice and leveraging my own career to help others than anything else.

When a colleague tells me that I have had a positive impact on his or her life, professionally or personally, that is the best compliment and endorsement for me and my efforts. It validates my goals as a woman in business helping others and I truly could not be happier.

Pictured: Sally, her son, her granddaughter and her Father at her NJBIZ top 50 women award

Pictured: Sally's Father, Harold Leftwich.

Pictured: Sally with two of her children and her Father at the Northern New Jersey Visiting Nurses Gala, where she was an honoree.

CHERYL GOLDHART

An internationally renowned and award-winning Family Law Lawyer, Cheryl is a true Alpha entrepreneur. A law school graduate at the top of her class, Cheryl went on to work in a big Bay Street law firm before founding her own firm.

Cheryl's generosity to family and friends is beyond measure, both in terms of skill, time, love and advice. As a teacher and mentor she gives back to the profession and is highly respected for her negotiation, mediation, and arbitration skills. The first of her family to go to University, Cheryl earned a B.A. from York University, an L.L.B. from the University of Western Ontario and an M.A. in counseling from University of Toronto (O.I.S.E).

POUND ON!!

CHERYL GOLDHART

From Comedy Shop to Courtroom

Having practiced family law for more than thirty years, I can tell you that it's sort of like being a nun – you either have a calling to do this work, or you shouldn't be doing it at all. It also brings with it a better understanding of yourself and the family you grew up with.

My parents met in Toronto when they were teenagers, after my grandparents emigrated from eastern Europe to Canada at the turn of the century.

My father's father, from what I can remember, was the kind of guy who would figure out how much money he needed that day and would quit working if he had earned it by 10 a.m. He lived a long, stress-free life. My father worked for a hardworking uncle who had built a large international auto parts company, and his work ethic was much different. After leading a highly successful division of the business for many years, he ultimately inherited the company in the 1980s when his uncle died and continued running it until he retired, and it was sold.

My mother, though born into a more financially secure family than my father, also ran her own business. As she did not enjoy being an isolated housewife, raising a family in a rather undeveloped area of Toronto, she started a jewelry and antique business out of the home, despite lacking any business training.

Soon, loyal customers would repeatedly visit her for her advice on all things bejeweled and beautiful, as she grew to become a fabulous marketer of shiny vintage items. So, at a time when few mothers worked, my entrepreneurial mother built and sustained a thriving, well-known retail business, which she quickly relocated to a retail store in an upscale Toronto neighborhood.

This is the kind of success I would look up to and the work ethic I was encouraged to achieve. Education would never be a priority in our home, as neither of my parents attended college, but working hard to make money was.

Still, childhood came first. I remember visiting our family's cottage each summer , with my mother, sister and I staying for days at a time while my father and the other men joined us on Friday evenings for big family dinners. I also remember my sister and I spending a lot of weekends with my aunt, who was a therapist, my blind uncle and our older cousins, which offered quite a different experience than my own nuclear family had.

I also had a lot of friends in school and in the neighborhood, but never of the popular kind. I attended all sorts of lessons from ballet to piano, but I wasn't very good at anything, much to the dismay of my talented mother.

Then, when I was a teenager, I found standup comedy. A place called Yuk Yuks had started up in the basement of a church and I used to go with friends to open mic nights, in which comedians such as Jim Carrey and Howie Mandel would perform. I also spent a lot of time trying it myself, which was interesting and fun. But my father, being completely unimpressed with my comedic ambitions, repeatedly discouraged me by telling me how little comedians earned and that I would never make any money.

This was not exactly the best thing for a lazy, misdirected, floundering soul to hear, especially when I wasn't the greatest or the most motivated of students. So, naturally, I dropped out of high school during grade twelve. There was quite an argument with my parents about my decision, but ultimately, I went to work in my mother's shop.

For nearly a year I would work during the day and perform stand-up comedy at night. Then, one day a wealthy regular came in to browse, speak with my mother, and perhaps purchase a bauble. I distinctly remember her Persian lamb suit with mink fur accents and the beautiful brand-new Rolls Royce she had parked outside. When I asked her if I could take a look at her car, she said, "Sure, honey, and while you're at it, you can wash it for me, too!"

I nearly collapsed under the weight of that insult. Determined never to allow anyone to treat me like that again, I decided to go back to school and learn something so that I would never again be in such a position.

I attended night school and summer school to catch back up and chose my courses more carefully so that I would be more interested in the subject matter. For example, I developed a particular interest in sociology and psychology because people who go into psychotherapy typically have issues themselves that they need to work out. I thought maybe I could help people help themselves (even though I learned later in life that most people cannot).

I worked so hard that I got a scholarship to earn my Bachelor of Arts in the subject from York University in 1982. However, I earned my undergraduate degree while living at home, and I eventually felt the need to leave to make something of myself. So, I applied to Western University Law, two hours from Toronto.

I knew no one who was a lawyer. I didn't even really know what a lawyer did, exactly. The most I ever learned about the law was from my cousin, whose exploits regularly required the services of a criminal lawyer. So, I never in a million years dreamed that I would be accepted, but I thought, why not try? I was shocked to have received an acceptance letter. I thought someone had made a huge mistake in letting me in. Were they really going to let me be a lawyer? I apparently was not the only one who felt this way. One of the first things I heard in law school was a male student telling me that I had taken away a spot at the university from another man. And, to make matters worse, everything about the coursework was indeed completely foreign to me.

In law school, you are always under some kind of deadline or pressure, because that is what the actual workload is like. That is why the Law School Admission Test has a time limit, so that you are forced to get the questions right while struggling to keep up. The skillset requires being able to absorb tons of information within a short amount of time to then apply it to a problem.

Needless to say, my first year of law school was extremely stressful. However, I soon met my husband, Harvey, who helped teach me how to study properly – and I met Professor Jay McLeod. Widely known as the brilliant family law expert of my generation, Jay was a rather unkempt, polarizing kind of instructor, but given my interest in psychology and sociology (let alone the complexities of my own family dynamics), I always found his courses appealing and fascinating. I found him to be funny while others found him to be difficult, and I happened to do well in his classes. So, I of course took every class he offered.

After making it through my first year, the second year was better, and, quite to my own complete shock, I truly excelled in my third. I was stunned out of mind that I could do this, but graduate I did with a Bachelor of Laws in 1985. I was no longer that high school dropout – I was going to be a lawyer and I was actually going to make a living.

Articling nearly killed that dream. I completed my required 10-month apprenticeship at a large downtown firm in Toronto, but it was a fate worse than death. Yes, it was highly competitive; yes, we worked extremely long hours with little respect; and, of course the work was boring. But mostly, I didn't like the people I had to work with. You see, my father was in the middle of selling his company at the time, and my law firm coincidentally would be representing the sale. Everyone therefore knew my business and either dealt with me with "kid gloves" or would treat me poorly because they assumed I got the job solely because my father was a huge client. Every day grew increasingly uncomfortable. Then, to make matters worse, Harvey called off our engagement three weeks before our impending wedding (but more on this later).

I was so demoralized by the entire experience that I decided to return to my previous interest in psychology and go back to school to earn my master's degree in counseling, which I would ultimately earn from the University of Toronto in 1986. I thought I would become a mediator, and so, when I ran into Jay at a conference, I asked for his advice. Could I start a mediation practice for family law? Was there work? Could I make a living?

Jay didn't think there was enough business, and the gentleman he was sitting with, Stephen Grant, told me that I couldn't be a good mediator without having practiced family law. Having also been my bar admission course instructor, Stephen and I chatted further as we boarded an escalator at the conference. Then, he offered me a job. I didn't even really know who he was, but his large downtown firm was looking to hire, and I said, okay! I worked at Gowlings, Strathy and Hendersen (later Gowlings) for seventeen years, working my way up to partner under the mentorship of Stephen, who was one of the major players in the area at the time.

Stephen was the first to teach me to start crafting a good reputation from day one because that is all you have. Being a good and respectable lawyer means not always taking your clients' positions just because that is what your client says to do. I mostly learned by osmosis while watching Stephen in a courtroom.

I had an immediate credibility with judges and other lawyers simply by being associated with Stephen and was therefore able to interact with the most senior members of the bar. I also was protected – no one started up with me because they knew they would have to deal with him. He was a rainmaker at the firm, and I was under his umbrella.

But while Stephen taught me to be a barrister, it was Karon Bales who taught me the skills of a solicitor. Karon, a daughter of a well-known politician in Toronto, took over his law practice and gracefully handled whatever it was that came across her desk with a stiff upper lip. When she gave birth to her children, she returned from maternity leave within two days, despite not believing it was right. She was a woman who certainly worked to earn the credibility she deserved.

You see, women in law at the time had to be even more organized and direct than normal but still were expected not to rock the boat too much. You had to overcome being a shrinking violet without being rude while also being able to tell people what you want and what you believe is right without appearing inappropriate. It was a delicate balancing act.

Still, I learned everything I needed to learn to be the lawyer I am today from my time at Gowlings, while balancing all of my personal responsibilities in a way that worked best for the most important people in my life.

I gave birth to my twins in 1990 with my first husband, whom I abruptly dated, too quickly married and ultimately divorced after my engagement to Harvey was called off. My youngest, however, was born in 1996 with Harvey, whom I had previously avoided as we had worked in the same building – but that could only last so long. When we saw each other again, we knew, and we took it from where we left off to get married in 1994.

While I now have an extremely good marriage for someone who is a family lawyer, I learned during my time at Gowlings that you simply cannot do it all. Harvey and I, for example, both worked full-time and therefore needed to hire a nanny. That's what worked for us and we were okay with it. You simply cannot be the best mother, the best in your career, and have a great social life – to push yourself to do and have it all is a mistake because something will eventually give. It might be your marriage, or your kids might be messed up, or you won't do well at work, but if you can realize early on how to designate the time and effort that works for you to each of these things, everything can remain balanced. Heck, I even found the time to serve as both the Family Law Executive Chair for the Ontario Bar Association and as a member of the Canadian Bar Association, as well as sitting on numerous other committees during this time. It can be done, and I had figured it out!

But then I started talking to Avra Rosen. Avra and I had been friends in high school (her first husband was actually my first boyfriend), and though we went our separate ways in university, we both ended up working in family law in Toronto. So, Avra and I got back in touch, she had started her own practice and she encouraged me to do the same.

For a long time, though, I was too afraid. I was well supported by a firm, after all, who handled all the accounting, photocopying, word processing and more. These were things I never even had to think about. But still, Avra persisted in her encouragement.

When I expressed an interest in leaving to my partners at Gowlings, they were more than happy to continue supporting me in my journey. After all, family law in a big law firm was not as profitable, and the business model typically wasn't a great fit.

So, when I said that I wanted to strike out on my own and start my own firm, they told me to take all of my clients with me. And, because of my work with Stephen, I was able to develop a high net worth clientele.

So, I hit the ground running as president of Goldhart & Associates in 2004, sharing office space with Avra and working with just one associate and two assistants. I even found that the minute I left I made double the money!

Looking back, I was able to strategically use the lucky parts of my life to my advantage. Yes, I was strangely accepted into law school, but I went and did well. Yes, Stephen offered me a job, but I took it and worked hard to make a name for myself. I took every opportunity to build on my luck toward success and have done everything expected of me and more.

Today, I am a practiced litigator, mediator and arbitrator, spending nearly half of my time helping to resolve disputes or make decisions instead of bringing a case to court in front of a judge. My multimillion-dollar family law firm is larger than typical with a staff of fifteen, but many times over, I have encouraged associates to do as

I did to become my own lawyer, because why sit second chair their whole lives? I must be an advocate.

I thought, perhaps, that I might become a judge after leaving Gowlings, but judges in Canada report to a boss – the chief justice and Canadian government. And, when I started my own practice, I thought, why didn't I do this years ago? So, although I have been presented with opportunities to pursue this line of work over the last few years, I would now rather spend my "spare" time mentoring and supervising my staff to make them better at what they do. There is far too much value in being your own boss.

However, because of my unlikely financial success as a family lawyer in Toronto, I also make it a point to give back. For example, I currently serve on the Family Law Bench and Bar Committee, which acts as a liaison between judges, the courts and the family law bar in Ontario; the Family Law Arbitration Executive Committee; the Unified Family Court Expansion Group; the Attorney General Committee, which develops protocols for reform regarding complaints against assessors; as Chair of the Dispute Resolution Officer Program, which runs a group of lawyers who conduct conferences at the court to resolve and narrow issues in cases, which conducts education and training; and, most recently was appointed by Canadian Parliament to serve on the Judicial Advisory Committee, which reviews and recommends candidates for judicial appointment.

I really enjoy the committee work because I love to do things that assist the court, other family lawyers, and most importantly, families in Ontario. I also am a frequent guest speaker and instructor in all matters regarding family law, including the issues of mediation, physical and emotional abuse, spousal and child support, power imbalances, wills and estates, custody agreements and more.

All of this has led to me being the only family lawyer in Ontario to be awarded the Lexpert Zenith Award in 2014 and my earning the Ontario Bar Association's Award for Excellence in Family Law in 2016. Named in honor of Jay, earning this prestigious award has been the highlight of my legal career, and I am extremely proud and humbled to have accepted it in front of my children and parents.

When people ask what I do, I like to say that I help people as opposed to saying I am a lawyer. I do my best work when I am able to help people get through difficult situations, using my skills to move them through a very difficult process while getting them what they need and what they are entitled to and causing the least damage to their loved ones as possible.

After all, you do the best you can with the cards you are dealt, and to get through it without being damaged yourself or damaging anyone else is certainly an achievement – one I know all too well.

Harvey retired from his career as a lawyer nearly three years ago and we travel more frequently than we ever had to places such as Europe and Asia. Though we live in Toronto , we often summer at a cottage up north and winter in Florida.

My younger sister, who married her high school sweetheart and settled closer to home, now runs my mother's store. Though we pursued very different dreams, we are now much closer than we used to be.

My youngest daughter, now in her second year of law school at Western University, sometimes comes home on the weekends to visit, and I also try to spend as much time as possible vacationing with my other two children and three grandchildren.

Overall, I am thankful to be in a good place today despite my own past obstacles, and I would say that my life, now, is truly blessed.

POUND ON!!

LEE INNOCENTI

A true Alpha and entrepreneur, Dr. Lee Innocenti is the Founder and Principal of Performance Strategies, Ltd., a 30 - year old firm specializing in organizational development, training and executive coaching, primarily in financial services, pharmaceutical and entertainment firms.

The first member of her family to go to college, Lee holds an Ed.D. in Education Administration from Yeshiva University (NYC), an MA in Psychology from Manhattan College (NYC), and a B.A. in Mathematics from the College of Mt. St. Vincent (NYC).

LEE INNOCENTI

Leadership Lessons Learned Early

Looking back on my life's journey, I realize that the attitudes and skills I used in business I learned as a child. Once learned, these skills served to form a foundation upon which I would build other skills that carried me through all my relationships, both personal and professional. For example, with the help of wonderful mentors, I learned various business skills that, combined with earlier life lessons, gave me a set of "leadership skills" that helped me attain the top corporate position in my function. It is the awareness of lessons learned and layering one lesson on top of another that created a complex, nuanced set of behaviors that allowed for agile problem solving, regardless of the situation. Also, the support of many coworkers was an invaluable contribution to the development of my leadership skills.

I was five years old when I realized that I wanted to make as much money as possible. How? I set my mind to figure it out at FIVE! My parents never discussed money as they were not especially ambitious. But I sure was, and I began observing how my parents managed money. Mom had a shiny, blue tin box with eight compartments, each with its own labeled lid: rent, food, medical, savings, clothing, gifts, charity, and children's allowance. When we would go shopping, I would watch Mom go to the tin and take out what she needed. If one compartment was empty, after much deliberation, she would carefully take money from one compartment and move it to another. The savings compartment built up until the money went into the bank. Dad was the breadwinner in the family but Mom managed the money. I sensed women had power even then.

I received a small allowance for a series of tasks I had to complete. I had to make my bed each morning before going to school, empty the garbage, and wash or dry the dishes every night. Only on one occasion, when I was perhaps six or seven, I refused to make my bed and Mom warned me that she would charge my allowance if she was going to do my work. It was not clear to me what "charge" meant, but I still would not make my bed that day.

At the end of the week, my allowance was ten cents short of the twenty-five cents I usually earned! I was shocked and annoyed but I liked the fairness of it and I never missed completing a task again. To this day, I budget my money and am a resolute saver. I learned responsibility early. I also learned that if I didn't work, I would not get paid. Later, as a manager, I used a consequences and rewards system to motivate resistant people. I was lucky to learn all of this at such a young age.

When I was five or six years old, I asked my Mom how I could increase my allowance. It's not that I needed the money, rather, I decided that money was a way to measure my productivity and I liked measuring my progress. I was always a very competitive child; I competed with myself if there was no one else to compete with. By this time, I had several piggy banks that mimicked Mom's tin box. Allowance and holiday monies were divided among my piggy banks. I had one for savings, one for family/gifts, one for college (I knew from this exercise that I would be going to college) and one piggy bank for me. I put 50% of my money into savings and divided the rest into thirds. I learned simple division and fractions! Mom said I could volunteer to do extra tasks around the house and I would be paid additional money. She, or I, would identify potential work opportunities and we would negotiate the pay for the extra tasks. Every day I looked for ways I could help and earn more. Cleaning the oven was big pay -- a dollar! Weeding the garden was less. I learned math, to show initiative, and negotiation skills all at once.

At about seven years old, I kept thinking of how to increase my revenue and decided to open a library in my basement for the local kids. The public library was at least 15 miles away and many parents were too busy to take their children there. I saw a perfect opportunity to meet a neighborhood need, and we always had an abundance of books. Kids could borrow my books for free but had to pay a daily penny late fee if they did not return the books on time. I prayed they would be late returning books. Running this library required crude record keeping or I would not be paid. So, I learned how to organize books and data at this early age. I also had an unpaid library assistant, a best friend who just wanted to do whatever I was doing. From this I learned that people will work to be part of a meaningful or fun project.

When I was 12 years old, I wanted to go on a trip with the Girl Scouts to Washington, DC. The cost was $25, and Mom said I could go if I earned the money; she would not pay. After much deliberation about what people would buy and what I could sell, I decided to make fashion pins out of flat toothpicks glued together, painted with leftover "paint by number" paint, and then embellished with the buyer's name made from alphabet soup letters. I charged twenty-five cents a pin. My grandmother, a supervisor of the AT&T phone cafeteria, placed my handmade marketing sign by the cash register and brought home orders every night. My girlfriend in another school was conscripted to sell my wares to her school friends, for which she was paid nothing; I did not know about pyramid marketing at that time! I made my $25 quickly and had extra money for trinkets on the trip. Only years later did I ever make it up to my girlfriend for all her efforts. I learned about marketing, sales, and production. It was clear I could not be a success without help from others.

As I got older, other schemes included a lemonade stand which I set up near our home where the trolley stopped, so thirsty travelers would be in ready supply. I learned about supply and demand. Mom packed the most wonderful lunches with sandwiches, candy, fruit, nuts, and veggies. If I felt full, I would sell some of this at lunch time. Homework came easily to me, and kids would ask me for answers so they would not have to do the work. I knew from early lessons that if someone else does your work, you were "charged", so the children I thought were smart enough to do the work themselves but were lazy, I charged for each answer. If I thought they were not capable, I gave away the answers. Unconsciously, I created my own crude kind of charity which I knew was important.

I came home one day and told my mom about Jan who had "cooties". No one liked her or would play with her. Mom made me imagine how Jan felt being treated this way. I resisted this because I did not want to be like Jan. Eventually, though, I could feel her immense sadness and self-loathing whenever she would hear such name calling. In the end, Mom suggested a play date with Jan to help her feel included. I worried that if the other kids found out, I would have cooties, too. I clearly remember Mom sitting next to me, supervising my call to Jan to invite her over after school. To my surprise, Jan was a lovely girl and we became friends. Her cooties went away and they did not rub off on me. I learned not to judge people and to have compassion for others. This memory still comes up for me as I navigate transactions with some less popular colleagues.

I began to read when I was four, as my parents read to me each night. I would point to the pictures and letters and try to decipher the symbols. One day, as the family gathered around on a Sunday afternoon, I read haltingly to my grandmother and everyone was so happy, and admired my achievement. I learned being good at schoolwork would get me much admiration and attention. I decided then that I would be the best in school whenever I finally enrolled.

My parents did not send us to summer camp. My Mother wanted to spend time with us in the summer. We would go away to the mountains with Dad for two weeks as a family. Otherwise, Mom amused us during the day. Mom and Dad were Catholic, as were Dad's parents. My Mom's mother worshiped at the Episcopalian church because her preferred Presbyterian church was too far away. Mom's father was Jewish, yet Mom enrolled us, with our Baptist friends, in a free Baptist summer camp because it had a bus to pick up and return the children each day. When I questioned why I was going to a camp of a different religion, Mom explained that it was all the same to God, and I should learn how people worship differently. That sounded good to me, and I loved every minute of it. To this day, I can still sing the songs we learned in this camp when I was, maybe, eight years old. I learned great acceptance and appreciation of various religions and I still study comparative religion.

My Supportive Family Unit

My sister, Beth, is three years older than me. We had a lovely childhood together, but, given the age difference, she had her friends and I had mine. Her choice was to be a housewife and she gave our family four lovely children and eight grandchildren. Her children provided me with many hours of being a loving aunt, which satisfied all my maternal needs.

I was the first college graduate in our immediate family. My maternal grandparents married young. My maternal grandmother did not finish high school and I am not sure if my maternal grandfather did. My wealthy, Orthodox Jewish, maternal grandfather, was disowned for marrying a Presbyterian woman, and he was denied any further education by his parents. He was, however, allowed to work in the family business of hardware stores, movie theaters, and catering. He eventually, painfully, abandoned his wife and children, leaving them penniless and out on the street after being evicted for nonpayment of rent. When my mom was 17 years old, she was horrified to find her furniture on the curb when she returned home from school one day. My grandfather was a nonperson in my life. My mom and her brother deprived him of ever knowing his grandchildren, and from the day he left the house, they had nothing to do with him. In those days, there were no requirements for alimony or child support. To support the family, my grandmother went to work as a waitress in a tea shop until she moved to the AT&T cafeteria where she worked her way up from the kitchen to supervisor of the employee dining room.

My grandmother was fifth or sixth generation American with English, French Canadian, and American Indian heritage, with English traditions being dominant. My grandfather was of Russian and Hungarian descent and was second generation American. These grandparents were from Yonkers, NY. Though I did not know my grandfather, I did meet his siblings who were wonderful, and we developed a warm friendship when I was in my twenties. I learned that spouses can abandon you, that there are big disappointments in life, and that I'd best have a backup plan of self-sufficiency.

My Catholic, paternal grandparents were from Italy. At 13 years of age, my grandfather, Nono, having left behind his entire family in Florence, arrived in boat steerage and headed to Michigan to be with distant relatives. I assume he left Italy because there was no work or food, but I am not sure. He worked as a coal miner until he lost his eye due to a mining accident. My grandmother, Nona, landed on Ellis Island with her abandoned mother when she was 18 years old; they arrived from Primaluna (near Lake Como). She, too, headed to Michigan where there were relatives. My grandmother worked as a maid and her mother as a seamstress. Her father had left the family to find work in Argentina but never returned. We have no idea what happened to him. Neither my grandmother nor grandfather went beyond 6th grade in school, yet they could both read and write in two languages (Italian and English). Together, even during the Great Depression in the late 1930s, they were able to buy two homes by means of extreme penny-pinching, and funds from taking in boarders. I knew them as apartment building superintendents in later years. I learned to take pride in the immigrant experience which reinforced working hard and saving money as principles to live by.

Seeing two families abandoned by breadwinners, forcing uneducated women to survive on their own by working for low wages, I vowed I would be well educated and always be able to support myself. I would depend upon NO ONE for my food or shelter.

My mom graduated high school but turned down a college scholarship since she had to go to work to help support her family.

My Dad also graduated high school and was a successful salesman who ultimately quit his job after more than 20 years because his firm wanted him to travel and Dad would not leave my Mom at night. I learned that family always comes first.

As a salesman, my Dad had to submit expense reports every week to his company, and I would ride with him to the post office every Sunday when he submitted his report. He explained to me that though he was a successful salesman, his expenses were lower than those of the other salesmen. When I asked why, he explained that many business people falsely added extra expenses to their report so they could have more money refunded to them; that was dishonest -- a form of stealing. I learned expense reports were an indication of integrity in business. When I lost one of my hard contact lenses, I suggested to Dad that he use the insurance he had purchased for my lenses so that he would not have to buy me a new lens. He explained the insurance was for "damaged" lenses, not lost ones, even though the insurance company would never know the difference. He explained that this, too, would be dishonest. I learned integrity was a very big deal in life and it was better to spend money in order to preserve your honesty.

My parents and grandparents were my first mentors who gave me life lessons. The women in my family were strong, hardworking, capable matriarchs of the family. In those days, most women did not work outside of the home, so all the working women in my family were pathfinders ahead of me who inspired me to find a career instead of merely finding jobs. The men in my family (except one grandfather and perhaps one great-grandfather) were very loving of their women and children, supportive of the family unit, and willing to let the women manage the household. My Dad was so proud of me. He cheered for each childhood achievement, and attended every school event. He taught me sports and played with me outside. We were pals and I loved him dearly. It was my Mom, however, who, day after day, actively attended to my every challenge and event, and did all the disciplining of us children. I love her deeply, too. I liked seeing women in an equal position with men, if only in the home. Today Mom is 103 and lives with me; she is still my best friend.

High School Success

As I made my way through school, I discovered, to my dismay, that I was not the sharpest knife in the drawer. I was popular and in the top

10% of my classes. But, I had to work harder than the really smart kids to get the same good grades. I enjoyed working hard but it stung, given my out-sized ambition, to realize that I was not, nor would I ever be, number 1. I learned that I needed to work harder than most to get ahead or just achieve the same results. I was disappointed with my raw, native intelligence but satisfied with my achievements thus far, so I didn't know what to think of myself. Oddly, I won many academic awards in school even though my grades were not the best. I asked some teachers why they awarded the prize to me when clearly someone else had achieved better performance in class. They explained that I was an enthusiastic learner, willing to help others and that counted as much as the actual academic achievement. I learned that passion and helping others can differentiate performance.

By the time I got to high school, my lessons learned enabled me to be elected for various leadership roles, such as vice president of our sorority, participant in school plays, editor of the school paper and leader of various team events. I suspect it was because I completed what was required, worked hard, always respected people's feelings, never missed a deadline, thanked people profusely for their help, made projects fun, and was honest in my transactions.

I donated my time for various charities, like working as a volunteer in a hospital, to fulfill my need to help others. The principles I learned early were paying off.

I did not win any big scholarship, reinforcing that I was not as smart as I'd hoped. I was awarded a small scholarship which made me feel better. I had good grades and would get accepted by many colleges, but my parents could not afford tuition and room and board. Neither my parents nor I wanted to take on college loans; accumulating debt was shunned in my family. Since they could afford tuition only, I became a day-hop to a small Catholic college (College of Mount Saint Vincent), in the Bronx, NY. It was well known locally but not outside a 150-mile radius; nor was it competitive with any Ivy League schools. I spent those four years studying very hard to demonstrate my gratitude to my parents for their investment in me. I would go out on dates only on Saturday nights because I studied the rest of the time. I graduated with a 3.35 GPA which was the best I could achieve, even with all my diligent studying. In defense of my GPA, I had to take religion, philosophy, and Italian -- a total of 16 classes! I competed with first generation Italian girls who went to Catholic school, and were fluent in both religion and language. I did not stand a chance as a public school kid and these required courses brought my average down. The day I graduated was the last day I took money from my father, as I now knew that I would be a very good earner, even if I wasn't sure how. I was ready for independence.

Early Career Advice

My parents' greatest hope was that I would achieve more than they had, which was much more than their parents had. We were "upwardly mobile." They knew of only two careers where women were well regarded: nursing and teaching. They honestly knew of no other professional jobs open to women. I, too, had no idea there might be other options as the few, professional women we knew were teachers. Computer classes, which were brand new in my college, were closed to women; it was deemed that women would never have a technical career. The sight of blood frightened me, so I opted, reluctantly, for teaching as a career. I majored in mathematics, which I loved, and education. I graduated qualified to teach K-6 or 7-12 in mathematics. I thought two options for work would double my chances of employment. With a full-time job as a public school teacher in the Yonkers, NY system, I pursued a Master's of Psychology degree at Manhattan College, also in the Bronx, NY. I thought having the option of being a counselor would be a third option I could add to my career possibilities. I graduated as a licensed psychologist.

I got my first taste of leadership as an adult when the school superintendent selected me to join the "high potential" group of future administrators. Though I loved the children, we were in the middle of integrating the schools and the parents were rabid. Also, the school system was bankrupt, making it hard to get even pencils for children. We experienced four strikes in seven years (by teachers, administrators, custodians, and secretaries). It was very hard to teach before, during, and after the strikes that represented months of time out of the school year. I taught for only three years and was promoted to the Human Relations function (helping teachers and students figure out how to work with one another) before I went into business.

Don, my supervisor in the school system, became my first mentor, when amid stiff competition, I was selected to join his Human Resource Department. He taught me the craft of organizational development and training adults. Don was fabulous; the best Organizational Development/Training professional I have ever seen. For three years he gave me feedback EVERY single day, for a minimum of 30 minutes. No detail of my behavior was exempt from his discerning eye: my body language, my clothing, the timber of my voice, my choice of words, key points I was making, and my pedagogical methods were all grist for the mill. I listened with rapt attention to his advice, learned what a gift feedback was, and developed my technical skills while I pursued my EdD at night. Because Don was outspoken about being African American, I began to have all African American friends for a few years. Learning about this culture was both fascinating and heartbreaking: "No, we don't trust white people, not even you." Don also sent me to many external workshops to learn about myself, my behavior, and my motivations. I started reading metaphysical books to try to understand what my purpose should be in this life, but I did not find the answer at that time. I was Don's shadow, his clone; with his care and feeding I grew very rapidly. He crafted state of the art interventions to help the children, teachers, and parents integrate and I could see changes in the behavior of children, parents, and teachers after working with us. We were having an effect. Don left the school system to go into business, leaving me in tears and to find my own way. I decided that I, too, must leave and go into business. I would follow in his footsteps and secure a job in business, but in a different company.

Business Mentors Were All Around

In a school system, many women are administrators (school management staff). They earn the same salary as their male counterparts. I had heard it was different in business. I now needed business mentors to help me navigate and understand this new environment and I found several devoted, caring men to help me.

I started as an Organizational Development/Training specialist for Automatic Data Processing. In the beginning, I had no idea how I would find my voice, be heard, and be invited into important discussions. We had more than 100 regional offices that were profit centers. These profit centers received a report card every month on about 20 dimensions that were published worldwide to all management, with a winner declared for the month. Always looking for a way to measure my contribution, I thought if I could improve one or more of the criteria on the report card, I would add value to the business. In the company, women in leadership positions were rare, and I knew I had to earn entry into the "boys club" by demonstrating that I could help their business. With my staff, we started doing team interventions around the country, and to our surprise and delight, the offices where we worked always won the award for the month's best overall performance and continued to perform well thereafter. I had found a way to demonstrate competence that the men would acknowledge as very helpful. Thereafter, I was admitted to senior level meetings with relative ease. I had found my voice and my team's voice in this predominantly male company.

The company was very proud of itself when it made me the first corporate female vice president. I was thrilled, and my coworkers seemed genuinely happy for me. My corner office was huge, and seemingly, too big for someone like me. I moved my desk where coworkers walking by could not see me in this large office, lest anyone realize I really did not belong in such a lofty space. Did I deserve this title? Was I a fraud? I wasn't sure. In the meantime, I made sure that when you walked by my office you could only see the important visitors, and I hoped observers would wonder who owned this office to attract such august people. It took me about a year to rearrange my office so that my desk was again visible. I learned many women felt this way as they started to achieve success.

I now needed no mentor for my craft, as Don was so thorough, and I could grow in my technical skills through various seminars and conferences. I was not prepared for the politics of business, and did not understand how it all worked. Here I needed much help. Various executives asked me if I ever played sports. What? In those days, there were NO intramural sports for girls, only cheerleading or twirling. What did this have to do with leading? My first business supervisor, Bernie, was a very talented executive who seemed to be able to get anything approved and was liked by everyone. His staff, including me, adored him. We would do anything for him, and I was inspired to be just like him. I decided he would be my mentor who would decipher sports questions and all things political for me.

I watched him in meetings, going toe to toe with other men. While I admired his guts and fast thinking, I instinctively knew that, as a woman, I could not behave the same way he did; at times he used profanity, raised his voice, or was threatening. Yet, there were no women executives to guide me. Bernie and I had many discussions about how to influence people in the organization. I listened and watched carefully, picking out bits of behavior I thought I could use.

Cleverly, I thought, I will use my staff to train me on how to be a good manager and leader, while also developing their technical skills. Every six months, the newest team member would gather anonymous data, which is a skill, from all my staff, a few peers, and my supervisor. After, he or she would consolidate the data (a skill) and prepare a professional report for me to share with my supervisor (a skill). Lastly, he or she would deliver the feedback to me (a skill) and, then, deliver the feedback to my staff and me in a joint meeting (a skill). Admittedly, I was often disappointed with my feedback, as I hoped I was so much better than what the report said. However, I could not deny the examples proffered. I enlisted my team and my supervisor to help me improve some specific leadership/ management behaviors of mine during the next six months and they were empowered to give me feedback anytime about my behavior -- and they did! I did this twice a year for many years. Not only was I becoming a better leader, but my staff was becoming better at their craft, too. Life was so good. I was passionate about my job, my staff, and my company. I was learning to lead by following advice from my team. Individuals may be wrong about something, but rarely is the entire group wrong. My staff became my loud, vocal compass. Constant feedback was the lifeblood of success.

Along the way, after each major project, I asked for feedback from my stakeholders. I listened carefully to how I, and my team, could improve and how we could be more effective. Bernie would weigh in with his opinions on my competence, and I always had a set of goals to achieve for the department and for him. There were layoffs in the company over the years, and people were threatened with losing their job, though I was rather sanguine about not being let go. Bernie assured me my job security was in my skill set, my reputation, and my network. And he believed that, were I to be eliminated, I would land somewhere good. So I did not lose sleep over cutbacks. I imbued my staff with the same sense of confidence in themselves. We were never let go. After working many years together, Bernie retired and I was again bereft of a "godfather" figure.

I enjoyed working with my next supervisor for two years. He was very politically supportive of my initiatives but was recruited away to another firm. My third boss, to my dismay, was devoid of integrity or a moral compass. I found him grossly cheating on his expense report, blaming his wonderful secretary every time he was late for a meeting, and lying when it served him. To remain silent would have been the politically correct thing to do, but I could not let him think that we were all so stupid that we did not notice his lapses of integrity and moral judgment. When I confronted him on his expense report and verbal abuse of his secretary (she was an icon of efficiency and effectiveness), I knew I was deciding my fate. I would not work for someone I did not respect and, therefore, would leave this company I loved to start my own business. It was time for my services to produce revenue for my own consulting firm, instead of being an "expense" to a firm.

During those eleven years I learned:

1. You can work people hard, but you must never deny them their dignity.
2. A successful termination is when the employee is able to say, "Thank you for helping me leave a place where I do not fit in."
3. Caring for the whole employee (their family, health, career, and emotional well-being) is critical to gaining their loyalty.

4. A manager may be best friends with her employees, but must maintain a position of respect and leadership.
5. Honesty is paramount in all dialogue; it allows one to speak about her feelings and thoughts authentically in small or large group settings.
6. If you are going to do something that might harm a person's career, you must warn them. Invite them to the meeting where the matter will be discussed so that they have an opportunity to make a defense. As an example, I had a 50-year-old, married, purchasing vice president who was having an affair with his new secretary; she was 25 years old. The problem was not the affair per se. The problem was that he was falsifying her time card so that they could have long, leisurely lunches, take three-day weekends, and travel overseas on business trips without his professional staff. The 15 other young, professional women working for him were furious about his duplicity and that he awarded perks based on sexual relations. The young women told me of their plan to discuss his affair with his wife. They would also initiate a class action lawsuit if he didn't end the time card fraud and if he didn't stop awarding perks unfairly. I was

hired to improve team relationships. My concern was that once the women coalesced, they might bring this action against the company for discrimination. I showed the VP three pages of examples of illegal and inappropriate behavior with his secretary. He admitted the allegations were true but, shockingly, he refused to modify his behavior! I explained to him that his behavior put our large, international, and well-known retail company at risk for a lawsuit. I asked him if he wanted to be present when I discussed the information with Corporate. I explained that my intent was not to harm him, but to protect the company from a lawsuit initiated by his staff and to create a well-functioning team. As a consultant, I had knowledge of a possible class action lawsuit being brought against the company, and I was obligated to share that fact with corporate staff so that they could mitigate the situation. Together, we set a meeting date, and I related to him the exact information I would present to Corporate so that he could prepare his defense. While we never became best friends, he had a chance to defend himself before Corporate, my integrity was left intact, and the lawsuit was avoided. In the end, the VP was moved to a different role with no direct reports, and a new VP was brought in to take over the department and restore integrity. The secretary was reassigned and ultimately, they married a few years later.

7. If you generously acknowledge your team's contribution to the department's accomplishments, privately and publicly, the team solidifies and team members' political value increases. Basically, your employees will shine, and you will glow in their light.
8. Promote your best employees, even though you will hate losing them. Having these valuable advocates for you operating throughout the organization will make negotiating various items throughout the company easier for you in the long run.
9. A competent team is essential. Help poor performers to improve or let them go. Allowing poor performers to linger helps no one, least of all yourself.
10. You owe employees direct, specific feedback for every performance, good or bad. Employees should also be reviewed twice a year, whether mandated or not.
11. If you can't offer advancement yourself, be a part of your employees' career development planning, even if that means

encouraging them to leave the company to work for the competition.

12. If you can't be loyal to your supervisor, look for work under a different supervisor or leave. You shouldn't work for someone you can't support.

Jumping Off the Cliff with a Parachute

ADP was reorganizing and I saw an opportunity to leave gracefully. I offered to resign, along with some of my staff, if we were given generous severance packages. My unpleasant supervisor was eager to bring in his own people who would ignore his transgressions, and he quickly agreed to make a deal with me. He even threw in more money if I could get my sick employee to leave with me. We were jubilant with our generous severance packages.

I had kept an "alumni" list of executives who had left the company in the previous four years, and thought I would start my own consulting firm with these alumni as potential clients. Many were now presidents of Fortune 500 companies, heads of Human Resources, and vice presidents of various operations departments. Before my last day at ADP, I had secured 100 days of consulting work with one client, and I had my severance package. So my transition, though scary, was financially secure; at least for the first two years.

Selling was new to me. Now my job was to figure out what services to market, what my unique service proposition would be, market my services, find work, sign deals, develop consulting materials for training programs or organizational development interventions, deliver the programs, and, on the weekends, do all the administrative work. 80-hour work weeks were the norm and I loved it. There was no work-life balance. My supportive husband had his own business and was busy working crazy hours too. We both traveled. Our weekend rendezvous were exciting and sustaining. Mutually, we agreed that a life with no children would suit us both and allow us to focus on our beloved work.

Clients referred their friends to me; I was passed from one friend to another, gaining clients and growing revenue. As my firm grew, some of my previous employees from ADP joined us. So I could again work, travel the world, and have fun with my dear friends, while we supported ourselves very well. My focus was financial services firms, pharmaceuticals, and entertainment -- money, drugs, and rock and roll. Everything I learned up to this point I used to grow and sustain my business. In the first twenty-five years, I did not have one unsold consulting day. Sometimes I would be so weary from work, but I always knew I was lucky to have found my niche.

My Purpose Finally Revealed

Many years after I left ADP, former female colleagues called me to catch up. To my surprise, each referred to me as her mentor. I had done no such thing that I was aware of. All those times that I had lunch, coffee, or took phone calls from mostly younger women, discussing their business dilemmas, they saw as mentoring. I saw it as just being a friend. It is true that anyone who wanted some help or advice could always get some of my time. To this day, I spend about two hours a week helping others, which is a huge source of satisfaction and joy for me. Just a little bit, I like to think, I help the world turn. Now that I am semi-retired, I find myself helping the children of my former colleagues and clients with their resumés, their networking, or their job-hunting process. No one makes it in business without significant help. I have been blessed.

Lee, Grandmother, and sister Beth

Lee, Beth and their Father

Lee and Jan

Lee and Bernie

Lee and her Mother

Typical executive offsite.

AMY LIEBSCHUTZ LONDON

Raised in Cincinnati Ohio in a musical family, Amy London followed her (mother's) dream to New York City and abroad to establish her powerful career as a jazz singer, performer and teacher. Well-respected by the jazz community around the globe, Amy developed music programs and teaches jazz in New York City and in jazz camps all over the world.

An Alpha to the core, Amy raised her family while juggling the demands of a performing career under the bright lights, mostly in New York. A brilliant networker whose courage on stage is truly remarkable, Amy sang with her sisters growing up and earned a music degree from Syracuse University before embarking on her stage career.

POUND ON!!

AMY LIEBSCHUTZ LONDON

Dispelling The Myth Of The Chick Singer

I was born a chick singer, there was no avoiding it. Music was pervasive in my house when I arrived. I am the youngest of 3 daughters, and my Mom's family was and still is full of musicians. My Mom, Edith Leshner, was a radio actress in the 1940s and played piano. My Mom's youngest brother, Uncle Gene, at 90 plus, is still a tenor sax player, and in his youth traveled with the Ray Anthony and Johnny Long Big Bands. My Mom's second youngest brother, Uncle Don, was a jazz DJ and voiceover actor. I even heard his most famous commercial in NYC in the early 90s, "Kahn's Wieners: The Weiner The World Awaited!" Mom's older brother, my Uncle Saul, sang songs. His big hit was "I Left My Heart In San Francisco" with which he regaled us with at every holiday. He also told jokes a la Henny Youngman. All 5 of my Uncle Saul's kids are professional or amateur musicians. My elder sister Linda is a professional singer, who was the first call choral alto in San Fransisco throughout the 80s, 90s and 00s, and is on a variety of early music recordings from those years, with the San Francisco Symphony Chorus, American Bach Soloists, Arvo Paert, and others. My middle sister Patty possesses little singing talent, and certainly never pursued music professionally like Linda and I did. The joke amongst the 3 of us is, my email is amylondonsings, Linda's is liebsings, and Patty's is patdontsing!

My Dad, David Liebschutz, always claimed to be tone deaf, and that there was no musical talent on his side at all, except that his Uncle Harry improvised on the organ at the movie theaters for Silent Films. Perhaps that is the only glimmer of musical talent on his side.

I am on the tail end of the Baby Boomers, born into a very comfortable middle class Jewish family in Cincinnati, Ohio. My maternal Grandma, Anna Leshner (nee Sonya Vogel) was a refugee from the Ukraine, and barely survived the ethnic cleansing of Jews that was happening around the turn of the century in Russia. At the age of 14 or 15, her parents booked her passage on a ship to Ellis

Island, probably around 1910, and she was orphaned the moment she said goodbye to them, much like the scene in 'Fiddler on the Roof,' when Hodel sings 'Far From The Home I Love' and says goodbye to her father Tevye and her little shtetl, then boards a train to Siberia to join her husband, Perchik. The difference is that instead of joining Perchik the Revolutionary at a gulag, Grandma Anna came to New York City, lived briefly with her half brother Max Vogel in the Bronx, and worked at a sweat shop in Lower Manhattan.

Grandma Anna did not like busy, crowded NYC, or working in a sweat shop, so she traveled to Cincinnati to become the cleaning woman for her wealthy cousins, the Safers. There she met my Grandfather Sam Leshner, also a refugee from Russia. He was born in Kiev, and probably emigrated around the same time as Grandma, but was luckier: he and his 3 brothers and a sister made it safely to Ohio, and were actually able to go back to Kiev and later bring their mother to America.

Grandma's maiden name was Sonia Vogel, and it was changed at Ellis Island, like so many others, to Anna Vogel. Grandpa Sam's real last name was Leschtiner, thus Leshner in America. Grandma and Grandpa were very poor, but very happy. They settled in rural

Hamilton, Ohio, just half an hour outside of Cincinnati, in a house in the country that probably looked a lot more like Grandma's shtetl in Komenetz Poldolsk than the tenements of New York City did.

Grandma had a beautiful, naturally operatic voice. My memories of her are wonderful; she was so sweet, so loving, always so happy to see all of us. She made her incredible butter cookies so often that her hands always smelled like butter. She would caress my face and say, "Shayne punim" and kiss me. She is so beloved in our family, that all 4 of our girls, my two daughters, and Linda's two daughters, are named after her: Linda's Shoshanna and Amara, my Sofia and Anna.

Grandma Anna never learned to read or write English, but she was a wizard of a homemaker. She never once made a mistake at the grocery store, she made delicious matzo ball soup, gefilte fish from scratch for Passover, and the aforementioned cookies as well as a wonderful honey cake for Rosh Hashanah. She was always in the kitchen singing as she cooked. When my Mom was a teen, she and Grandma used to go to downtown Cincinnati, look in the fancy dress shop windows, my Mom would choose what she liked, and Grandma would go home and make the clothing for her from scratch, no pattern.

Grandpa Sam had a gorgeous high baritone voice, and was a well-trained Yeshiva boy. In shule, he would stand next to the rabbi and sing the entire torah and haftorah, like a cantor, even though by trade he was a used car salesman. Grandma and Grandpa Leshner were poor, but they had a loving, happy family. In my memory, Grandma never spoke about the horrors she witnessed when Jews around her in her village were being slaughtered. She was just happy all the time, and no doubt so grateful to have this beautiful family, and food on the table. The only thing she complained about was that Grandpa Sam was constantly bringing strangers home to eat at their house; he had so much empathy for those struggling, and this was during the Depression.

My Dad's parents were descendants of German refugees that arrived in Cincinnati in 1851, when there was a huge influx of Germans to Ohio and all over the midwest, both Jewish and non-Jewish. To this day, you can still look in the phone book in Cincinnati, and see a lot of German names. My Dad's ancestors, Leon Safdi, from Egypt, and Carolyn Bertelheimer, from Germany, were married in Cincinnati in the mid 1800s. My Dad was a merchant, like so many of his friends, and as was typical for a successful Jewish businessman, he was in the 'shmata' business. He owned a string of high end women's clothing stores in Cincinnati, called 'Martins' Town and Country.' (He certainly wasn't going to call the stores 'Liebschutz's!'.) His family, having lived there for several generations, was able to establish itself financially as successful merchants. He was not a first generation child. Instead, his father gave him a millinery store (hat and gloves) to run when he was only sixteen years old.

When my Dad met my Mom, a beautiful svelte gal I refer to as a 'Jewish fox,' she became a living model for his fashions, along with her two sisters-in-law, and thus began our family: A first generation pretty Jewish woman married to a successful businessman, and a very comfortable home in a comfortable neighborhood. We weren't super rich, nor were we super spoiled, but we lacked for nothing.

TV and record players were very big in our house. We grew up in the era of Ed Sullivan, The Flintstones, Patty Duke, The Twilight Zone, Bewitched, etc. In the mail we regularly received newly marketed convenience food samples from Proctor and Gamble, which was the big industry in Cincinnati, (think 1 2 3 Jell-O, Velveeta cheese and SpaghettiOs. Serious junk food!) There were two cars in every driveway, pink and turquoise kitchens were the norm, and a piano in every living room. The piano was in the house before I was born. Baldwin Piano Company was based in Cincinnati, and we had a Baldwin Acrosonic Upright piano, which I still have in my home today. I am very sentimentally attached to it. When we were little girls, my Mom had a favorite song, "Forest of the Flowers," that she would play and we would skip and dance around the living room. She also played "Body and Soul." And that was about it. She never practiced, and as the years went by she would lose a few bars of this, a few bars of that, always complaining that she couldn't do it anymore, but never willing to practice to retain it.

Dad was a very distant personality, perhaps a typical post WW II man. He was fiscally responsible, but left the child rearing and home keeping to Mom. He came home from work every night at 10:00 p.m., and Mom always had to make a second dinner just for him. He had no idea how to deal with a house full of noisy, mouthy, opinionated little girls, so he basically shut us out. I know that he meant well, but after two failed marriages, I know that my lack of any kind of emotional connection to my Dad had a huge impact on my ability to choose the right partners. It is only now, in my early 60s, and after decades of therapy, that I have finally figured out how to ask for what I need in a relationship, that I can't fix what was wrong with the relationship with my father, and also how to avoid the wrong types of men.

My Mom overcompensated for our lack of any relationship with our Dad, and for his explosive temper. We were generally afraid of him; at 6' 3" he was quite an imposing and sometimes frightening figure. If we ever needed anything from him, Mom was our filter. As I said, she came from this raucous, funny, fun loving musical family. She was an actress and pianist in her youth, and as a teen she was the star of the dramas in her high school. She used to love to tell us how she was the character actress in Clifford Odet's "Waiting for Lefty." She was so good at pulling off a Brooklyn accent, that one day, in the stall in the girls' bathroom at her high school, she overheard some younger girls talking about her, wondering if she really was from Brooklyn and talked like that! She was so proud of that. After high school, from the late 1930s through the 40s, my Mom was in a quartet of actors who performed live on the radio every Friday night. It must have been such a thrill for my grandparents and uncles to turn on the radio and hear her weekly. No doubt she was a small town celebrity in Hamilton, Ohio.

So this was the atmosphere that formed me: A fun loving, beautiful warm and funny Mom who took care of everything, a distant but successful father, the most adorable, sweet and wonderful Russian immigrant grandparents who adored us, and spoke Yiddish as their first language. My Dad's mother, Goldie, was wonderful and loving, and unfortunately died of cancer when I was only 5. Dad's father Leon was generally grumpy and nasty, and Dad told us that when he was a little boy, he was not allowed to speak at the dinner table.

Grandpa Leon, who had to be 5' 5" at the most, had an enormous appetite and was round as a globe. He had a white mustache, a ring of white hair around his bald head, and always wore those super high waisted men's pants, I remember he favored brown pants, with a thin brown leather belt and a white shirt tucked in. He looked like a cross between Humpty Dumpty and a globe, his belt the circumference between the northern and southern hemispheres. How he fathered 3 tall, slender good looking men is beyond me, and Grandma was a saint - it certainly wasn't the mailman! I remember Mom always had him over for Sunday dinners; he lived 10 years past Grandma Goldie. One Sunday dinner while we were eating, I remember him making a snide comment about my big appetite. I regret to this day that I didn't have the chutzpah to say, "Gee, Grandpa, I wonder who I inherited it from!!" But I was about 8, and generally terrified of him.

I had my own room in our house as a kid, and my own bathroom, too. It was the smallest of 4 bedrooms, as the youngest child usually gets the smallest room. Considering the attached bathroom, I probably was living in the maid's room. I was a girly girl, my bedroom was pink, and I was probably OCD, the neatest child anyone could imagine. I was so obsessive compulsive about tidiness, that my underwear, socks and wardrobe were color coded, and I used to line my stuffed animals along the wall, and kiss them each good night, every night.

But other than this extraordinary neatness, which from a psychological view was probably my attempt to maintain control in a somewhat dysfunctional, chaotic household, the MOST important thing in my room was my clock radio. I had that radio on constantly, and sang along with it and memorized songs from birth. When I was two years old, my favorite songs were "Johnny Angel" and "I Wanna be

Bobby's Girl." A few years later, my two older sisters, Patty and Linda and I watched the Beatles' debut performance on the Ed Sullivan show, jumping up and down on my parents' bed and witnessing this historic performance on their black and white Zenith TV. At the age of 6, I was harmonizing with Linda, age 12, as she played guitar and sang folk songs of the day. At the age of 8, I began reading music, and I was probably the only kid in 3rd grade who loved playing the recorder, and being in choir. I also began piano lessons at age 8, and I was reading music in choir all the way through high school. I am one of the lucky Americans who grew up in a time when serious music was still cherished and well supported in the public school system. I have been reading music since age 8, and between that and my piano skills, I developed musical ability at a very early age.

At age 12, one day my sister Patty brought home Laura Nyro's Eli and the 13th Confession. I absolutely flipped out when I heard it. I still have that scratched LP that I played constantly for years. Up until that time, I was a decent pianist for my age, and singing in choir. Thanks to Laura, I discovered how to sing and express myself as a solo singer. Fortunately, some wise music book publisher released a songbook of 4 of her records and my Mom bought it for me. That dog-eared copy is still on my piano. Thanks to my sight-reading abilities at the piano, I was able to play through Laura's entire repertoire and play the arrangements on the piano that were very close to what she played on her recordings. For some reason, I was able to imitate her voice pretty accurately. Every single day after school, I would come home, and sit at the piano for a few hours, playing her music and singing my heart out.

Laura Nyro is a combination of many elements that spoke to me at the time. She was a prodigy that grew up in the Bronx in a house of left wing Jews. Her aunt turned her on to opera, but she was also very heavily influenced by a cappella singing, and would hang out in the subways and sing in groups with her friends when she was growing up. She was also very influenced by jazz. There is a very famous photo of Miles Davis hanging out with her at her recording session at Columbia records in the late 60s. Laura was half Eastern European Jewish/half Italian, she had a full figure and long flowing black hair. She described herself floating around NYC in her long skirts and hippy blouses, writing songs about what she saw and observed on the streets. She went to Music and Art High school, and before she graduated, she had already written some hits, such as

Wedding Bell Blues and Stoned Soul Picnic, which were hits for the Fifth Dimension, and Stoney End, a hit for Barbra Streisand, And When I Die, a hit for Three Dog Night. She was so successful in her late teens and early 20s that she retired from the music business in her mid 20s. She was a pure artist, so brilliant and such a soulful singer, she hated the business and moved out of the city to a house in the countryside in Connecticut. We unfortunately lost her in 1996, she died from Ovarian Cancer at age 49, same as her mother.

During my teen angst years, Laura's soulfulness and deeply expressive, powerful voice answered all the loneliness and insecurity I was experiencing. I never felt like I was one of the pretty girls, but I always knew that I could sing circles around anyone. Thanks to my innate musical talent, the fact that I was surrounded by a musical family, and growing up in the feminist era, with such female musical heroes as Laura Nyro, Joni Mitchell and Carole King, I found an identity that not only determined my entire adult life, but gave me the confidence that I needed to feel good about myself.

Growing up in the 60s and 70s was such a mixed bag: there were the civil rights and feminist movements, which were such a strong influence on me. I don't know if it was my lively, verbose and funny Mom's family, or if it was the feistiness of the times, but I have been an outspoken, opinionated gal since childhood. I remember standing on my teacher's desk in 8th grade, giving a speech about Women's Liberation, while the boys threw paper airplanes at each other in the back of the room. I remember putting on a black armband as a little girl, and marching in protests against the Vietnam War. I walked the 8 miles to school on Earth Day to save on auto exhaust.

Even though my Dad was emotionally vacant, he always supported our endeavors to achieve. He was, in his own way, an early male feminist. There were several female shop owners on his side of the family in Cincinnati, his first cousin Roz Epstein was one of the first doctors in her community, having become a doctor in the 1930's. My Dad was very proud of the fact that he attended the ordination of the first woman rabbi in America, Sally Priesand. Rabbi Priesand was ordained in 1972 at our Reform Jewish Synagogue, Plum Street Temple, a stunning Moorish style architectural masterpiece on the National Historic Landmark Registry, built in 1865.

On the flip side was the constant pressure in our family to look good and be junior models of the fashions of Martins', Dad's store. The three of us couldn't have rebelled more against that concept. First of all, Linda and I were not born tall and skinny, even though middle sister Patty is tall and skinny, so any kind of modeling was out for me. Considering the fact that Patty has been a card carrying communist her entire life, she could not have rebelled more against being a junior model for Martins'.

I always refer to my parents as 'Jewish Mad Men.' They hung out with other good looking, successful Jewish couples. The wives were all housewives, no career women, and they were all perfect looking, thin, fashionable. They all went out together every Saturday night, the men smoking their cigars, the women with their weekly visits to the beauty parlor, big diamond rings and fur coats.

My sisters and I, at very early ages, made a decision to not grow up and be that way. We all escaped from that insular world as soon as we could. Linda became a hippie the moment she went to college, Patty moved out in 11th grade, and I couldn't wait to get away from that stifling environment. I always had friends of all colors, religions and sexual orientation, and I was drawn to the jazz world as a 12 year old. Aside from the spectacular music, the jazz community is open to all people, regardless of race or religion.

The other big influence in media at that time was Twiggy, and the mod movement from London. Twiggy was a freak of nature, no doubt she was anorexic to maintain that look. The entire pop/op art, mod movement was pervasive in those days, all over the covers of Glamour and Seventeen magazine, on TV, everywhere you could find ads and commercials. As impressionable young women, these images of tall skinny Twiggy and others that looked like her were seared in our brains. Being born into a zoftig Jewish family, where big boobs and big, child bearing, bales-of-hay-lifting hips were the norm, this was an impossible image to match physically, and caused so many of us in our generation to develop serious body dysmorphia problems.

As a result, and also because the message the 3 of us got from our father that we were not pretty and that we were too fat, I had little confidence in my physical attractiveness. Granted all this, I really was a beautiful child, but I always felt ugly.

Mix all of this together, rebelling against the status quo of the model woman, the hippie and revolutionary movements and the arrival on the scene of Laura Nyro, Shirley Chisolm and Gloria Steinem, the outcome was what I became: a really great singer. I knew that even though I wasn't the prettiest or thinnest girl in my high school, but I could sing circles around just about every other girl in the school.

My main identity in high school became the girl who could sing and play like Laura Nyro and Carole King, and I was also an accomplished choral singer, making my way into the elite Walnut Hills High School 16 Voice Ensemble. Naturally, when applying to colleges, I decided I wanted to be a professional singer and majored in voice in college. My parents naively said ok, they never once gave me that 'Don't you think you should major in music education?" speech. I honestly think they figured that, like my Mom, I would perform a little bit, and then move back to Cincinnati and marry some nice, rich Jewish doctor or lawyer.

However, this rebellious, smart, talented mouthy gal was having none of that. My Mom shipped me and my sister off to Dr. Sidney Peerless, the plastic surgeon who did all the Jewish girls' nose jobs in Cincinnati, the minute the 3 of us got our periods. Mom was gorgeous, and had a big nose, and was always kvetching about her nose. The 3 of us were brainwashed that our noses were ugly, so off I went at 15 for my nose job. By the time I got to college, always a place where one can start over and redefine, I had a little fake shiksa nose, long blonde hair, and learned how to do my makeup, instead of looking like a hippie all the time.

I flourished in college. I sang with bands the entire time I was there, was in several musicals and the lead in 'Candide' my senior year. I was a musical theatre major my Freshman year, but got out after I saw how the talent deficient skinny bottle blonde Barbie Doll types got cast in plays and I did not, because they were sleeping with the drama director, or looked like soap opera stars. Funny, that is still so much in play in show biz today.

I had a wonderful voice teacher, classical bass baritone Donald Miller. I stuck with him all 4 years at college. The first thing I learned was Bel Canto singing, a method of singing developed by Italians 500 years ago that is the basis for voice lessons globally. Mr. Miller helped me develop my opera sound. I started off with the classic 'Caro Mio Ben' everybody's first song - a love song in Italian from the 17th century. I fell in love with the Italian language, took two years of Italian Language in college, and spent my junior Spring semester in Florence, Italy. This was a life changing experience. Once I learned that I could get by in a foreign country all by myself, and speak enough of the language to explore Italy and get on a bus or a train, get back to the place I was staying, or walk into a market and negotiate a price in Italian, I knew that I could go anywhere in the world and be fine. This definitely gave me the courage to leave safe Ohio and move to New York City.

In my sophomore year at college, there was an audition to be the singer with the Syracuse University Big Band. The director, Steve Marcone, who is now in the music dept. at William Paterson College in NJ, told the 3 of us girls auditioning for the job to "Go find 'Shiny Stockings' and come back next week and sing it," kind of like the Wizard of Oz telling Dorothy to find the broomstick of the Wicked Witch of the West. I immediately went to a record store in downtown Syracuse, and bought a recording of Ella Fitzgerald singing 'Shiny Stockings' with The Count Basie Orchestra. I memorized it, went back the following week, and sang it for Mr. Marcone, and got the gig. The other two girls showed up, unprepared, not knowing the song, and asked me how I knew it. I said, "I went and found it!" This was a defining moment for me, proving that with hard work and smarts, I could get ahead and get the gig. It also led to 3 years of keeping the gig, and having the opportunity to sing with jazz legends Thad Jones, Mel Lewis and Phil Woods, who all visited Syracuse to do workshops with the students and perform with the big band.

After college, I had another defining moment which showed me that chutzpah and perseverance can work. There was a production of 'Fiddler on the Roof' being produced at a professional dinner theatre near my hometown. This was hands down my favorite musical since Hodel was the life story of Grandma Anna. I had always wanted to play Hodel, so the minute I heard there were auditions, I ran to the theater and auditioned with Hodel's beautifully sad song, 'Far From the Home I Love,' which I had just sung at my graduation voice recital at SU.

The director did not like me, and did not offer me the part. I was devastated, but a few days later, I went to a show at Playhouse in the Park, a renowned professional theatre in Cincinnati, and low and behold, the musical director/pianist for 'Fiddler on the Roof', Kristen Blodgett (she went on after that to work for Andrew Lloyd Weber for many years) was sitting right behind me. I overheard her say to the person she was with that she was involved with 'Fiddler', and that they had not yet cast Hodel or Tzeitel. I turned around and said, 'Excuse me, I just graduated from college with a degree in opera, I would love to audition for 'Fiddler.' She gave me the name of the producer, I called him and went for a second audition. Kristen was there at the piano, and the producer was there, but the director was not there. They both loved me, and offered me my choice of Tzeitel or Hodel. I of course took the part of Hodel. The show, an Equity production, ran from September to December, 1979, 8 shows a week, and we received excellent reviews in all of the local papers. The harshest critic in the Cincinnati Enquirer said that I was a 'marvelous Hodel with a mesmerizing voice.' Needless to say, the director wasn't too happy with me the whole time. It turned out he was just another sleazy director that wanted to get into girls' pants, and at the audition it was probably very clear that that wasn't going to happen with me.

After Fiddler closed, Hodel and Tzeitel hopped into Hodel's Honda wagon and drove from Cincinnati to NYC. I spent 10 days in New York, and absolutely fell in love with it, and decided to move here. I had another performing job waiting for me as a singing waitress in Florida for 6 months after 'Fiddler' closed. It was my first 'dues' job. The owners of the restaurant called the job a 'college semester,' did not pay us any salary, packed the joint with 300 alta cockers from Century Village 6-nights-a-week who only tipped a nickel. We only made tips, with the carrot hanging in front of our noses that we would get $1000 if we made it to the end of the 'semester.' My friend, Equity actor from NYC Johnny Kudan, who played Perchik in Fiddler, told me I needed $3000 to move to NYC, so I was determined to earn it.

I was the worst waitress on the planet. I did not make good tips, but I managed to get the $3000 I needed, and in August, 1980, I came to NYC to look for an apartment, and I have been here ever since. That was almost 39 years ago. When I first moved here, I was very ambitious, overly confident, somewhat naive, and pursued every little tiny lead of singing work that I could find. I immediately got hired to sing in the Trinity Church choir, on Wall Street and met jazz singer Judy Niemack there, who introduced me to the jazz scene. I got gigs in clubs right away, and started to meet lots of other singers and instrumentalists, and developed a community of peers instantly. I still sing and play with some of those wonderful musicians to this day.

My social life has always been going out to jazz clubs with my peers and friends to listen to music, and to perform it. This started way back in Cincinnati. I first heard live jazz as a 7th grader at Walnut Hills High School. We had a fantastic big band, and the minute I heard them, I was hooked on jazz for life. The director, Gary Johnston and I are now Facebook friends! There were some renowned musicians that came out of that big band, most notably pianist/composer Fred Hersch, who also moved to NYC, and has led a very productive life of recordings and compositions. He has been nominated for Grammy's countless times, and is one of the most respected pianists on the jazz scene. Marc Wolfley held down the drum chair, and has been the principal drummer with the Cincinnati Pops Orchestra since the 1980s.

In NYC, I hung out at all the clubs I could possibly go to. The 1980's were cooking with live jazz. There was a club called Bradley's on University at 11th Street, that was THE hangout for all jazz musicians, open until 4:00 a.m. If the cats weren't playing there, they would come by after their own gigs. Judy Niemack and I used to go there all the time. We saw many legends such as pianists Tommy Flannigan, Hank Jones, Michel Petrucianni and so many more, and many legendary bass players. One night, Phyllis Diller came bursting into the club, very loaded, and ran over to the piano, pushing the pianist off the bench, saying 'Lemme play the piano…." And she did!

She was a good pianist. That was a fun celebrity sighting - one of many more to come!

I worked as a jazz singer regularly, and also sang at a lot of weddings, which was good money, plus whatever singing jobs I could find. I sang in several a cappella vocal groups that performed at schools and whenever there was a vocal jazz group job, I seemed to get the call. In August of 1989, I got a phone call from John Miller, a bassist who has booked the orchestras for Broadway shows for decades. He told me that Cy Coleman had written a new show, "City of Angels," and that Cy wanted a vocal jazz quartet in the show ala Manhattan Transfer. I knew that this was a great call for me and I knew I was 'right' for the show. I went to the audition and aced it immediately (this was after many other auditions and gigs that I did not get.) At the audition table were Cy Coleman, playwright Larry Gelbart, musical director for the quartet Yaron Gershovsky (Manhattan Transfer's music director for more than 40 years now) and David Zippel, the lyricist.

I sang "On The Sunny Side of the Street" and "Moody's Mood for Love" for my audition, went out into the hall, expected to just go home, but instead was invited back into the room numerous times to sing with a combination of other singers. Finally, Cy Coleman looked me and said, "Amy, will you be the soprano?" Thankfully, I had been in show biz long enough to know that an offer to be in a Broadway show should be answered with a resounding "Yes!"

I was out of my mind with joy! I remember heading uptown, getting off the train at Columbus Circle, calling my mom collect from a payphone and shouting, 'Mom, guess what, I'm going to be in a Broadway show!!!' My parents of course were overjoyed, and saw the show many times. I have to say, even though the show was a huge hit, nominated for 11 Tony Awards and winning 6, the best and most fun part of the entire experience was the rehearsal process. We would receive new music every day since the authors were constantly editing, so there would be daily changes. The other 3 singers in the quartet were also great readers, so we had a lot of fun reading through this very challenging music. The show was magnificent, the cast was amazing, and it was pure joy to be in the presence of such top shelf actors, Cy, Larry and David. Working with Yaron was a dream. Mom and Dad came up for opening night. My Mom bumped right into Paul Newman and Joanne Woodward after the show when she was on her way up to my dressing room. I bumped into Angela Lansbury back stage, who told me I was "Marvelous!" My reply was, of course,

"YOU'RE marvelous!" Bill and Hillary were at opening night, and there was a constant stream of celebs and luminaries coming by to see the show. It was a grand time in my life, and a huge feather in my cap. I felt so very lucky to have that job, but I also felt that I won it and that I deserved it.

When I first moved to NYC, even though I had performing work right away, it wasn't enough to cover my expenses, so considering what a sucky waitress I was, I got a job as a prep cook in a restaurant, including working for Suzanne Levine, owner of the famous Sarabeth's. (I was a migrant fruit cutter. I used to spend days prepping the fruit for those adorable Ball jars of jam that she still sells.) I have to say, I learned so much watching her work so hard and grow that business, she is so successful, and was a great role model. I had several of these types of jobs for the first 4 years I lived in NYC. At the time, they paid $5 an hour under the table, and I could eat on the job as well as take food home, so I had very low grocery bills, and combined with my music work, I got by.

One day in 1984, Judy Niemack said to me, "Amy, why don't you teach?" I had never thought about being a voice teacher, but I thought it was a good idea, so I went down to the New School, and got a job teaching at The Guitar Study Center, a rock and roll school lodged at the New School, founded by Eddie Simon, Paul's brother. Around that time, I was at a jam session at The Angry Squire, a club that used to be on Seventh Avenue and 22 Street. The pianist invited me to sit in, I called a tune, the key, counted it in and off I went. It was fine, everybody liked it. Then, another singer got up to sing. She called the tune, and the pianist said,'What key?" and she giggled and said "I dunno,' so the pianist rolled his eyes and shouted to the bass player, "Eb." Then he said, can you count us in, and she giggled and said 'I dunno....' so he counted her in, 1, 2, 1234.

This was a pivotal moment for me. My mouth dropped open, I couldn't believe my eyes, that a singer would get up on a stage in NYC and not know what she was doing, instilling the wrath of the band who had to now babysit her. This is what I call, "The Chick Singer Mentality." It's the old stereotype of the girl singer not knowing what to do, behaving unprofessionally, and having to lean on the band to do her job as well as theirs, resulting in the disdain and disrespect of the band. This leads them to the opinion that singers don't know shit, and perpetuates the myth of the woman as a sex object - just a pretty girl propped up on the bandstand to look good fronting the band.

At that moment, my future life was instantly defined. I set out on a path as a vocal jazz educator to teach singers to 'know their shit,' as we say in the jazz world and this is how I have made my living my entire life since that moment. I have been an adjunct professor at The New School for Jazz and Contemporary Music since then; I am in my 33rd year there. I have been adjunct professor at City College Jazz for 6 years, and I created the vocal department at the enormously successful after school program for teens, Jazz House Kids, in Montclair, NJ, which is run by dynamo woman Melissa Walker, and her husband Christian McBride, one of the most successful bassists in the world. Christian has won 6 Grammys for his own recordings as a leader, is on hundreds of other records as a side man, is on Sirius radio, NPR Live From Lincoln Center Jazz and directs both the Newport Jazz Festival and NJPAC jazz series.

Throughout my teaching career of 36 years, I have taught hundreds of singers, predominantly young women, to be well prepared and educated jazz singing professionals, ready to be equal players on the band stand, and to earn their reputations on their merits, and not have to be propped up by the band. Thus the title, 'Dispelling the Myth of the Chick Singer.' I have devoted my entire teaching career to it.

Over the span of nearly 39 years on the jazz scene in NYC, I have performed and recorded a fair amount. I have 5 recordings as a leader, and I am singing on many other records as a 'sidewoman.' I have performed on Broadway, traveled the world to sing at jazz clubs in Russia, Turkey, Greece, England, Italy, France, Belgium, Brazil, Puerto Rico, Canada, more, and all around the US. Not only am I a world renowned jazz educator, but I have led summer jazz camps and workshops globally for 15 years. I have sung on several film scores and TV commercials, and on several educational books and DVDs.

Perhaps the recording I am most proud of is The Royal Bopsters Project, my 3rd recording on the Motema record label. This was a 5 year project, from start to finish, released in 2015, the idea for which I came up with - singing in a vocal quartet alongside some of our greatest living bebop singing heroes. The recording features 5 vocal jazz legends: Mark Murphy, Jon Hendricks and Bob Dorough, now departed and sorely missed, and the female jazz singing heroines

Annie Ross and Sheila Jordan. I sing soprano in the quartet along with my pals Holli Ross, alto, Pete McGuinness, tenor and Dylan Pramuk, bass. This project was my idea; I was the creative director and executive producer of it, and it made a big splash on the jazz scene.

We have released our second recording, and performed at the Newport Jazz Festival, in August 2019. We performed in Athens, Greece and in London, England. I am also proud of my solo singing CD, 'Bridges', which represents my recordings form the late 1980s and early 1990s, with a stellar cast of jazz musicians, Both of these recordings still receive regular airplay on WBGO, years after their releases. WBGO is the largest jazz radio station in the world, and a very important component of the jazz scene here in NYC.

In conjunction with my nearly 39-year career in NYC, I have raised two amazing, independent and socially conscious daughters, Sofia and Anna, both in their 20s. My children grew up hearing the best music; a combination of the greatest jazz singers such as Ella Fitzgerald, Billie Holiday, Mark Murphy, Joe Williams, Teri Thornton Lambert, Hendricks and Ross, as well as the great Broadway cast recordings featuring such legends as Ethel Merman, Judy Garland, Julie Andrews, Fred Astaire, Bonnie's father John Raitt and Jerry

Orbach. My girls were both born in NYC. We were living in a medium-sized apartment, but when it came time to be a school chaser, and I learned that my two-year-old daughter would have to be tested to go to nursery school, I decided to take the suburban plunge to avoid the madness that is getting your child into the 'right' schools in NYC. I looked for houses in the 'suburban ring' for about a year - Westchester, Bergen County, Essex County. I focused on some of the more arty fartsy areas, such as Ossining, Dobbs Ferry, Hastings in Westchester, and Montclair, Maplewood, Engelwood and Teaneck in NJ. I settled on Teaneck, not only for its proximity to NYC and ease of driving into town, but because Teaneck was the first public school system in the US to voluntarily integrate. Teaneck has a history of African American jazz musicians moving there to raise their families in a friendly, accepting community of lovely homes and a good school system, so we moved to Teaneck when the girls were very small. They went to Teaneck public schools for nearly all of Elementary, Middle and High school. Their circle of friends included kids of every color, religion and sexual orientation, which is what I envisioned for them. I did look at houses in lily white suburban areas and made the decision that I did not want my kids raised in that world. As a result, they are both very well adjusted to the world, and still have friends of all stripes. This was my dream for them, more important to me than their grades, or their achievements in their careers. The most important thing in life is to be able to get along with people, all people, and to not segregate oneself in some insular community. My children live successfully in the world, are compassionate, smart, open minded, artistic and funny. I could not be more proud of both of them.

In conclusion, and to reflect on some of the choices I have made in my life, what I have accomplished, and who my greatest role models are, I will start with my parents. Though I rejected my parents' insular Jewish community that was very segregated and one dimensional, they were both hard workers and ethical people, and I inherited a great work ethic from both of them. My Dad in particular, although emotionally distant, was a self-starter, very creative and smart, and worked very, very hard and diligently. He took care of our family in the only way he knew how. He brought home the 'corned beef,' (instead of bacon, we were semi-Kosher!) and was very committed to my mother and to us, in spite of the fact that he had no idea how to talk to us. My mom was warm, funny, smart and extraordinarily kind and generous. She was very popular and highly trusted amongst her large community in Cincinnati, so well respected and loved in our extended family, and had a way of making strangers feel instantly welcomed. I credit my Mom with unknowingly giving me the ability to walk into a room of strangers and immediately make friends and feel at ease. She took great care of us, and taught me how to be a good mom and take care of my family. She also schlepped me to 5 million piano, voice, dance and drama lessons, skills which I use in my adult life on a daily basis.

I knew from the age of 12 that I wanted to be a professional singer. Once I heard Laura Nyro's records, and saw the big band at school, my path was set for life. I consider myself very lucky to have achieved this on several counts: my parents had enough money to finance my education, and support me in my endeavors. They were absolutely supportive of my performing career, and were always thrilled with my accomplishments. I know that this is not the case for lots of people, and I am extremely grateful for the unconditional love and support I received from my parents.

I am very grateful to have been able to spend my entire life in the world of jazz and on the stage. I have worked hard for this, and I feel that I have earned what I have been rewarded with. I have had to tolerate a lot of bullshit and rejection, both professional and personal, I still do - it is ever present. I did not deal with rejection well at all when I first started out, I have learned to develop a very thick skin about it, and also recognize that there are always more opportunities out there. You just have to find them, or create them.

You have to be willing to hang in there and do whatever it takes to get what you want. It is very important to me that my goals have not involved hurting anyone. I feel proud that I have managed to be successful without leaving any dead bodies on the side of the road. Also, perhaps the experience of feeling a little bit like an outsider, never feeling like I was one of the 'pretty girls' who just had things handed to them because they looked good, was actually a positive experience for me. It forced me to look outside the box and find my own path, maybe around the obstacles, instead of confronting them, but still leading to my goals.

My advice for young women: stay the course. Keep in mind exactly what it is you want, while constantly re-examining yourself and being open to changes here and there. Be ethical. Don't kill other people to get what you want, because at the end of the day, you have to look in the mirror and be ok with yourself. Be willing to accept defeat when it comes, give yourself a little break to recuperate and re-energize, and get back on the horse.

NEVER believe someone when they tell you if you sleep with them you will get jobs x, y and z. It never works out, ever, usually it backfires, because word gets around. You have to earn your own credentials, and base your reputation and your work on your skills and knowledge, not your looks and sex appeal.

Lastly, follow your instincts and don't second guess yourself. You can second guess yourself into complete disaster and depression. Your instincts are usually right. Follow them, stand by them and work hard to complete what needs to be done. NEVER let anyone tell you you're not good enough, or you can't do this or that. If people treat you that way, they are trying to manipulate you and stop you from achieving, because they are weak and jealous. We always have the power to do what we want, even if it takes an unusual path to get there. Stick to your guns, and believe in yourself, because if you don't believe in yourself, nobody else will.

COMMON THEMES

We are Very Different but Have A Lot in Common...

All of my Alphas are extremely successful, impressive women. I enjoyed all of our discussions and looked so forward to our talks and interviews. Each was incredibly open, reflective and generous in sharing her experiences and I was truly awed by the grit, determination and perseverance I heard in their stories. I have known some of my Alphas for decades, but didn't know their whole story, what motivated them, who influenced them, and why they ended up where they are now. Every Alpha told me they found this reflective exercise to be very cathartic. They had never taken the time to understand themselves in this way, or to deeply examine where they came from and where they derived their power. They also immensely enjoyed the trip down memory lane, conjuring up long-lost relatives and memories, and reliving the safe, earlier times in their lives.

Their memories and mine were not always pleasant or positive, and their tenacity in "pounding on" surprised them. They would tell me in our talks that they couldn't believe how much they had done, and how much they had been through. Step by step we advanced through adversity and change, often without stopping long enough to savor the moment. There simply wasn't time, and there was too much to do. We have all learned at some level to stop and smell the roses, but it's really not our nature.

We all came from different places with different experiences, but as I chatted with each Alpha I started to see and hear some common themes emerge. No matter how different our paths, we shared some commonalities which I now proudly and humbly share with you.

1. Hard work really does pay off

It should really go without saying, but I'll say it anyway: hard work really does pay off. All my Alphas are amazingly hard workers. We have defined goals and tasks, and high expectations of what we need to accomplish every day. Every day is a precious gift and experience, and no Alpha wants to waste it or not meet her goals.

Every Alpha chose a profession where success is impossible without hard work. Several became lawyers which requires years of study, countless hours of reading, exams and qualifying programs which are rigorous to say the least. We have Alphas who built their own businesses from scratch, who dared many years ago to take the risk of walking away from secure jobs and high salaries to venture out on their own. Being self-employed sounds empowering and glamorous, but takes days, weeks, months and years of hard work to succeed. Our Alphas did it with families and many other responsibilities. Those of us who held demanding jobs in large companies devoted thousands of woman hours to the betterment of those entities, often toiling away at great personal expense. We each had our own reasons to find the drive and passion to work this way, but work this way we did. Great success, even positive, attainable success, takes hard work, and lots of it.

2. We were born lucky

All Alphas featured in this book were born lucky. We didn't have to fight to survive as young children. We were all born into families where we were loved, cherished, and cared for, mostly by close relatives. Our families were by no means perfect, and some dysfunction would require therapy to fix (like my father wanting a boy), but we had secure homes and relatively secure family relationships as small children. All of us had well-furnished homes, running water and food on the table. Worries about the basics of survival were not our collective experience. Those types of struggles were endured by the generations before us, many of whom emigrated from far-away places and came to North America with very little. With the exception of Irene who was born in Taiwan, we were born in either Canada or the United States, as were most of our parents and some of our grandparents.

It is abundantly clear that our early nurturing environments allowed us to grow and thrive without concern for our own survival. Our environments allowed us the freedom to focus on higher level needs like relationships in our families, celebrations, social relationships, sports and fun activities, and then the privilege of going to school. It's not like we had to worry about having money for groceries - our devoted families took care of those worries for us. It was only later and upon reflection that we can see how very lucky we were to have had families who took such good care of us.

I was once part of a panel at work where we were speaking to high school students about our backgrounds. A European colleague of mine made a comment about having a very "privileged" childhood because she had running water and food on the table every night. One of the American students told me afterward she'd expected my colleague to say that "she was a princess or something", when she said she was privileged. The girl had never thought about her good fortune in growing up in a middle-class family in the secure NJ suburbs. We Alphas probably never thought too much about it either. We were born lucky into families with means in a society where girls are permitted to go to school. Our strong families gave us a very strong start.

Along with providing us with basic sustenance and emotional support, we also got a lot of encouragement from our families for the things we wanted to do in life. While there was some independence and rebellion, like Lynda moving away, and me going to a school my family disapproved of, there was also a lot of family pride in our achievements and help along the way. My father told me he would help me, Amy 's parents encourage her musical and show biz aspirations, Sally's father employed her to help grow his business, and the list goes on. While we may not have always followed their advice, knowing that they were behind us early on made it much easier for us to follow our dreams.

3. Strong Family Values

Along with being born lucky in terms of the basics and then some, and having supportive encouraging parents, we Alphas also came from families with strong values and integrity. (Except maybe some of Cheryl Goldhart's interesting extended family!).

It took many of us a while in the workplace, and the experience of getting knocked down a few times, to understand that others don't have our integrity or share the values we were taught. Lee talks a lot about honesty. Lynda talks about office politics and sabotage by those who wanted her to fail. "Watch your back" she says in her story. No doubt a hard-fought lesson after growing up in families that would not have prepared us for such back-stabbing and ambushes.

4. Gratitude for the strong, loving women who came before us

We all know that role models set the stage for us and form our view of how to approach the world and our lives in general. Role models are everywhere - both good and bad - and are often seen in pop culture, movies, on tv and in music videos. They do not necessarily provide good values or models to live by, but they are most certainly everywhere we look. If we are smart, we can ignore the bad role models, or take them for what is a side effect of our modern-day technologies, Internet and information flows.

Technology has changed current role models with the advent of social media. Those channels provide platforms for all manner of influence and influencers, and have allowed some very odd, seedy characters to become wealthy as supporters of esoteric fashion and lifestyle brands. My Grandma Jeannie would be horrified. She was once handed a magazine on the Toronto waterfront. "I've never seen such filth in all my life!" she exclaimed. I often wonder what she would think of the things we now accept as the norm in pop culture.

We Alphas, on the other hand, all had very strong female influences and role models growing up. Our mothers and grandmothers took care of us and our families even if men abandoned them as they did in Lee's family. Lynda's family had a breadwinner "disappear" too. This left our ancestral women with great responsibility at a time when it was virtually impossible for a women to get a decent job, let alone earn a good living and support a family. Amy's grandmother came from persecution and poverty in Russia and chose domestic servitude in Cincinnati, Ohio over a sweatshop job in NYC. Some choice. No wonder she was so happy to be married, have a family, and be able to cook and care for her children and grandchildren. We can hardly imagine an experience like hers, or the women who were abandoned. How did they survive and end up so loving and dedicated to us? We are all very grateful.

We Alphas had the luxury of some economic stability as well as the benefit of living with and being loved by extraordinary "ordinary" women. They taught us perseverance and independence, resourcefulness, and how to love. They also left an indelible mark on how we face life's challenges. Incredibly, we Alphas have all modeled our lives to honor them in some way; whether it's through following their lessons or emulating their values, our hard work and tenacity honors them every day. We are all keenly aware of what they did for us, and of the legacy they left behind. We all feel the need to pay it forward. It is also very clear that we all still feel their loss and think them often and with gratitude. Our attainable careers would have made them proud, and we all wish we could have shared more time with them. I often say I would give everything I own for one more day with my mother. I mean it.

Regardless of their lack of physical presence today, our strong ancestral Alpha women live on in our hearts and in the lessons we teach our own daughters. We all benefit from the perseverance and love of the early Alpha women who helped shape our lives.

All my Alphas try to be good role models. We feel an enormous responsibility to the women coming up behind us to leave our world and companies better places than we found them. By being good role models we not only honor our ancestral matriarchs, we continue the legacy of their work.

5. The Mean Girls and other bullies

To my great surprise I found during the Alpha interviews that many of us had negative social experiences for a variety of reasons in many settings. All my Alphas are very well-adjusted adults with large networks of friends, colleagues and acquaintances. However, each of us learned something about early social rejection and feeling excluded from "cool" or accepted groups throughout our developmental years.

Socialization and feeling part of a broader social order is a fundamental, basic human need. It is third on the Maslow hierarchy of needs after physiology and safety, and is termed "love and belonging". Animals ostracized or lost from their packs can't survive in the wild. Similarly, in the jungle of schools and workplaces, being ignored, sidelined or excluded can have devastating and long-lasting psychological impacts. Clicks of girls who are "in" and girls who are "out" start early in childhood. Girls with valued traits are generally the ringleaders - those with good looks, some kind of special talent, or simply the ability to attract and influence others. It's the attraction that is often so mysterious. What is it about the leaders of the "cool crowd" that allows them to attract others to follow them blindly into the river like the Pied Piper? To an outsider, the attraction is not understood, but is very visibly observed. It's like John Travolta's character in the movie Grease - the coolest, albeit simple-minded, bad boy in the town from the proverbial wrong side of the tracks, who gets the cutest, incredibly beautiful painfully skinny and perfect wealthy girl. I always thought that there was an inverse relationship between the coolest kids and basic human intelligence; intelligence dropped as coolness increased. The cool kids were street smart, kind of like pack animals, but seemed not to have much intellect. Maybe that was just my "sour grapes" coming through after being excluded and bullied. "If you don't want us, that's fine -- you're not smart enough for us anyway." Looking back, I think the mean girls were probably even more insecure than I was. They just covered it up with lipstick, trendy clothes and bravado.

In talking with my Alphas, I found that many of us were socially excluded, especially in our teen years. If we were good at school, the books and attendant success were our friends. The kids of the in crowd generally didn't do that well in school, and spent more time socializing as an outlet for acceptance and gratification. Social success was their validation. Except for Lee, who had lots of friends, the rest of us found our validation and salvation in our book reports, high marks and good test scores. School was our friend, she accepted us. Every day, no matter how we were treated socially, school welcomed us with open arms, reinforced our intellectual capability, and was there for us through thick and thin with objective approval.

The mean girls, however, were everywhere in high school, and followed us into the workplace as well. I experienced the mean girls first at summer camp as a 10-year-old. Lynda was surrounded by them in Thunder Bay, Ontario growing up where they even tricked her into thinking they had a "playdate" organized. It doesn't end with childhood. As a young adult, a few of the mean girls from camp tried to lose me en route to one of their houses and then wouldn't answer the doorbell when I got there. All these years later these events form indelible bad memories. They were early lessons in rejection and exclusion which leave profound scars in the ability to trust and form strong bonds of friendship. You just never knew what you were going to get (or not get). We learn to move past them once we find like-minded people and have positive social experiences, but it's a tough start.

Exclusion can be mean in other ways as well. Take Amy, who is beautiful and immensely talented, but not "Twiggy" as she describes herself. Being in show business and coping with this kind of meanness and rejection could have crippled her. Instead, she educated herself, turned to school, and made herself better informed, skilled and capable than the skinny giggly "accepted girls". Way to

Pound On!!, but those feelings of exclusion have stuck with her all these years after too, and could have had lasting negative effects on her self-confidence and self-esteem.

The mean girls and other exclusion affected us Alphas deeply. Mean girl treatment shaped our view of social relationships and where we fit in to the order of things, whether at camp, school, show business or the workplace. These experiences taught us what it feels like to be left out, and that we should, rather, include people and treat them with kindness so that no one would feel like we did, at least not if we can help it.

I understand now how profoundly the nasty mean girls and other bullies affected us. In a sense, though, they did us all a favor. Without their "approval and acceptance" we had to find success and validation (i.e. love and belonging) in other ways. We learned to cope in difficult situations that the mean girls wouldn't potentially confront for decades. Their early social success was in some ways to their detriment. It caused many to compromise their educations or plans for the future. They chose the in crowd over school and future career planning because it wasn't cool to do well in school. In those pre-teen and teenaged moments, your friends and social click are everything.

With maturity, we learn that they are not. There are many more important things in life like good health, loving spouses, and happy children.

Social success and acceptance in high school or college is no predictor of any kind of success later on. Workplaces are also fraught with other kinds of "mean girls" and unkind people (we'll get to that when we talk about women mentors) many of whom don't succeed or aren't happy either. We Alphas were more prepared than others to deal with these people given our early social experiences. In the end, the mean girls were just a blip on our radar screen as we've ascended through our lives and left them behind. We should recognize what we learned from these lessons and Pound On!!

6. The Three R's Mattered - Getting a good education was important to us and to our families

All of my Alphas have extremely impressive academic credentials, most of us with several university degrees and accreditations. Education is the gateway and foundation to opportunity in our society. Educational success is highly valued in most families, and academic success is celebrated and rewarded. Get an "A" and you'll get a prize, we would often hear. Reading, writing and 'rithmetic set us up to get good jobs later in life. Our parents, notably our mothers, got us off to school every morning with the tools for success - lunch or lunch money, books and supplies, breakfast and completed homework and supplies. And they were (or many of them were) there when we got home, or sent us to capable babysitters. We got help with our homework, projects, assignments and presentations. They also carted us around to our extra-curricular activities which formed part of and enhanced our educations. My mother took us to all our music and dance lessons, sports and activities. Amy's mother, who had two other daughters, took her to all manner of voice and music lessons. Lynda learned piano and to ski outside of school where she always had her nose in a book or novel of some kind -- even hidden in her math book in class. Clearly our parents and grandparents saw the value of education of all kinds both inside and outside the traditional classroom. They encouraged and supported us, as well as invested time and money in our development and enjoyment of school and other interests.

School and education is a ticket out; out of poverty, out of mundane jobs and careers, out of small towns we want to escape, and big cities we felt lost in. Lynda came to the big city to go to school, as Amy did to pursue her Broadway dreams. I fled the big city for a smaller venue where I thought I'd fit in better and could leave behind the painful loss of my mother.

Interestingly, many of my Alphas were the first in their families to go to University. Cheryl was working in her mother's jewelry and antique store when an insult ("Go wash my Rolls") by a wealthy client catapulted her back to finish high school. Lynda's family members had educations, especially the women, but not at the high level of hers. Similarly, Lee's parents did not have the means to pursue higher education opportunities.

The common thread and theme, however, is that we all knew a great education would afford us independence and self-determination. With a job and our own money, we would be independent and could make our own decisions. Education provided us that gateway, and we were determined to get in. How and where we got our educations varies. Some of us stayed close to home while others ventured far away. Early work experiences, like Lynda's bad moments in law, drove her back to school to re-examine her choices. Cheryl had a similar unhappy experience and went back to school to study psychology. My first career in teaching wasn't satisfying enough for me, so I went to law school. Lee continued her education for many years so she could better help her consulting clients after she bravely formed her own consulting business. All interesting choices but with one strong commonality - when we wanted to change our lives and upgrade our positions, we went back to school.

We all worked very hard for our educations and professional designations and training. They took years to complete, but allowed us immeasurable career opportunities and choices. Our paper chase gave us our fine start to climbing the walls.

7. Our Women Mentors at work - or lack of them

In addition to having a lack of professional women mentors in school, and very little social acceptance by girls in our early experiences, our workplaces did little to provide women mentors either.

When we Alphas were in professional schools, the proportion of women in those programs was very low. Our first workplaces (and some now) were no different. There were very few women outside of the administrative staff and very few role models or potential mentors. Lee talks about having great mentors and sponsors, but they were men. Sally had her father as her first boss and mentor. The rest of us describe a somewhat different experience.

Those of us who started in professional firms found very few women there. If there were women in the firm, they made it very clear that they had no interest in helping any of us. We never expected the men to help us, but the women not helping us was a disappointing surprise. Mentoring and its benefits were not really widely understood in those days. Engagement of young talent was not seen as the task of employers or more senior professionals. We were told we were lucky to have jobs, and we honestly believed that, at least at first. Not wanting to rock the boat led us to put up with a lot of crap and lousy treatment. Without the support and protection of the women who were there before us, we were left to fend for ourselves with the unruly men in their boys' clubs. The more senior women felt no obligation or desire to help us, and they said so. They thought that since they had paid their dues, that we should too. We see this theme in my story, Lynda's, Cheryl 's, and in a different way in Amy's show biz story. This blatant lack of care for women coming up behind us still persists in some environments with some women. I once had a very senior European woman tell me - "While I'm here in the US I don't intend to do anything for the women here, so don't ask me". Another woman more recently honored for professional accomplishments admonished those who wanted to congratulate her for being the first woman to win a prestigious award. She didn't think gender had anything to do with it, which was really not the case or the real message. The first woman to win a prestigious STEM award should be celebrated as an example and role model for the next generation. Not wanting to be a role model in that circumstance does not help the women who are currently making career choices. Denying it cheats everyone and undermines progress.

The behavior of the senior women we encountered was very exclusionary and discouraging. These days, diversity and inclusion is well-recognized as essential to business success. Customers need to have confidence that their suppliers operate with integrity and respect, and many require certain diversity standards or they won't do business with you. The behavior of women at the top not wanting to help us flies in the face of these objectives. We never felt included in the culture of the places we worked at the beginning of our careers, which truly hurt everyone. We looked up and saw very few people like us, or people we wanted to be like. This led all of us in different directions. I went in-house to a big corporation, Cheryl opened her own law firm, Lynda left and worked in other environments and opened her own firm. Our decisions might have been different had we been included, and had our female "role models" stepped in and stepped up. It cost them - firms and companies make big investments in training when they bring in employees who are early in career. When we leave after a few years we take everything we learned with us, and rightfully so. Mentoring keeps good people. Feeling included does too. Not having good senior female role models hurt everyone, and is a common refrain in our stories.

8. Gender Discrimination and Sexual Harassment

The purpose of this book is to tell positive stories of success for us Alphas. Many of us had early loss, struggles and problems along the way, but we persevered, worked hard, used what we had, and achieved. We are voracious students of our chosen fields, and have the desire to help others in meaningful ways. Since this book and our stories are meant to be a positive chronicle (albeit truthful, and not all recounts are blissful) to inspire and help give other women the courage to pursue their dreams, I don't want to focus too much on gender discrimination and sexual harassment as part of our stories. I have a later section of the book that talks about concepts, which outlines the impact and presence of gender discrimination in the workplace, pay inequity, and some other issues women face at work because of gender. There are many, and there is still much work to be done. However, for this topic, in this work, suffice it to say that all Alphas have experienced various forms of gender discrimination whether in sabotage, lack of opportunity, getting less interesting work, or having to overcome a "chick singer" mentality. We rose above all of it, found our voices, or voted with our feet if it got unbearable.

I would like us to focus more on how we deal with such topics, rather than on the incidents or events themselves. Let's look at how we coped, what we learned, and how we can continue to effect change. With this focus we recognize these problems and tackle them with our eyes wide open. Together, we blaze the trail so that those coming up behind us can more easily walk through the jungle, and metaphorically climb the walls. We thereby pull them up to join us in pounding on the glass ceiling.

Most importantly we need to raise our voices and speak up for ourselves and other women. Silence perpetuates the problems of discrimination and harassment and shames the victims. We should encourage women to come forward if there are issues, support each other through a journey of healing, and hold perpetrators accountable for their words and deeds.

9. We accomplish nothing alone -- it takes a village

We've heard it over and over again, especially when it comes to raising children: it takes a village. Whether we came from families with means or not, there were hundreds of people and extensive resources involved in raising us. Our extended families -- parents, grandparents, aunts, uncles, cousins and siblings were there from the beginning, shaping us, caring for us, and giving us guidance and guideposts along the way. Then came a broader more extended world of educators, both secular and non-secular. We all went to school, most of us had religious training, and those fortunate enough had activities, lessons, camps and groups we joined. All of these groups, lessons, teachers, artists, athletes, artisans and role models were part of our village. We remember our early teachers, and what a strong influence they had on us. Amy, Lynda and I had a myriad of instructors for all of our activities and lessons. Many of us had "villages" which included getting back to nature. Summer camps are full of peer and teenaged teachers who mentored and guided some of us in skills of privilege like boating and horse back riding. Lynda skied with friends and had a family camp up north. I went to summer camps and a Toronto boating club. This exposure and its benefits took a true army of many dedicated people year after year. Some were relatives, some volunteers, others paid instructors, but what they taught us is woven into the fabric of our childhoods and teenaged years, through and into college and university programs. All the people who taught us and exposed us to these great experiences were part of our villages, and it didn't stop there.

Our careers have taken a village to build, construct and maintain too. Our towns, camps, cottages, neighborhoods and schools all converged into our workplaces where we found another "village". There were many people along the way we learned from, lessons both good and bad, but influences nonetheless. Our projects and assignments were mostly done in teams. We started out as individual contributors working alone, but this changed as time went on. When the work got more complex and we ascended and got more experience, we needed teams of people to help drive success. We learned, some of us the hard way, that we don't do anything alone. To accomplish anything we needed to inspire, motivate, drive, supervise and sometimes even discipline our teams. It took that whole village to get us where we are, and it takes our continuing village of networks to sustain us here as well. We've built relationships in our professional villages and leveraged them to enhance our careers. This also takes strategic input, drive and opportunity, often provided by other Alphas.

The town "villages" remained important to us even once we entered the workforce. We have children and parents. We've all had a spouse, some of us more than one. We've needed villages to balance and juggle our careers and families along our journeys. If we've had the means we've had nannies and housekeepers. Many of us have at least needed babysitters and afterschool programs. Our children had activities which required organization and transportation. Our parents have their own villages for support as well, like Lee's 103-year-old (amazing) mother. I've often reflected on how all the people who help me in my life required payment of some kind. Even the woman who walks my dog. Our careers allow us to hire resources to take care of everyone, but it still takes a village to do it.

All these "villages" from early childhood to our career networks, our children's and parents' villages have all gotten us to where we are now. We are very grateful for them all.

10. Give back and forward - to others and to ourselves

We Alphas know that we were all born lucky. Whether we came from families with wealth, or middle class means, we know we started a step ahead and with many advantages others don't have. We know these advantages in love, care and education formed us and allowed us to become Alphas. Without these advantages we might have gotten here, but it would have been much less likely and a lot harder.

All of us talk about giving back. We give back to earlier in career women, our families, friends, network and peers. We have strong consciences which make sure we help others as part of our life's mission. Lee jumped in with ideas as soon as I told her about this project. Cheryl has helped me immeasurably with personal legal matters. I like to think I helped her through tough times as well. Lynda saved me from the trials and tribulations we encountered as early lawyers by sharing the journey with me. Sally helped me establish a network when I moved to the US and started a new job.

I reconnected with Amy, a childhood friend, when I moved to New Jersey. She reconnected me to our childhoods.

We have helped and guided each other through careers, marriages, divorces, children and many other life events. I hope I've given back as well. When I told Lee about this book, she said, "All the good karma you've put into the world will come back to you now." I must have given some, because I've already gotten back 1000 fold more than I ever thought I gave.

All of us understand that we need to pay forward as well as back. We work on paving the way for the next generation, and try to live in ways that keep the planet sustained. We are all involved in mentoring and teaching. We sit on boards and participate in our communities. We find time to spend with those who ask and those in need. I am awed by the work of my Alphas, and how they make time for everyone and everything. I hope they make time for themselves.

Paying it back and forward is not just for others, our communities and our planet. It is for each and every one of us all. We need to care for ourselves and nurture our needs and desires, or we won't be able to care for anyone or anything else. This important lesson usually comes to us late. It is in our nature to nurture and care for others, but not really to care for ourselves. How many times do we say "I'll go to the gym tomorrow, or next week"....or "I'll take a vacation soon and try to unplug"...which always turns out to be an impossibility. We need to pay back, pay forward, and pay ourselves too. If we don't take care of ourselves we won't be able to take charge or take care of anyone else.

ALPHA(S) RULE(S)

Make your own life decisions even if others disagree.

Speak up for yourself and others.

Live your life balance.

Take on meaningful work, whatever that means to you.

Earn your own money (i.e. learn to type so you won't starve).

Find your voice early and use it often.

Help other women whenever you can, especially women who are early in their career who can learn from your example.

Self-evaluate every day and try to do better every tomorrow.

Remember that failure shouldn't be an option. Learn from it if it is.

Be proud of how you behave.

If it doesn't feel right, don't do it.

Be true to yourself.

Show empathy, not softness.

Remember that others are not like you and accept it.

Don't try to fix other people or their problems.

Share and seek personal information wisely and sparingly.

Don't say anything behind people's backs that you wouldn't say to their face – especially your boss.

Pretend your boss is looking over your shoulder before you hit "send".

Be fair, just and honest.

Embrace change and new challenges.

Get the question right.

Feel the room and react.

Demand and give respect.

Don't get pushed around.

Give back with gratitude.

Make your own rules.

POUND ON!!

HOW TO CLIMB THE WALLS

Barriers, Obstacles and (the rare) Helping Hands: What the research shows about gender norms in the workplace and how to overcome them

This chapter is meant as an overview of concepts which appear in the research literature around gender and leadership. I've touched on the various concepts in my Alpha stories. This information is a high level introduction to give you a vocabulary for discussion of the issues women face in the workforce. Take it as part of the instruction guide to ensure that we all feel supported on our climb, understand the reasons for our challenges, and find the helping hands we need to give and receive along the way.

It is clear from the research that women and men experience the workplace quite differently, and are viewed very differently within it. Without the helping hands of other women, we have largely been left on our own to navigate through the maze of gender norms and unwritten rules ourselves. Sadly for us Alphas, we would have fared much better with any support from other women, both leaders and peers alike. Our stories all indicate very little female support on our climbs. Even a very recent study by the University of Notre Dame and Northwestern University revealed that women with a solid support group of other women are more likely to attain high-ranking leadership positions[1]. Our ascents were all made much more difficult because we were unknowingly threatening the existing male-dominated power structure. Also without knowing it, we were walking a tightrope. Read on.

The Double-Bind: Walking the Tightrope

Women leaders face the need to be seen as warm and nice, as well as competent and tough at the same time[2]. Researchers say that this creates a "double bind" or a "catch-22" for women leaders who are either seen as "bimbos" or "bitches". I would take this even further and say we really have a triple bind. To say we have to be nice and warm or strong and tough is only part of the equation. The third part, or the triplet part of the bind is being underestimated or assumed incompetent for the task or job in the first place. To say we struggle with deciding on appearing too nice or too strong overlooks the fundamental issue of whether we are seen to even have a right to be in the job. We need to prove that we are worthy of the job in the first place. Think about our Alpha stories. I was continually underestimated as an early in career lawyer as either being too young, too inexperienced or lacking the capability to do the job, and was repeatedly told so by clients and lawyers alike. Amy had to overcome the "chick singer" stereotypes through education and capability. Both Cheryl and Lynda had such poor early validation as lawyers that they questioned whether law was the right career for them and took different paths for a while. This is a disappointing reflection after spending years training for entry into the profession. Never underestimate the impact of underestimating someone else. It hurts, and hurts our confidence, but in the end it made us Alphas even more determined to prove ourselves. I'm not sure why we had the tenacity to persevere, but we did. Again, the third arm of the triple bind is being underestimated and/or perceived as unworthy of being in the position. Too nice or too tough only matters if people think you should be there in the first place.

Emily Bazelon interviewed Katherine Phillips of Columbia University and Shelley Correll of Stanford for a recent article in the New York Times Magazine[3]. Bazelon also talks about the "double bind" as the distinction between taking care and taking charge. She examines the impact of the "bind" on salary negotiations, and in particular, indicates that women settle for lower salaries than men when negotiating. Furthermore, those women who negotiate for high salaries are not positively viewed upon entry into the jobs[3]. This fits with my additional third point or "triple bind" - being underestimated and assumed unworthy of the job in the first place. With little validation or encouragement, we are our own worst enemies on the ascent. Women didn't help us, and we were severely underestimated by others, as well as by ourselves.

Zheng, et al. talk about the "demanding yet caring" contrast as the first of four paradoxes, or as part of a balancing act. The need to be demanding yet caring is the first paradox. Our feedback may not be positive after driving hard, and we question whether a man would have gotten the same comments. Who knows, but I submit that it is highly unlikely. The second paradox centers on the need to be authoritative yet participative at the same time.[2]

In a similar vein to the first paradox, women in the study felt a strong need to be collaborative at the same time as being confident and assertive. Paradox three is not much more encouraging -- the need to advocate for ourselves while serving others. Are we waitresses seeking a higher wage? And the fourth is equally difficult -- to maintain a distance while still being approachable. How is that really possible, I ask myself? We start sounding like superwomen -- which ordinary woman could possibly navigate all these contradictions and paradoxes?[2]

How can we be distant and approachable, an authority figure and a participant, serve as well as advocate and care for others while we take charge? And all of this while questioning whether we should be in the job in the first place, which is the third or triplet piece of the bind. It's enough to make you want to strangle yourself on the rope of impossibility. Zheng, et al, do have some strategies to manage this myriad of demands, which I'll refer to and comment on next. [2]

Zheng sets out some practical advice, like adapt to the situation, by not always sitting at the head of the table, for example. Try to be nice first and then tough, i.e. build relationships and establish trust before getting too directive. Look for wins, focus on the tasks, and try to reinforce the positive. All good advice, but I sum it all up as saying "be human". We are Alphas, true, but we are not Super Woman, Wonder Woman, a female version of the Hulk, a dragon lady, Dorothy of the Wizard of Oz or Alice in Wonderland. All of this research should recognize that we are human too, trying to do a difficult job in difficult circumstances with very little support or respect.[2]

All of this further underscores the need for women to help each other as we climb the walls, something that all of us Alphas now aspire to do. We need to give back and forward and lend a hand to the women coming up behind us so that their path is easier than ours was. At some level, all of us with our stories in this work have encountered some, if not all, of the paradoxes so aptly set out by Zheng.[2] I still contend that the third aspect of the bind, that of being underestimated and unwelcome is actually the biggest barrier and probably the biggest paradox of them all: being underestimated while ensuring we are exceptionally qualified. I'm not sure how to reconcile all of this, except to be aware of it, make your own rules and

Pound On!!

The Queen Bee Phenomenon - Has she died off?

Along with women not helping each other generally, there is the issue of what top women leaders do for other women once they get to high level positions. I've already talked about the women who refused to help us in law firms, or help other women in the corporate world. Our Alpha experiences were a long time ago but the problem still persists. Some research indicates that the Queen Bee phenomenon has died off, but our experience, while limited, contradicts this. Let's first explore the phenomenon and what it means, and then explore whether the phenomenon still exists.

There is an assumption that there can be only one "Queen Bee" in an organization. She rises to the top, but guards her precarious position deftly not wanting other women to join her. Anne Welsh McNulty writes about this in her article in Harvard Business Review "Don't Underestimate the Power of Women Supporting Each Other at Work," where she talks about her career experiences at an investment bank[4]. McNulty recounts an experience where she tried to have lunch with the only woman senior to her, who turned down her invitation. Not only did the senior woman turn her down, she clearly told McNulty that they were not going "to be friends" as there was room for only one senior woman partner in the firm. Not too inviting, and still extremely common. This, says McNulty, is the Queen Bee phenomenon, where some senior women distance themselves from other more junior women. Perhaps this isolation is designed to make the Queen Bee more accepted by her male peers, she theorizes, or is an attempt by the Queen Bee to separate herself from a marginalized group[4]. By contrast, men are more likely (46%) to have an advocate of a higher rank (Sylvia Ann Hewlett is quoted in this regard).

The marginalization that McNulty experienced led her to isolate herself. Until other women started leaving the firm they didn't realize their common experience. Other women were having the same issues, but they weren't talking to each other about it. In the end, McNulty resolved never to let this happen to her again.

While other research casts doubt on the continued existence of the Queen Bee "Syndrome[5]", the stories of our Alphas suggest otherwise. Our other stories suggest that help from more senior women is a rare exception. I encountered a sole woman partner who was determined to sabotage the early in career women lawyers, and Lynda recounts similar stories. In fact, the poor treatment of women toward each other seems to begin in early childhood. Both Lynda and I recount stories of "mean girls" who were cruel to us. Lee talks about befriending a girl others had isolated. This lack of early role models for helping each other as girls followed us into the workplace decades later. It didn't stop when one woman succeeded; she still didn't want to help others.

Another question which arises in the research is whether there is an implicit quota for women at the top. In other words, once there is a Queen Bee, is the job of the organization done? Palmquist questions whether the presence of one top woman executive actually hinders the chances that another woman will get a similar appointment. He postulates that it's not the Queen Bee phenomenon alone in that women don't help each other, but that there's an implicit quota for top female executives. One woman might be invested in and promoted, he theorizes, in order to "put a face[5]" on gender diversity, but this limitation of women at the top preserves the status of the male-dominated power structure.

Palmquist refers to a study of women in senior positions at 1500 firms over a 20-year time frame. They found that the probability of a woman holding a leading role in a company is 51%

lower if there is another woman in the top management group. They call this "the negative spillover effect" i.e. appointing one woman at the top has a negative effect on the opportunities for other women in the firm. Some small "positive" spillover effects existed, but largely with respect to supporting professional roles, not to promotions to positions with higher levels of responsibility. In other words, any power is dispersed and doesn't change or threaten the company's fundamental power structure. They did find that the "CEO Queen Bee" brought in other women moreso than women further down in the organization.

Frankly, I still need to see the death and extinction of the Queen Bee to truly believe it. My experiences, and those of our Alphas, would suggest that she is still alive and well, quotas or not.

The Glass Ceiling and Other Glass Barriers

All my reading and research leads me to think that there are a lot of glass barriers in women's ways as we ascend the corporate ladder. I reference glass ceilings, glass cliffs, glass borders, glass staircases, escalators and labyrinths. I was struck by all of these so-called "invisible" barriers to our success, and began to wonder when we stopped chasing the handsome prince and the proverbial glass slipper, and started seeking our own "impeded" success instead.

When my daughter was a little girl I'd read her fairytales at night. The happy endings described a handsome prince, sometimes with a glass slipper in hand, rescuing the helpless girl and whisking her away to her happily ever after, likely on a white horse with her hair flying behind her. That, in a nutshell, was the fairytale. There was no dream of a great career equal to a man's, nor the ability to take care of ourselves throughout our lives. I always changed the endings of the nighttime stories. Instead of the handsome prince coming to the damsel's rescue I told my daughter: "Don't wait for a handsome prince. Get a good education, find a good job, and rescue yourself!!" I wanted her to be able to buy her own glass slippers. At the time, I was a young lawyer still climbing the walls. I was just starting to learn about all the invisible obstacles in my path. Hence the name of this book: "From the Glass Slipper to the Glass Ceiling". I wanted to share my rewritten fairytale, and describe what career pursuits are really like, both good and bad.

The Glass Ceiling is now a metaphor cemented into the common parlance of women and our careers. I still contend that we are not welcome in the first place, and that all these barriers, invisible and otherwise, are descriptions of mechanisms which protect existing power structures.

I do wish to state again, that this book is not meant as an academic treatise and is intended as a positive chronicle of women in attainable careers, sharing our lessons learned for other women to learn, especially those women coming up behind us. It is still important, however, to understand these "glass" concepts and barriers, especially as we collectively move to shatter them all.

The term the Glass Ceiling is attributed to Carol Hymowitz and Timothy Schellhardt of the Wall Street Journal. In 1986, when addressing the question of why there are so few women in the C-Suite[6] their answer was that women "could not break through the glass ceiling", meaning the invisible barrier between managerial positions and the C-Suite. (The concept was also outlined in the Corporate Woman, 1986, Kanter 1977 Morrison, White and Van Velsor 1987). While some previous opposition and constraints to women's careers had been legal in nature (see our timelines) opinions preventing women's advancement were loudly voiced even as late as the 1970s. Take former President Richard Nixon who would not consider appointing a woman to the United States Supreme Court[6] as he deemed women "erratic and emotional" moreso than men, and therefore considered women unsuited for "any government job whatsoever". (From the White House audio tapes made public through the Freedom of Information Act). With the most recent elected women in Congress he must be spinning in his grave.

Eagly & Carli contend that "times have changed"[6]. I'm not so sure about that. Times are different, but I'm not sure they've really changed all that much. While a few of us have made it into the C-Suite at corporations like me and Lee, others have formed our own companies and made our own C-Suites, like Cheryl and Lynda. What is absolutely certain is that we are subject to extreme scrutiny as we take these positions. I got comments that I was "under a microscope" as I took a C-level job. Male co-workers felt free to comment on everything from my clothing to my nail polish. Other Alphas were subjected to the same scrutiny, like Lynda, in law firms where she was objectified. Increased scrutiny of women is well-documented in the literature and in studies[7].

Let's take a closer look.

The Glass Cliff

While reading and researching women's career experiences, I came upon many articles which documented a disturbing phenomenon called "the Glass Cliff". It seems less well known than the Glass Ceiling concept, at least in non-academic circles, but may have unfortunate negative effects on future Alphas and their careers.

The concept of the Glass Cliff was first officially recognized by Michelle Ryan and Alex Haslam in 2005 and is cited in many subsequent works and articles, including much more recent ones[8]. The theory goes like this. Women encounter the invisible barrier of the Glass Ceiling and earn well-deserved senior leadership positions. However, many of these leadership positions are "precarious" in that they are inherently unstable. In other words, we are offered senior positions in organizations which are not doing well. Women are therefore destined to fail, and we create a self-fulfilling prophecy that women lack leadership capability even though their failure was inevitable. This cements the notion that women are not suited for C-Suite jobs even though they inherited precarious and unstable businesses which could not be fixed regardless of leadership gender[9]. The Glass Cliff also diminishes women's confidence and makes organizations reluctant to put women in executive positions.

Fraud syndrome, or imposter syndrome then becomes an issue with women in senior level jobs, a topic which we should further explore as well. Research conducted after Ryan and Haslam's work demonstrates that the Glass Cliff phenomenon is widespread and is not unique to any location or industry. Also disturbing is that most of such failures are internal hires who may have felt obligated to take on an "impossible" challenge[8].

None of these phenomena mean that we should shy away from opportunities. Quite the contrary. We should, however, take on tasks with our eyes wide open, and ask for coaching and support. Ongoing support and mentoring would help women succeed and make a lasting impact with reduced risk of negative career implications. To have real influence we need real power, and not just when times are bad[10].

The Leadership Labyrinth

In 2007, Eagly and Carli wrote about a concept which takes the glass ceiling barrier even further. Believing that the metaphor may be changing, they felt that the glass ceiling concept failed to capture the variety of complex challenges faced by women on our leadership journeys. They note that women disappear from leadership at many points along our climb to the glass ceiling. They feel that women face walls all around, or a labyrinth of barriers with various twists and turns along the way. While the "goal" might be attainable through various routes, some of the twists and turns are expected, and some are not. Among the obstacles faced, the authors name several, including vestiges of prejudice in that men earn more and are promoted faster than women, i.e. gender pay gaps exist where women earn approximately 81 cents for every dollar earned by men. Promotions come more slowly for women than for men, and this advantage grows for men throughout their careers. Gender bias has even been shown in essay evaluation, e.g. the Goldberg Paradigm in 1968 where names were changed on essays and male writers received higher grades than women for the same work[6].

Eagly and Carli found that the gender bias against women still exists at all levels, not just at the top, and that resistance to women's leadership continues. People associate men and women with different traits, and that more traits connoting leadership are associated with men than women i.e. agentic traits of aggression and assertion, rather than more communal traits which are more closely associated with women, i.e. compassion and caring. Similar to the double bind where women have to be tough and likable at the same time, these findings show that dominant behavior can be more damaging to women as these traits are not commonly associated with women. It is the same with self-promotion[6].

Demands of family life can also present twists and turns for women as we are more likely to interrupt our careers for family reasons. The bulk of domestic work still falls on women's shoulders. Women also have very little time for socializing with colleagues and building social networks. We Alphas all evaluated how to manage our careers and families. Some of us stepped away for a while, like me and Lynda, Cheryl hired a nanny, and Lee enjoyed her role as an aunt[6].

In the labyrinth of leadership there are many challenges for women along the way. The authors suggest that certain actions can help address the problems. They suggest, among other things, to increase awareness, change the long-hours norm, and ensure that women are in executive positions. Mentors and family-friendly policies will also help, especially welcoming women back who have taken leaves of absence[6].

In other words, look at the whole path and the maze to see solutions. That way, we can "stop the leaks in the lower floors of the building" and not just see the glass ceiling as the problem[6].

Hear hear.

CONCLUSIONS

I sat for a long time, trying to figure out what to say to close this book out. It's tough to let go of the idea that this creation is nearly done; I've worked on it for so long, and thought we all had so much to say. The more I wrote this book, the more I realized that there will always be more to learn, and more to say. Hence I need to conclude with a few parting words (until we meet again).

This book is partly an historical journey, and partly a forward-looking pathfinder. I thought it was important to look at where women have been, how far we've come, and how much work there is left to do. The Timelines showcase earlier times in our history, and the injustices women faced. They also show how far we have traveled, and the rights we are still looking to earn.

The Stories are heartfelt accounts from wonderful Alpha Women who generously poured out their life reflections and learnings. There are many positive lessons to learn, as well as poignant accounts of survival and challenges. Their stories of perseverance and tenacity are lessons for Alphas at all stages and phases of our journeys. Savor them and imagine their paths. Model your paths after whichever journeys most inspire you.

I was surprised and heartened at the things all of the Alphas have in common. Thus, the chapter on the Common Themes. We grew up in different places under different circumstances, but had some common elements to our lives and childhoods. We were really all born lucky, and capitalized on this luck with determination and hard work. We all feel truly blessed and are grateful for our lives so far.

The Concepts are meant to provide an overview, not an academic treatise. As I've said throughout, this work is not meant as a textbook or test case; it is accounts of positive stories of Alpha Women meant to inspire, motivate and help other Alphas pursue their dreams. Take the interview questions and use them. Ask other Alphas to share their stories. Continue to learn from them and understand their wisdom and how they earned it. So too with the Rules. Read mine, and make your own. Use the Rotenberg Axis to see where you are on your journey, and examine what you must do to attain the next level. Dream big and never give up. Above all else, be true to yourself and Pound On!! You can do this, I know you can.

POUND ON!!

POUND ON

EPILOGUE

As I write this, I am contemplating my next project, and where I can take my experience and Alpha knowledge next. I am hopeful that sharing these positive stories will truly inspire a next generation of Alpha Women, and give some hope and guidance along the way.

This will definitely NOT be my last book. It took my life so far to write this first one, but I intend to continue teaching and learning, sharing and listening, and giving back. There is always more to be done.

Stay tuned...

POUND ON

COMMENTS

From My Husband

When I first learned that my beautiful wife Robin was going to write a book about Alpha Women I thought that it would involve a new superhero aptly named Alpha Woman, who would fight evil and criminal elements with help from her sisters Wonder Woman, Super Woman and Bat Woman.

My imagination lit up with great expectations for future movie rights, cartoons, a clothing line, and toy figures all designed to establish and market the identity of this invulnerable character who could soothe the savage beast, while at the same time selectively destroy impediments that stand in her way.

After some research and thoughtful reflection I came to the realization that the concept of the Alpha had long been based upon the law of the jungle involving the survival of the fittest and control of the herd. In fact, Robin has long advised anyone who would listen that in our lives, we can either behave as sheep or leaders. Perhaps it was that view of life that ultimately gave rise to this book.

POUND ON

In truth, I never thought about my wife being either an Alpha, Beta or any other creature of the human jungle. Rather, it was her love, kindness and concern for others that helped to propel me towards her. I always knew that the drive, ambition and toughness was inside of her and would be unleashed at the appropriate time.

Ultimately, we are all shaped by our experiences and it is those seminal life events that make us into leaders, or sheep. Robin had the terrible misfortune of losing her mom at a very young age and it was that difficult challenge that likely made her the sweet, graceful, yet forceful survivor that I married.

Alpha is the first letter of the Greek alphabet and while being first is generally advisable, it is not meant for everyone. The more ancient and perhaps deeper meaning of Alpha is found in the Hebrew and Phoenician letter Aleph which means not merely a leader, but an ox. These incredible strong creatures toiled and worked hard to achieve their reputation as being indispensable. So perhaps Alpha Woman is a super hero. They toil in the fields of career, family and life in general, not as sheep, but leaders.

From My Daughter

One of my earliest memories is my mom telling me she loves me "more than anything". I got more "any's" as I got older, to make sure I got more than anybody else. Now I get 3 - she loves me more than "any any any thing".....Others may get 1 or 2, but she always makes sure I get the most. If my mom were an animal, she would be a swan. She is elegant and beautiful, serene and calm, at least above the surface. What you don't see is her paddling like mad underneath. And if you cross her or try to hurt me, she'll peck your head off. I always said, "You don't want to mess with my mom". I know she always has my back.

My mom is the strongest woman I know. No matter what is going on, I know she will hold her head high and keep going. She would do anything to help me and my son Carter. I'm really proud and happy that she wrote this book to tell her amazing story, and the stories of her friends and colleagues. She has achieved a lot in the corporate world, but worked really hard when I was growing up to take care of me and build her career at the same time. Her jobs were tough, and she didn't have much help. I really don't know how she did it all. I don't know where I would be without my mom. I love you mamas. More than anything. Love Taryn. xo

ACKNOWLEDGMENTS

First and foremost, I'd like to thank my family. While their initial skepticism was palpable, they came around to the idea that I might have something valuable to contribute to the women coming up behind me. They do keep me grounded, and definitely keep my head from swelling.

To be more specific:

To the love of my life - my husband Mitch - You are my destiny, my ultimate partner, my true and complete love. Always and forever.

To my beautiful daughter Taryn - You are my dream come true, an answered prayer, and my over the rainbow.

To my sweet Grandson Carter, who has no idea that I've ever written anything other than his name in letters on the fridge - words cannot express the joy and happiness you bring to my life. The mere thought of you melts my heart and fills me with gratitude.

To my Mother and Grandmothers who watch over me. You taught me how to live, love and persevere. I try to honor you every day and hope I make you proud.

To all my Alphas - my deepest appreciation for opening your hearts, embracing this project and sharing your amazing journeys so far. You spent many hours writing and telling your stories to complete your chapters. You have my total respect and admiration.

This work was inspired by my good friend and colleague Cris Brito, a native of Brazil, who is the consummate Alpha Woman. She generously coached and coaxed me into the idea of writing this book. I am grateful for her creativity and support.

Acknowledgments

This book would not have been possible without my Project Manager Marilyn Brady who from the start has tolerated my many changes and somewhat crazy ideas. I am eternally grateful to Rebecca Best of Emineo Marketing who used her great skill, ability and patience to bring my brand to life with her brilliant marketing ideas and creativity. My editor Meg Fry was instrumental in perfecting the Alpha Stories, making them more readable. Special thanks to the Groton Teacher Stacey Spring and her students who helped edit and footnote the Timelines.

Thanks also to my extended family and friends for their enthusiasm, support and encouragement.

POUND ON

A

ENDNOTES: TIMELINE OF WOMEN'S RIGHTS UNITED STATES OF AMERICA

1. Lewis, Jone Johnson. "The Blackstone Commentaries and Women's Rights." ThoughtCo, Feb. 11, 2020, thoughtco.com/blackstone-commentaries-profile-3525208.

2. Sir William Blackstone, Commentaries on the Laws of England, Book the First: Chapter the Fifteenth: Of Husband and Wife. 4 vols. Oxford: Printed at the New-York Historical Society Clarendon Press, 1765–1769.

3. "Timeline for Women's Rights." Topic Timeline, Digital History, 2019, www.digitalhistory.uh.edu/timelines/timelinetopics.cfm?tltopicid=3.

4. The Editors of Encyclopedia Britannica. "Married Women's Property Acts." Encyclopedia Britannica, Encyclopedia Britannica, Inc., 8 Sept. 2010, www.britannica.com/event/Married-Womens-Property-Acts-United-States-1839.

5. The Editors of Encyclopedia Britannica. "Seneca Falls Convention." Encyclopedia Britannica, Encyclopdia Britannica, Inc., 7 Feb. 2020, www.britannica.com/event/Seneca-Falls-Convention.

6. The Editors of Encyclopedia Britannica. "Fourteenth Amendment." Encyclopedia Britannica, Encycloedia Britannica, Inc., 27 Sept. 2019, www.britannica.com/topic/Fourteenth-Amendment.

7. The Editors of Encyclopedia Britannica. "Arabella Mansfield." Encyclopedia Britannica, Encyclopedia Britannica, Inc., 29 July 2019, www.britannica.com/biography/Arabella-Mansfield.

8. The Editors of Encyclopedia Britannica. "Women's Suffrage." Encyclopedia Britannica, Encyclopedia Britannica, Inc., 24 Mar. 2020, www.britannica.com/topic/woman-suffrage.

9. "Timeline for Women's Rights." Digital History, 2019, www.digitalhistory.uh.edu/timelines/timelinetopics.cfm?tltopicid=3.

10. "Timeline for Women's Rights." Digital History, 2019, www.digitalhistory.uh.edu/timelines/timelinetopics.cfm?tltopicid=3.

11. Linder, Douglas. "The trial of Susan B. Anthony for Illegal Voting" http//IJURIST.LAW.PITT.EDU/TRIALS14.HTM (2001)

12. "Timeline for Women's Rights." Digital History, 2019, www.digitalhistory.uh.edu/timelines/timelinetopics.cfm?tltopicid=3.

13. "Timeline for Women's Rights." Digital History, 2019, www.digitalhistory.uh.edu/timelines/timelinetopics.cfm?tltopicid=3.

14. "Susanna Madora Salter." Emily Taylor Center for Women & Gender Equity, University of Kansas, 22 May 2013, emilytaylorcenter.ku.edu/pioneer-woman/salter.

15. Milligan, Susan. "Stepping Through History." U.S. News & World Report, U.S. News & World Report, 20 Jan. 2017, www.usnews.com/news/the-report/articles/2017-01-20/timeline-the-womens-rights-movement-in-the-us.

16. National Constitution Center - Centuries of Citizenship - Map: States Grant Women the Right to Vote, constitutioncenter.org/timeline/html/cw08_12159.html.

17. Milligan, Susan. "Stepping Through History." U.S. News & World Report, U.S. News & World Report, 20 Jan. 2017, www.usnews.com/news/the-report/articles/2017-01-20/timeline-the-womens-rights-movement-in-the-us.

18. Milligan, Susan. "Stepping Through History." U.S. News & World Report, U.S. News & World Report, 20 Jan. 2017, www.usnews.com/news/the-report/articles/2017-01-20/timeline-the-womens-rights-movement-in-the-us.

19. "Birth Control Organizations." The Margaret Sanger Papers Project, MSPP / About Sanger / Birth Control Organizations, www.nyu.edu/projects/sanger/aboutms/organization_ppfa.php.

20. Joint Resolution of Congress proposing a constitutional amendment extending the right of suffrage to women, approved June 4, 1919.; Ratified Amendments, 1795-1992; General Records of the United States Government; Record Group 11; National Archives.

21. "Women's Rights Movement." National Women's History Alliance, The National Women's History Alliance and Endorsed by National and State Organizations, nationalwomenshistoryalliance.org/resources/womens-rights-movement/.

22. "Women in the United States Senate." Wikipedia, Wikimedia Foundation, 2 May 2020, en.wikipedia.org/wiki/Women_in_the_United_States_Senate.

23. Breitman, Jessica. "Honoring the Achievements of FDR's Secretary of Labor." FDR Presidential Library and Museum, www.fdrlibrary.org/perkins.

24. "Lettie Pate Evans ." Lettie Pate Evans Foundation, lpevans.org/about/lettie-pate-evans/.

25. Sanger, Margaret. "The Status of Birth Control: 1938." The New Republic, The New Republic Magazine, 20 Apr. 1938, newrepublic.com/article/100850/the-status-birth-control-1938.

26. "The FDA Approves the Pill." PBS, Public Broadcasting Service, www.pbs.org/wgbh/americanexperience/features/pill-us-food-and-drug-administration-approves-pill/.

27. Jewish Women's Archive. "Publication of "The Feminine Mystique" by Betty Friedan." , https://jwa.org/thisweek/feb/17/1963/betty-friedan

28. "The Equal Pay Act of 1963." U.S. Equal Employment Opportunity Commission, www.eeoc.gov/statutes/equal-pay-act-1963.

29. "The Civil Rights Act of 1964." Constitutional Rights Foundation, www.crf-usa.org/black-history-month/the-civil-rights-act-of-1964.

30. "Title VII of the Civil Rights Act of 1964." U.S. Equal Employment Opportunity Commission, www.eeoc.gov/laws/statutes/titlevii.cfm.

31. "Timeline of Important EEOC Events." U.S. Equal Employment Opportunity Commission, www.eeoc.gov/youth/timeline-important-eeoc-events.

32. "History of the Abortion Debate." NPR.org, National Public Radio (NPR), www.npr.org/news/specials/roevwade/timeline.html.

33. "Timeline of Important EEOC Events." U.S. Equal Employment Opportunity Commission, www.eeoc.gov/youth/timeline-important-eeoc-events.

34. Wilcox, W. Bradford. "The Evolution of Divorce." National Affairs, 2009, nationalaffairs.com/publications/detail/the-evolution-of-divorce.

35. Michals, Debra, PhD. "Shirley Chisholm." National Women's History Museum, 2015, www.womenshistory.org/education-resources/biographies/shirley-chisholm.

36. "Phillips v. Martin Marietta Corporation." Oyez, www.oyez.org/cases/1970/73.

37. "ERA History." EqualRightsAmendment.org, www equalrightsamendment.org/history.

38. "The Civil Rights Act of 1964 and the Equal Employment Opportunity Commission". National Archives. 2016-08-15. Archived from the original on 2017-10-20.

39. "Eisenstadt v. Baird, 405 U.S. 438 (1972)." Justia Law, supreme.justia.com/cases/federal/us/405/438/.

40. The Editors of Encyclopedia Britannica. "Juanita Morris Kreps." Encyclopedia Britannica, Encyclopedia Britannica, Inc., 7 Jan. 2020, www.britannica.com/biography/Juanita-Morris-Kreps.

41. "Roe v. Wade." Oyez, www.oyez.org/cases/1971/70-18.

42. "Fair Housing Act and Amendments." www.nolo.com, 20 June 2012, www.nolo.com/legal-encyclopedia/content/fair-housing-act.html.

43. "The Fair Housing Act." The United States Department of Justice, 21 Dec. 2017, www.justice.gov/crt/fair-housing-act-1#sex.

44. "Cleveland Board of Education v. LaFleur." Oyez, www.oyez.org/cases/1973/72-777.

45. "A Reflection on the History of Sexual Assault Laws in the United States." The Arkansas Journal of Social Change and Public Service, 20 Apr. 2019, ualr.edu/socialchange/2018/04/15/reflection-history-sexual-assault-laws-united-states/.

46. "The Pregnancy Discrimination Act of 1978." U.S. Equal Employment Opportunity Commission, www.eeoc.gov/statutes/pregnancy-discrimination-act-1978.

47. "Paula Fickes Hawkins," in Women in Congress, 1917-2006. Prepared under the direction of the Committee on House Administration by the Office of History & Preservation, U.S. House of Representatives. Washington, D.C.: Government Printing Office, 2006.

48. "Women in the Senate." Senate.gov, United States Senate, 27 Jan. 2020, www.senate.gov/artandhistory/history/common/briefing/women_senators.htm.

49. Smentkowski, Brian P. "Sandra Day O'Connor." Encyclopedia Britannica, Encyclopedia Britannica, Inc., 22 Mar. 2020, www.britannica.com/biography/Sandra-Day-OConnor.

50. Anderson, Ashlee. Sally Ride. 16 Aug. 2018, www.womenshistory.org/education-resources/biographies/sally-ride.

51. "Geraldine Anne Ferraro." US House of Representatives: History, Art & Archives, U.S. House of Representatives, history.house.gov/People/Detail/13081.

52. Dagley, David L. "Meritor Savings Bank v. Vinson." Encyclopedia Britannica, Encyclopedia Britannica, Inc., 9 Jan. 2020, www.britannica.com/topic/Meritor-Savings-Bank-v-Vinson.

53. "The Year of the Woman, 1992: US House of Representatives: History, Art & Archives." Year of the Woman, 1992 | US House of Representatives: History, Art & Archives, history.house.gov/Exhibitions-and-Publications/WIC/Historical-Essays/Assembling-Amplifying-Ascending/Women-Decade/.

54. Tikkanen, Amy. "Anita Hill." Encyclopedia Britannica, Encyclopedia Britannica, Inc., 12 Apr. 2019, www.britannica.com/biography/Anita-Hill.

55. "Violence Against Women Act of 1993 (S.11 - 103rd Congress (1993-1994))." Congress.gov, www.congress.gov/bill/103rd-congress/senate-bill/11.

56. "United States v. Virginia." Oyez, www.oyez.org/cases/1995/94-1941.

57. The Editors of Encyclopaedia Britannica. "Madeleine Albright." Encyclopedia Britannica, Encyclopedia Britannica, Inc., 23 Apr. 2020, www.britannica.com/biography/Madeleine-Albright.

58. Norwood, Arlisha. "Condoleezza Rice." National Women's History Museum. National Women's History Museum, 2017.

59. The Editors of Encyclopedia Britannica. "Nancy Pelosi." Encyclopedia Britannica, Encyclopedia Britannica, Inc., 22 Mar. 2020, www.britannica.com/biography/Nancy-Pelosi.

60. The Editors of Encyclopaedia Britannica. "Sarah Palin." Encyclopædia Britannica, Encyclopædia Britannica, Inc., 7 Feb. 2020, www.britannica.com/biography/Sarah-Heath-Palin.

61. Londoño, Ernesto. "Pentagon Removes Ban on Women in Combat." The Washington Post, WP Company, 24 Jan. 2013, www.washingtonpost.com/world/national-security/pentagon-to-remove-ban-on-women-in-combat/2013/01/23/6cba86f6-659e-11e2-85f5-a8a9228e55e7_story.html?utm_term=471c91c2a526.

62. Patrick, Jeanette. "Hillary Rodham Clinton." National Women's History Museum. National Women's History Museum, 2016.

63. "Women in the United States Army." The United States Army, www.army.mil/women/history/.

64. Dailey, Daniel A., et al. "U.S. Army." U.S. Army, https://www.army.mil/e2/downloads/rv7/women/full_integration_of_women_in_the_army.pdf.

65. "Women in U.S. Congress 2017." Center for American Women and Politics, Rutgers Eagleton Institute of Politics, 8 Feb. 2018, cawp.rutgers.edu/women-us-congress-2017.

66. Sheth, Sonam. "More than 3 Million People Believed to Have Protested on the Day after Trump's Inauguration." Business Insider, Business Insider, 25 Jan. 2017, www.businessinsider.com/more-than-3-million-people-marched-on-saturday-for-the-womens-march-2017-1.

Appendix B

ENDNOTES: TIMELINE OF WOMEN'S RIGHTS CANADA

1. "Canadian History of Women's Rights." The Nellie McClung Foundation, www.ournellie.com/learn/womens-suffrage/canadian-history-of-womens-rights/.

2. "Harriet Tubman and Women's Rights." Harriet Tubman

   Historical Society, www.harriet-tubman.org/women-rights-suffrage/.

3. "Mary Ann Shadd." Wikipedia, Wikimedia Foundation, 21 Apr. 2020, en.wikipedia.org/wiki/Mary_Ann_Shadd.

4. Specia, Megan. "Overlooked No More: How Mary Ann Shadd Cary Shook Up the Abolitionist Movement." The New York Times, The New York Times, 6 June 2018, www.nytimes.com/2018/06/06/obituaries/mary-ann-shadd-cary-abolitionist-overlooked.html.

5. "Canadian History of Women's Rights." The Nellie McClung Foundation, www.ournellie.com/learn/womens-suffrage/canadian-history-of-womens-rights/.

6. "Canadian History of Women's Rights." The Nellie McClung Foundation, www.ournellie.com/learn/womens-suffrage/canadian-history-of-womens-rights/.

7. "Canadian History of Women's Rights." The Nellie McClung Foundation, www.ournellie.com/learn/womens-suffrage/canadian-history-of-womens-rights/.
8. "Timeline: Status of Canadian Women." Osstftoronta.ca, 21 June 2013, osstftoronto/ca/wp-content/uploads/2013/11/Womans-Timeline.pdf.

9. Blackhouse, Constance. "MARTIN, CLARA BRETT." Dictionary of Canadian Biography, Vol. 15, University of Toronto/Université Laval, 2005, www.biographi.ca/en/bio/martin_clara_brett_15E.html.

10. Blackwell, John D.. "Clara Brett Martin". The Canadian Encyclopedia, 04 March 2015, Historica Canada. https://www.thecanadianencyclopedia.ca/en/article/clara-brett-martin. .

11. Smirle, Corinne. "Emma Sophia Baker." Psychology's Feminist Voices, 2012, www.feministvoices.com/emma-sophia-baker/.

12. "A History of Canadian Sexual Assault Legislation 1900-2000." Constance Backhouse: Abduction of an Heiress, www.constancebackhouse.ca/fileadmin/website/abducth.htm.

13. MacGregor, Mary. "Proving a Rustling Charge." Proving a Rustling Charge, Beef in B.C., 1989, 2006, www.marymacgregor.ca/article40.htm.

14. "A History of Canadian Sexual Assault Legislation 1900-2000." Constance Backhouse, www.constancebackhouse.ca/fileadmin/website/1909.htm.

15. Strong-Boag, Veronica. "Women's Suffrage in Canada". The Canadian Encyclopedia, 25 August 2016, Historica Canada. https://www.thecanadianencyclopedia.ca/en/article/suffrage.

16. "Women's Suffrage in Saskatchewan." Women's Suffrage in Saskatchewan | Provincial Archives of Saskatchewan, 2011, www.saskarchives.com/Suffrage.

17. Strong-Boag, Veronica. "Women's Suffrage in Canada". The Canadian Encyclopedia, 25 August 2016, Historica Canada. https://www.thecanadianencyclopedia.ca/en/article/suffrage. Accessed 06 May 2020.

18. Pettinger, Tejvan. "Biography of Emily Murphy", Oxford, www.biographyonline.net Published 1 February 2010. Last updated: 12 February 2018.

19. Culbertson, Debbie. "Roberta MacAdams Price". The Canadian Encyclopedia, 31 March 2015, Historica Canada. https://www.thecanadianencyclopedia.ca/en/article/roberta-macadams-price

20. "The Evolution of the Federal Franchise." Elections Canada, Dec. 2014, www.elections.ca/content.aspx?section=vot&dir=bkg&:document=ec90785&lang=e.

21. "Women's Suffrage in Atlantic Canada." The Canadian Encyclopedia, Historica Canada, www.thecanadianencyclopedia.ca/en/timeline/womens-suffrage-in-atlantic-canada.

22. Kelly, Paula. "Looking for Mrs. Armstrong." Canada's History, 9 Jan. 2016, www.canadashistory.ca/explore/women/looking-for-mrs-armstrong.

23. Reilly, J. Nolan. "Winnipeg General Strike of 1919". The

Canadian Encyclopedia, 07 October 2019, Historica Canada. https://www.thecanadianencyclopedia.ca/en/article/winnipeg-general-strike.

24. Hallett, Mary E.. "Nellie McClung". The Canadian Encyclopedia, 03 October 2018, Historica Canada. https://www.thecanadianencyclopedia.ca/en/article/nellie-letitia-mcclung.

25. "Social Justice Reform for the Benefit of Women in British Columbia." Legislative Assembly of British Columbia, Legislative Assembly of British Columbia, www.leg.bc.ca/content-peo/Learning-Resources/WHM-2015-Part-2-Social-Justice-Reform-English.pdf.

26. Klowak, Sandy. "History Idol: Agnes Macphail." Canada's History, 30 Sept. 2010, www.canadashistory.ca/explore/women/history-idol-agnes-macphail.

27. Marshall, Tabitha. "Agnes Macphail". The Canadian Encyclopedia, 28 August 2015, Historica Canada. https://www.thecanadianencyclopedia.ca/en/article/agnes-macphail.

28. "Significant Dates in History of Women." Prince Edward Island Women in Government, PEI Coalition for Women In Government, 2010, www.peiwomeningovernment.ca/significant-dates-in-history.

29. "Divorces in Canada, 1925." Published by Authority of the Hon. J. A. Robb, M. P., Acting Miniter of Trade and Commerce, 1925.

30. Cavanaugh, Catherine and Susanna McLeod. "Irene Parlby". The Canadian Encyclopedia, 03 October 2018, Historica Canada. https://www.thecanadianencyclopedia.ca/en/article/mary-irene-parlby. Accessed 06 May 2020.

31. "Canadian Women's 150: 150 Years of Canadian Women's Accomplishments." Make It Our Business, Western Center for Research and Education on Violence Against Women, 28 June 2017, makeitourbusiness.ca/blog/canadian-womens-150-150-years-canadian-womens-accomplishments.

32. Marshall, Tabitha and David A. Cruickshank. "Persons Case". The Canadian Encyclopedia, 18 October 2019, Historica Canada. https://www.thecanadianencyclopedia.ca/en/article/persons-case.

33. Marshall, Tabitha and David A. Cruickshank. "Persons Case". The Canadian Encyclopedia, 18 October 2019, Historica Canada. https://www.thecanadianencyclopedia.ca/en/article/persons-case.

34. "INTERNATIONAL WOMEN'S DAY." Canadian Labour Institute, Canadian Foundation for Labour Rights, 14 Mar. 2018, www.canadianlabourinstitute.org/story/international-women%27s-day.

35. Strong-Boag, Veronica. "Women's Suffrage in Canada". The Canadian Encyclopedia, 25 August 2016, Historica Canada. https://www.thecanadianencyclopedia.ca/en/article/suffrage.

36. Ramkhalawansingh, Ceta. "Know Your History on Pay Equity." Policy Options, 11 Apr. 2017, policyoptions.irpp.org/magazines/april-2017/know-your-history-on-pay-equity/.

37. Williams, Patricia. "Ellen Fairclough". The Canadian Encyclopedia, 16 December 2013, Historica Canada. https://www.thecanadianencyclopedia.ca/en/article/ellen-fairclough.

38. "Women & The Right To Vote In Canada: An Important Clarification." CBCnews, CBC/Radio Canada, www.cbc.ca/strombo/news/women-the-right-to-vote-in-canada-an-important-clarification.html.

39. "Le Code Civil De Quebec." BibliotheQue, http://www.bibliotheque.assnat.qc.ca/guides/fr/le-code-civil-du-bas-canada-a-aujourd-hui/342-1964-bill-16?ref=93

40. "Birth-Control Pill Turns 50." CBCnews, The Canadian Press, 10 May 2010, www.cbc.ca/news/birth-control-pill-turns-50-1.908892.

41. "Abortion in Canada." Abortion in Canada | The Canadian Encyclopedia, www.thecanadianencyclopedia.ca/en/article/abortion.

42. "Unemployment Insurance Fund Gets Richer in 1971 - CBC Archives." CBCnews, CBC/Radio Canada, www.cbc.ca/archives/entry/employment-insurance-ui-gets-richer-in-1971.

43. Ito, Gail Arlene. "Rosemary Brown (1930-2003)." Welcome to Blackpast •, 20 Aug. 2019, www.blackpast.org/global-african-history/brown-rosemary-1930-2003/.

44. "Pauline Jewett Institute of Women's and Gender Studies." Women's and Gender Studies, The Pauline Jewett Institute, carleton.ca/womensstudies/about-us/pauline-jewett-bio/.

45. Macleod, R.C.. "Royal Canadian Mounted Police (RCMP)". The Canadian Encyclopedia, 15 November 2016, Historica Canada. https://www.thecanadianencyclopedia.ca/en/article/royal-canadian-mounted-police.

46. https:/vancouverisland.ctv.news.ca/vancouver-island-features/i-just-forged-ahead-the-story-of-one-of-canada-s-first-female-rcmp-officers-1.4277849

47. Anderssen, Erin. "No Memoirs for McDonough Yet." The Globe and Mail, 6 June 2002, www.theglobeandmail.com/news/national/no-memoirs-for-mcdonough-yet/article4135982/.

48. The Editors of Encyclopaedia Britannica. "Jeanne Mathilde Sauvé." Encyclopædia Britannica, Encyclopædia Britannica, Inc., 22 Apr. 2020, www.britannica.com/biography/Jeanne-Mathilde-Sauve.

49. Legislative Services Branch. "Consolidated Federal Laws of Canada, Access to Information Act." Legislative Services Branch, 1 May 2020, laws-lois.justice.gc.ca/eng/const/page-15.html.

50. The Editors of Encyclopaedia Britannica. “Bertha Wilson.” Encyclopædia Britannica, Encyclopædia Britannica, Inc., 24 Apr. 2020, www.britannica.com/biography/Bertha-Wilson.

51. “Bertha Wilson.” Bertha Wilson | The Canadian Encyclopedia, www.thecanadianencyclopedia.ca/en/article/bertha-wilson.

52. Alphonso, Caroline, and Marjan Farahbaksh. “Canadian Law Only Changed 26 Years Ago.” The Globe and Mail, 1 Apr. 2009, www.theglobeandmail.com/news/world/canadian-law-only-changed-26-years-ago/article1150644/.

53. “Sexual Harassment Persists in Canada.” Sexual Harassment Persists in Canada | Canadian Human Rights Commission, www.chrc-ccdp.gc.ca/eng/content/sexual-harassment-persists-canada.

54. Tremblay, Jean-noel. “Jeanne Sauvé”. The Canadian Encyclopedia, 26 February 2018, Historica Canada. https://www.thecanadianencyclopedia.ca/en/article/jeanne-mathilde-sauve.

55. “Bill C-31.” Indigenousfoundations, indigenousfoundations.arts.ubc.ca/bill_c-31/.

56. “Abortion Rights: Significant Moments in Canadian History | CBC News.” CBCnews, CBC/Radio Canada, 27 Mar. 2017, www.cbc.ca/news/canada/abortion-rights-significant-moments-in-canadian-history-1.787212.

57. “1989: Audrey McLaughlin Becomes First Woman to Lead a National Party - CBC Archives.” CBCnews, CBC/Radio Canada, www.cbc.ca/archives/entry/1989-audrey-mclaughlin-is-first-woman-to-lead-a-national-party.

58. National Defence. "Women in the Canadian Armed Forces." Backgrounder, 14 Aug. 2018, www.forces.gc.ca/en/news/article.page?doc=women-in-the-canadian-armed-forces/hie8w7rm.

59. The Editors of Encyclopaedia Britannica. "Kim Campbell." Encyclopædia Britannica, Encyclopædia Britannica, Inc., 6 Mar. 2020, www.britannica.com/biography/Kim-Campbell.

60. Calhoun, David. "Beverley McLachlin." Encyclopædia Britannica, Encyclopædia Britannica, Inc., 3 Sept. 2019, www.britannica.com/biography/Beverley-McLachlin.

61. "Louise Charron." Supreme Court of Canada, 4 Nov. 2011, www.scc-csc.ca/judges-juges/bio-eng.aspx?id=louise-charron.

62. Abella, Irving. "Rosalie Silberman Abella." Jewish Women's Archive, jwa.org/encyclopedia/article/abella-rosalie-silberman.

63. "Rosalie Silberman Abella." Supreme Court of Canada , 18 Mar. 2019, www.scc-csc.ca/judges-juges/bio-eng.aspx?id=rosalie-silberman-abella.

64. "Her Excellency the Right Honourable Michaëlle Jean, LL.D." University of Manitoba, 5 June 2007, umanitoba.ca/admin/governance/senate/hdr/848.html.

65. Martin, Michel. "Michaelle Jean: Canada's First Black Head Of State." NPR, 2 Apr. 2009.

66. Senate. "Senator Bev Busson." Senate of Canada, sencanada.ca/en/senators/busson-bev.

67. "Ontario New Democratic Party." GENi, www.geni.com/projects/Ontario-New-Democratic-Party/31378.

68. "Dunderdale Becomes 1st Woman to Lead N.L. | CBC News." CBCnews, CBC/Radio Canada, 3 Dec. 2010, www.cbc.ca/news/canada/newfoundland-labrador/dunderdale-becomes-1st-woman-to-lead-n-1-1.959039.

69. "Kathleen O. Wynne." Legislative Assembly of Ontario, www.ola.org/en/members/all/kathleen-o-wynne.

70. Leslie, Keith. "Parents Tell Kathleen Wynne Having Openly Gay Premier Makes Their Homosexual Kids Safer." CBCnews, CBC/Radio Canada, 9 Apr. 2015, www.cbc.ca/news/canada/kitchener-waterloo/parents-tell-kathleen-wynne-having-openly-gay-premier-makes-their-homosexual-kids-safer-1.3025842.

71. Munn-Rivard, Laura. "Women in Canada's Parliament." HillNotes, 4 Nov. 2015, hillnotes.ca/2015/11/04/women-in-canadas-parliament-making-progress-2/.

72. Murphy, Jessica. "Trudeau Gives Canada First Cabinet with Equal Number of Men and Women." The Guardian, Guardian News and Media, 4 Nov. 2015, www.theguardian.com/world/2015/nov/04/canada-cabinet-gender-diversity-justin-trudeau.

73. "Employment Standards." Government of Saskatchewan, www.saskatchewan.ca/business/employment-standards/vacations-holidays-leaves-and-absences/leaves-family-medical-and-service/interpersonal-violence-leave.

74. Przybyla, Heidi M., and Fredreka Schouten. "At 2.6 Million Strong, Women's Marches Crush Expectations." USA Today, Gannett Satellite Information Network, 22 Jan. 2017, www.usatoday.com/story/news/politics/2017/01/21/womens-march-aims-start-movement-trump-inauguration/96864158.

POUND ON

ENDNOTES: CONCEPTS

1. Locker, Melissa. "Women Need Other Women to Get Ahead in the Workplace, Says Science." Fast Company, Fast Company, 28 Jan. 2019, www.fastcompany.com/90297884/women-need-other-women-to-get-ahead-in-the-workplace-says-science.

2. Zheng, Wei, et al. "How Women Manage the Gendered Norms of Leadership." Harvard Business Review, 22 Nov. 2019, hbr.org/2018/11/how-women-manage-the-gendered-norms-of-leadership.

3. Bazelon, Emily. "Why Aren't Women Advancing More in Corporate America?" The New York Times, The New York Times, 21 Feb. 2019, www.nytimes.com/interactive/2019/02/21/magazine/women-corporate-america.html.

4. McNulty, Anne Welsh, et al. "Don't Underestimate the Power of Women Supporting Each Other at Work." Harvard Business Review, 3 Sept. 2018, hbr.org/2018/09/dont-underestimate-the-power-of-women-supporting-each-other-at-work.

5. Palmquist, Matt. "Why Are There So Few Women in the C-Suite?" Strategy Business, 17 Mar. 2016, www.strategy-business.com/blog/Why-Are-There-So-Few-Women-in-the-C-Suite?gko=9629d.

6. Eagly, Alice and Carli, L.L. Women and the Labyrinth of Leadership. Sept. 2007. Career Planning p. 2, 4, 5, 6-8 12, 16-20

7. (Early, Karau, Makhijani, 1995 as quoted in Ryan, Michelle, K, and Haslam, S. Alexander. The Glass Cliff: Evidence that women are over-represented in precarious leadership positions. British Journal of Management. Vol. 16, pp. 81-90 (2005))

8. Whawell, Susanna. "Women Are Shattering the Glass Ceiling Only to Fall off the Glass Cliff." The Conversation, 18 Feb. 2020, theconversation.com/women-are-shattering-the-glass-ceiling-only-to-fall-off-the-glass-cliff-94071.

9. Murrell, Audrey. "The New Wave Of Women Leaders: Breaking The Glass Ceiling Or Facing The Glass Cliff?" Forbes, Forbes Magazine, 9 Jan. 2019, www.forbes.com/sites/audreymurrell/2018/12/03/the-new-wave-of-women-leaders-breaking-the-glass-ceiling-or-facing-the-glass-cliff/#78d6d5431ddb.

10. Palmquist, Matt. "Female Directors and Their Impact on Strategic Change." Strategy Business, Harvard Business Review, 12 May 2014, www.strategy-business.com/blog/Female-Directors-and-Their-Impact-on-Strategic-Change?gko=e73b4.

NAVIGATING THE STORM

LESSONS LEARNED FROM A MENTAL HEALTH CRISIS

SHAYNE PETKIEWICZ

NEW DEGREE PRESS

NAVIGATING THE STORM
Lessons Learned from a Mental Health Crisis

ISBN 978-1-63730-438-9 *Paperback*
978-1-63730-533-1 *Kindle Ebook*
978-1-63730-534-8 *Ebook*

DEDICATION

To Mom, Dad, and Didi.

Thank you.

Contents

Introduction

Dear Shayne – 2019,

You are about to experience some of the most challenging moments of your life. These moments will yield a new depth of grief, loss, and pain. You will feel very alone, scared, and the future will seem bleak; a darkness will hover over you, linger, and at times feel inescapable.

I share this with you not to warn or cause apprehension, but rather to provide a level of comfort. I understand what you are about to go through and can confidently say while overcoming these moments will not be easy, they will pass.

Know also while you may feel alone at times, you do have a tremendous support system. You have a family and many close friends who love you dearly and will care for you and offer a shoulder for you to lean on.

While it may be challenging to recognize at the time, these difficulties can also offer moments of joy, fulfillment, and growth. You will strengthen old relations and forge new ones.

And throughout this transition, you will also bring a sense of curiosity to this process that will enable you to better understand your sense of self, who you are, what you value, and what gives you meaning.

All of this will take time. It will not happen overnight. Actually, it will take much longer than what you would like. Please be patient. You will grow and rise, like a field of wildflowers after the first rain.

LOVE,

SHAYNE – 2020

I had just turned twenty-seven in the summer of 2019 and was enjoying my time living abroad in London. I originally moved there in the fall of 2015 to commence a twelve-month master's program at Imperial College London. Following my graduation, I was fortunate enough to continue living in London and began working at a start-up.

My life's trajectory, which seemed to be on such stable footing, fell out from underneath me almost without warning. In a matter of weeks, I announced my resignation at work, my long-term relationship ended, and I began preparations to move back to the US. Suddenly, I felt as if I had fallen into an abyss, an abyss I didn't even know was possible to reach—murky, dark, without direction, and no sense of where the bottom lay. Having not dealt with any significant mental health challenges, I then faced hardships that challenged the very core of my beliefs. My fraught transition brought me back home—to San Jose, California—where I had lived as a teenager, and introduced me to the world of mental health and therapy.

As a result of not having previously faced a mental health crisis, I knew very little about mental health and had never sought out therapy. I did not have time to prepare myself for how suddenly I needed help. So, I learned about therapy on the fly, from others and on my own, as it helped me deal with the traumas that precipitated my departure from London.

One step on my journey to recovery involved writing my letter. Doing so was a revelation. Throughout my path toward healing, I routinely wondered how things might have been different were I equipped then with the knowledge to deal with my mental health challenges I now have. My process of reflection and writing made clear I had, in fact, grown during my time in therapy. I was struck by the many lessons I had learned that aided me in my process. It occurred to me these same insights could help others become more prepared to overcome the traumas and suffering they were facing or may face.

As therapy helped me grapple with the traumas I experienced, I slowly became more comfortable sharing and voicing my story. I found myself speaking openly about my difficult moments—initially only with close friends and loved ones. In opening up, I was surprised by their responses and found they created the space for others to share their own traumas. My stories became a powerful way to connect with others.

I noticed many of these same people who had experienced trauma responded in one of two ways:

- They tried to deal with the trauma by themselves and didn't ask for help.
- They reached out for professional help only when facing a crisis.

I found this curious. There seemed to be a juxtaposition between how some of my friends were responding to their mental health challenges and what my therapist was recommending I do to address my tribulations. Many of my friends routinely spoke of the benefits of prioritizing and addressing mental health, yet many couldn't address their challenges in ways that were recommended by professionals and thought leaders in the field of mental health. Even more, very few actually accessed, or even knew how to access, the very services that could support their mental health when they need it most. The premise of this book is, it is one thing to be aware of and value mental health but it's a very different thing to be prepared to handle emotional traumas in a healthy manner.

This insight served as a genesis for what became this book and led me to try and help those dealing with their own proverbial valleys. As part of this effort, I had the incredible experience of meeting people from all walks of life and from across the globe. I spoke with leaders in the field of psychology and mental health, as well as many who shared their stories and traumas, all doing a fantastic job contributing to the conversation of mental health and working to make it a less taboo and more socially accepted topic. My discussions, secondary research, and personal experience touched on topics ranging from growth, anxiety, hope, loneliness, emotional intelligence, self-injury, and more.

Having these conversations also validated the importance of prioritizing mental health and raising awareness of this issue. I hope to contribute to this conversation by sharing my experiences in a very honest and transparent way. I will share many personal moments in which I was incredibly vulnerable. While I am nervous about opening up to such a wide audience, I believe conveying an authentic and true experience is necessary in order to reduce the stigma surrounding mental health.

As part of writing this book, I have routinely been asked, "What do you want readers to take away from this book?" It's a great question and one that took me some time to discern. My overarching goal is for this book to be a resource for anyone hoping to learn about and improve their mental health. Going to therapy has made a huge impact on my life, and I would like to share with you some of the lessons I learned in the hopes they might help you become more informed about mental health. My aim is by reading this book, you can leave with a set of tools at your disposal you can employ to help manage your own difficult moments, traumas, or crises and have the knowledge to access professional help if you so desire.

PART 1

TRAUMA

CHAPTER 1

Disequilibrium

Sunlight streamed through the window. I opened my eyes and saw the maple tree, its leaves bright green and in full bloom, framed by a clear blue sky.

It was already warm, and I pushed away the covers. London was in the midst of a heatwave, the kind where the humidity clings to your skin and gives pause to any would-be rider on London's non-air-conditioned Underground train lines. I yawned and stretched out in bed.

Had I made the right decision?

My stomach clenched.

Could things have been fixed?

I reached for my phone on my nightstand. Saturday. Only three days? It felt a lot longer.

How much effort would it have taken to fix?

My stomach remained clenched. Three days; I couldn't stop thinking about her.

Would things have been different if I wasn't moving?

All these questions raced through my head with few answers. Hoping journaling would help me organize my thoughts, I rode my bike to Hyde Park. The air was rich with the aroma of honeysuckle, but it did little to distract me from my questions. I docked my bike and found a secluded lawn bereft of people, most likely due to the overgrown grasses. Walking directly to the center, I sat down and attempted to process the many emotions swirling within me, hoping to gain some clarity.

In the span of a few weeks, my relationship of three and a half years with my partner, whom I had met shortly after arriving to London, suddenly ended; I announced my resignation at work, a start-up of which I was a founding member and had devoted over three years of my life to getting off the ground; and I was then being forced to consider leaving London, my home for the previous four years, and returning to the US. I had hoped to continue living in London and did apply to various jobs there, but as one recruiter told me, it was "difficult to offer a sponsorship visa in this political climate," referring to the political uncertainty created by Brexit, the United Kingdom's withdrawal from the European Union. Suddenly, a lifestyle I had cultivated for years ceased to be, as did the life I had envisioned for myself in the years to come. Sitting in the park, I was trying my best to keep things together and prevent my life from falling apart.

The journal rested lightly on my lap; a blank page stared back at me. Unsure of how to begin, I listed the many questions I had.

My face scrunched up, and I crossed out what I had written.

Why is it so hard to get a sense of why I'm feeling this way?

My eyes opened wide, and I furiously jotted down a few half-sentences.

- relationship
- living situation
- work/career decisions

The pen slipped out of my hands and fell to the ground. My shoulders felt heavy, and I hunched over my journal, staring at the three bullet points.

No wonder everything seems jumbled.

I found it hard to catch my breath. My heartbeat quickened. The heat shimmered on the walkways nearby and the air weighed down upon me.

I reached for my phone and called my friend.

Pick up! Pick up!

Nothing.

I tried calling a different friend; again, no answer.

Tossing my phone to the side, I looked back at the three bullet points. Beads of sweat streaked down my forehead.

Just at that moment, a Royal Parks Constabulary car—the police force tasked with policing the Royal Parks—stopped close by. Two officers stepped out, both heading in my direction. The younger officer, probably in his mid-thirties, led the way followed by a grizzled veteran. I assumed they wanted to speak with me as there wasn't anyone else around. Sitting cross-legged on the grass, I looked up toward the officers.

"Are you smoking?" asked the younger officer.

My brow furrowed. "No." I remembered the three bullet points. "I'm…I'm feeling overwhelmed."

Both officers stopped one meter away from me. Their hands rested on their belts.

The young officer cocked his head. "Overwhelmed with what?"

I lowered my head, closed my eyes, and muttered, "With life…"

Drops of water dotted my journal. Tears ran down my cheeks. My chest suddenly relaxed and I exhaled. Something had been triggered inside me, which released that wave of emotion. I continued crying, my head resting on my hands.

I took in some deep breaths and reached for a napkin in my pocket and blew my nose. The officers were no longer standing over me. Instead, the grizzled veteran was kneeling on the grass and the younger officer sat across from me with a look of concern. I guess after witnessing a grown man crying in public, they no longer felt I fit the bill as a recalcitrant drug fiend and decided to change tactics.

I explained my situation, of everything I was dealing with.

"Cheer up, man," said the veteran. "There are plenty of girls around; you should go have fun."

I chuckled. Thinking about other girls seemed inconceivable.

"Where are you from?" asked the younger officer.

"California."

"California? That's a nice place." The veteran looked up with a smile. "At least you don't have to go to a war-torn country."

I smiled feebly. While true, his comment did little to make me feel better.

For a short while, they continued trying to cheer me up. Regardless of whether or not I would heed their advice, I was very much thankful for their willingness to offer support. Sitting with them helped me feel less alone. At last, they stood up, waved, said their goodbyes, walked back to their car, and continued patrolling the park.

It took me a moment to process what had just happened, how unusual that moment was. Not known for being emotive, I suddenly found myself crying in front of two strangers. It felt cathartic. I was alone, feeling distraught, wanting to be able to speak with someone, and two men whom I had never met before helped me process that moment of grief. Speaking with the officers helped me feel less lonely, and I found it encouraging strangers were willing to help in my moment of need.

A new energy coursed within me. I put my journal in my pack and stood up. I walked back to my bike and noticed the officers gazing toward me. I smiled. They seemed to be looking out for me. I started biking back home, but not before stopping to treat myself with a smoothie; I felt I had earned it.

* * *

One year later, in the summer of 2020, I met my friend Matt for dinner at his apartment in Berkeley, California. We had just finished enjoying a delicious homemade mapo tofu—a Chinese dish consisting of spicy tofu with Szechuan peppercorns. We ate our fill, reclined in our chairs, and enjoyed the transition of a warm afternoon to a chilly evening brought about by the oncoming afternoon coastal fog typical for Berkeley at that time of year.

It had been years since we last saw each other, so I shared with him my experience in Hyde Park and spoke of the many difficulties I continued to deal with since returning to California. Finishing my story, I looked at Matt.

He sat pensively, his gaze fixed on the garden behind me. "Have you heard of the concept called punctuated equilibrium?"

I shook my head.

"I remember learning this in an undergraduate biology class. It's a theory that proposes new species evolve through periods of rapid transition. These moments of change are typically followed by longer periods of little change. These moments of quick change can be triggered by both internal and external forces."

I stopped picking at the rice with my fork and looked intently at Matt.

"Imagine you are a bacteria or fish living in a lake. Over time, the species found in the lake have developed a balance. Suddenly, the water level of the lake drops, and the entire lake ecosystem is abruptly changed. Everything from the amount of water, amount of food, temperature, to oxygen levels suddenly adjusts, and all of the species in the lake must adapt quickly and evolve to a new equilibrium or perish."

My eyes widened, and I leaned forward. A smile spread across my face as he finished explaining the concept of punctuated equilibrium. I couldn't help but notice parallels between it and my personal experience.

Had my life undergone a shift in equilibrium?

The sun had set at that point. The red hues in the sky had given way to the dark of night, and the vibrant greens, reds, and yellows in the garden were replaced by muted greys and long shadows. I thanked Matt for the dinner and biked home.

Was my afternoon in Hyde Park the first moment I began to realize my life had shifted? If so, what were the implications?

I awoke eagerly the next morning, hoping to research the theory of punctuated equilibrium. I learned it was first postulated by Stephen Jay Gould and Niles Eldredge in 1972.[1] Trained as natural historians, they were intrigued by the evolutionary pattern observed in the fossil record that species do not change much over time. They proposed, "The history of life is more adequately represented by a picture of 'punctuated equilibria'...The history of evolution is not one of stately unfolding, but a story of homeostatic equilibria, disturbed only 'rarely' by rapid and episodic events of speciation." This proved controversial, as their theory refuted the more accepted view of Darwinian natural selection—that "new species arise from the slow and steady transformation of entire populations."

Gould and Eldredge's theory on how species change began to influence fields of research outside of biology. Other researchers and academics used their framework to investigate how change itself takes place. UCLA professor Connie Gersick published "Revolutionary Change Theories" in the *Academy of Management Review* (1991), which explores whether the "punctuated equilibrium paradigm" can be applied to areas beyond the scope of evolutionary biology.[2] Driven by "the need to understand change processes," she set out to determine "how do individuals, groups, organizations, and industries evolve over time? How do they adapt or fail to adapt to changing environments?"

As part of "Revolutionary Change Theories," Gersick focused on six domains. I was particularly intrigued by her work on individual adult development. Underpinning her research was the belief adult development "centers on the same paradigm, or basic gestalt, of evolution: relatively long periods of stability (equilibrium) punctuated by compact periods of qualitative, metamorphic change (revolution). In every model, the interrelationship of these two modes is explained through the construct of a highly durable and underlying order or deep structure. This deep structure is what persists and limits change during equilibrium periods, and it is what disassembles, reconfigures, and enforces wholesale transformation during revolutionary punctuations."

As I became more familiar with Gersick's research, I couldn't help but wonder if my experience constituted a life transition. Had the end of my relationship, resignation from work, and relocation back to the US thrust me out of equilibrium into a period of revolutionary transition?

To determine this, I drew on Gersick's framework for revolutionary changes as a starting point. Gersick proposed for a system to transition from one state to the next, it must proceed through three distinct periods: an initial equilibrium, a revolutionary period, and a subsequent reordered equilibrium. Utilizing her definition of a period of equilibrium as having a "system's basic organization and activity patterns stay the same," I set about examining whether my life prior to these difficult moments fit this definition.

Upon reflecting on my four years in London, I noticed my work and my relationship were the central components of my life structure. This was made clear by my annual goals for 2017 and 2018:

Goals 2017	Goals 2018
-Grow professionally with start-up	-Grow professionally with start-up
-Improve French and get tutor (my partner was French, and I wanted to learn)	-Learn thirty new French words each month
-Keep traveling	-See sister and parents three times each in the next twelve months
	-Spend half a day per month volunteering at a homeless organization
	-Run one twenty-five-kilometer trail run

Professionally, my goals were identical. I viewed my development as being directly tied to the growth of the start-up. As the start-up expanded and reached new stages of development, so too did my roles and responsibilities within the company. I was very content with this alignment and only wanted to see it continue. Similarly, I was excited to be part of a loving relationship with my partner and had begun playing with the idea this relationship would be an enduring one. My interest in learning French was underpinned by my desire to be able to better communicate with her friends and family and pointed to my effort to be more engaged with her values and life. I derived much fulfillment from this life structure and created a day-to-day routine that helped maintain my commitment to both my work and my relationship.

Weekdays were centered on working at the start-up. I would routinely wake up at around 7:30 a.m., get ready, and enjoy the thirty-minute walk to work. While my responsibilities varied drastically from day to day and even hour to hour—client calls, team meetings, moving lab equipment, and preparing for investor presentations—they all fell under the umbrella of growing the new venture, thus feeling routine. Wrapping up my day's tasks, I would head back home.

My partner and I prioritized seeing each other on the weekends. As I lived in London and she in Oxford, we would alternate taking the roughly two-hour trip to visit each other. We would spend the weekends going for runs and hikes, enjoying new types of cuisine, visiting museums, and creating art. About once a month, we would also spend a weekend in an exciting city in Europe—considering the low price of airfare offered by low-cost carriers, the pound-euro exchange rate, and the fact that London is so expensive, what I spent during a weekend away from London was typically the same as a weekend in London. And so, you could typically find me rushing out of work on Fridays at around 5 p.m. to try to catch a train or plane and returning back to London on Sunday evenings.

It is important to note while I very much enjoyed the life structure I had built, it was not without misgivings, which was also evidenced by my goals. In 2017, I was enamored with traveling from city to city and country to country. Living in London, I felt as though the whole world was at my doorstep, and I wanted to take full advantage of it. Gradually, this desire began to ebb. I started to become aware of the fact that, in all my travels, I had sacrificed my ability to foster a community or friend group in London. I also was beginning to miss my family and community back in the US. So, by 2018, I began adjusting some of my priorities and worked to establish roots in London—through volunteering—and placing more effort in seeing my family. That being said, I was still very happy with my way of living and was hopeful of maintaining this balance for at least a few more years. With that in mind, I would argue my life did fall within Gersick's definition of a system at equilibrium.

It is no wonder, sitting by myself in Hyde Park, I felt so overwhelmed. It was in that moment I first began to feel and notice—not quite be aware of—my "deep structure" was facing the prospect of being completely dismantled. This also marked the beginning of an exceptionally difficult time. In a matter of weeks, the equilibrium I had developed over years of effort was suddenly subjected to significant upheaval—this held true for both my day-to-day routines as well as my life structure. Against my wishes, seemingly every aspect of my life was being uprooted, and it brought about a "period of uncertainty about the future." Such instability adversely impacted my mental and emotional health and inhibited my ability to find joy and fulfillment.

My disequilibrium lasted far longer than I had anticipated, taking almost two years to establish a new equilibrium. The rapid sequence of events, including the end of my relationship, loss of work, and relocation to the US, exposed me to a much deeper level of pain than I thought possible. The result was an overwhelming sense of uncertainty that required significant effort to address and often led me to question if I could reestablish a new life structure that would bring me contentment.

CHAPTER 2

History of Mental Health

What is mental health?

I think it is worthwhile asking this question as it is the primary focus and topic of this book. To treat and promote one's mental health implies the promotion of the health of someone's mind. But what does it mean to have a healthy mind?

At first glance, this seems to be a tall order to answer, as the mind can relate to our thoughts, feelings, and experiences. With so many factors and aspects that influence the mind, it is no wonder promoting a healthy mind feels like a more challenging task than maintaining a healthy toe or healthy teeth. The complexity of the mind, and subsequently mental health, is reflected in the World Health Organization's (WHO) definition of mental health as a "state of wellbeing in which every individual realizes his or her own potential, can cope with the normal stresses of life, can work productively and fruitfully, and is able to make a contribution to his or her community."[3] Coping with normal stress, working productively and fruitfully, and making a contribution in one's community are factors that are much more difficult to quantify or observe then, say, a broken bone. The consequence of this is mental health having a long history of stigma and misunderstanding.

As a term, it has only been around for two hundred years, but as a concept, it can date back ten thousand years.[4] Prehistoric skulls and cave art, dated to 6500 BC, have been found to depict the practice of trephination, which involves surgically drilling holes in skulls to allow the release of trapped spirits. Supernatural attributions to mental health disorders continued throughout the Middle Ages, where many turned to religious practices, astrology, and alchemy as solutions to such ailments.[5]

The turn of the seventeenth century brought about different forms of mental health treatment yet did little to destigmatize mental health. It became common practice in Europe for people suffering from mental health to be institutionalized. Many of these institutions—hospitals or asylums—forcibly restrained or left many in solitary confinement, leaving them in inhumane and unsanitary conditions. Such practices were believed to be the best form of treatment and were grounded in the view the mentally ill "did not have the capacity to reason and could not control themselves."[6]

Only in the eighteenth and nineteenth centuries, in response to the horrid conditions of these institutions, did there begin to be a concerted effort to improve the living conditions of the mentally ill. Notable individuals in Europe included

Italian physician Vincenzo Chiarugi (1759–1820), French physician Philippe Pinel (1745–1826), and English Quaker William Tuke (1732–1822). In the US, Dorothea Dix's (1802–1887) work to establish over thirty state hospitals and Clifford Beers' memoir *A Mind That Found Itself*, which was published in 1908 and recounted his time in an asylum, did much to raise awareness and spur action for improvement in mental health services.

At that same time, certain theoretical approaches were being developed to help inform our understanding of mental illness. Most notably, Austrian neurologist Sigmund Freud (1856–1939) proposed his theory of psychodynamics, which centered on the notion mental illness related to the interaction of different unconscious forces. His work led to the creation of more than four hundred schools of psychotherapy.[7]

In the latter half of the twentieth century, the combination of psychotherapy and the first psychotropic medications enabled the trend away from institutionalization. Now that various mental illnesses could be treated outside of an institution, community-based outpatient settings became more common as forms of treatment.[8] With this shift, there was a pronounced effort to help those dealing with mental health conditions in a humane way.

Having an improved understanding about mental health, as well as improved techniques to treat ailments, has done much to diminish the stigma surrounding this topic. A survey conducted by the American Psychological Association (APA) in 2019 found people in the US are becoming more open about mental health. Of the respondents, 87 percent agreed that having a mental health disorder is nothing to be ashamed of and 87 percent said they believe people with mental health disorders can get better. However, stigma persists, as 33 percent of respondents continue to fear mental health disorders and 39 percent say they would view someone differently if they knew that person had a mental health disorder.[9]

This challenge of stigma is also reflected on a global scale, where a significant fraction of the world's population feels embarrassed or ashamed of having a mental health condition or knowing a friend or family member facing a mental health condition. Unfortunately, many of the beliefs and practices that were so pervasive centuries ago continue to this day. A Human Rights Watch report titled "Living in Chains" (2020) reported hundreds of thousands of men, women, and children with mental health conditions were being shackled, chained, or locked in confined spaces in dozens of countries around the world.[10]

Removing the stigma surrounding mental health should be of the utmost priority, particularly when the WHO estimates one in ten people, or 792 million people, and one in five children have a mental health condition.[11] I count myself lucky to have received a tremendous amount of support while struggling with my mental health challenges, support that was provided both from loved ones and strangers, as was the case with the two officers in Hyde Park. I think it is critically important the estimated 792 million people who have a mental health condition receive the same level of care and assistance I have.

CHAPTER 3

Suicidal Ideation

Maybe I should kill myself.

The thought surprised me. It scared me too. I opened my eyes and looked around. The flight attendants were in the midst of handing out snacks. On my left, a man slept with his sleep mask on. On my right, a man absentmindedly flipped through the pages of the inflight magazine.

The air conditioning wasn't functioning properly, and the cabin felt hot and muggy. My shirt, dampened with sweat, weighed down on me. The seat upholstery clung to the backs of my legs, and I kept shifting my position, trying to get comfortable.

Remembering my thought, I closed my eyes and started taking deep breaths, hoping to calm the anxiety that had an iron grip over my psyche.

Maybe I should kill myself.

It popped up again, rising from a dark cloud, which felt as if it had taken over my entire being. There weren't any words emanating from this darkness, but I understood very clearly what it was trying to communicate.

I opened my eyes. This time I focused on the screen in front of me. My breaths became labored. It felt as if the air had been sucked out of the cabin.

Maybe I should kill myself.

It kept coming up! My body was frozen; I couldn't even bring myself to speak.

My eyes closed tightly, and creases appeared by my temples. I grimaced as I tried my best to form logical arguments about why I shouldn't end my life. However, they were no match for the darkness that pervaded every inch of my body.

Maybe I should kill myself.

I gripped the armrests and struggled to find any reason for why I shouldn't kill myself. Why was it so difficult to think of something positive?

Finally!

Mom, Dad, and I are laughing. I met them after work at a little French bistro close to my house in London. We have just finished our delicious meals and are enjoying the warmth of the indoors as we watch the rain outside.

The memory passed, fleetingly. It provided a brief reprieve.

I'm sitting on a bench, enjoying the warmth of the sun, savoring the delicious nectar of my slice of watermelon, and staring up at the snowcapped peaks of the Bernese Alps. The sky is a stunning blue, without a cloud in the sky, and I'm surrounded by the verdant beauty of the Lauterbrunnen Valley in Switzerland. My legs are tired and I'm proud of having completed a thirty-kilometer run from the town of Lauterbrunnen, up to the Kleine Scheidegg mountain peak train station, and down the Eiger mountain's north face to the town of Grindelwald.

Another temporary reprieve.

I opened my eyes. I adjusted the air conditioning unit, but it did little to slow the sweat beading on my forehead. The flight attendants had only served one or two additional rows in that time.

Maybe I should kill myself.

This time, a new thought.

I don't want anyone else to have to deal with this. If for no other reason, I can't kill myself so I can support others who are struggling with this.

For four hours on the flight, I clung desperately to those three thoughts as a defense against the continual tsunami of darkness.

* * *

Dark thoughts haunted me for over ten months, which reached a climax during the flight. I was scared by these ideas and did my best to lock them deep down within me. But the emotions had a way of fighting back. Everything seemed to be a trigger. The more I tried repressing the thought of killing myself, the harder it was for me to ignore it. Only after addressing those emotions was I able to step back and reflect on what brought me to that point, and to more generally ask the question, what compels people to end their lives?

Suicide is a complex topic, so much so even the task of agreeing to a set definition for suicide has proved challenging. The Institute of Mental Health first proposed a definition in the 1970s. The Centers for Disease Control developed their own "Operational Criteria for the Determination of Suicide" in 1988. This was followed by an attempt from the World Health Organization's EURO Multicentre Study to propose a unifying terminology. In Matthew Nock et al.'s comprehensive *Oxford Handbook of Suicide and Self-Injury* (2014), they define suicide as "death resulting from intentional behavior, associated with any intent to die as a result of the behavior. Importantly, intent can either be stated by the individual or inferred."[12]

Suicide, as a phenomenon, can be subdivided into three classes: (1) suicide, (2) suicide attempt, and (3) suicidal ideation.[13] While vaguely familiar with the first two classes, I wasn't entirely sure what suicidal ideation meant. According to an article published by Christopher Bagley in the *British Journal of Guidance & Counselling* (1975), suicidal ideation is defined as "having thoughts, ideas, and intentions about suicide" and can be further broken down into two categories—passive ideation and active ideation.[14] Passive ideation is a "desire rather than a plan," whereas active ideation is a "desire to make an active suicide attempt."[15]

After learning this, it became evident I struggled with a form of passive suicidal ideation. I never planned to attempt suicide, nor did I ever intend to actively attempt suicide. Instead, I was very scared of having suicidal thoughts and really fought to push them away. I couldn't understand why these ideas kept popping up and routinely found myself in situations where I didn't trust myself. This was due to the fact I wasn't sure what I would do impulsively once these ideas were triggered. Learning about the various classes of suicide did help allay my fears somewhat, but I still didn't understand what would bring someone to attempt suicide.

Renowned clinical psychologist Thomas Joiner argues in his work *Why People Die by Suicide* that three criteria must be met for a person to attempt suicide.[16]

- The feeling of being a burden on loved ones
- The sense of isolation
- The learned ability to hurt oneself

Expanding on the third point, Joiner proposes people must habituate themselves or "acquire the ability to commit suicide over time."[17] This can occur through various acts ranging from recurrent violence, intravenous drug use, eating disorders, self-injury, and more. This habituation, coupled with an individual's perceived burden on others and society, and "obliteration" of a person's sustaining connection to others can lead someone to die by suicide.[18]

Of the three criteria, the sense of isolation contributed most to my anxiety and suicidal ideation. Following my move back to California, I missed my lifestyle; I missed my friends, unsure if I would ever see them again; and I missed living in London. That being said, my parents were incredibly supportive and routinely offered their love and support when I moved back to California. I never felt like I was a burden to them—I can't imagine what my mental state would have been otherwise. I strongly believe it was the support of loved ones and friends that helped me through that moment and prevented me from progressing beyond suicidal ideation.

While I count myself lucky to not have met all three of Joiner's criteria, many unfortunately do. However, no one set of reasons can lead someone to attempt suicide. Instead, Nock et al. identified a plethora of reasons and offered several frameworks to understand someone's self-injurious behavior. Research has identified a wide set of factors ranging from genetic and developmental influences on social, cognitive, and cultural impacts.

Nock et al.'s summaries of proposed approaches[19]
Genetic and Neurobiological Approaches: Research suggests genetic factors and neurobiological processes can influence a person's susceptibility to suicidal behavior.
Developmental Approaches: Research indicates a strong correlation between age and risk of suicide. To further characterize this relationship, current efforts are aimed at determining a person's risk profile toward suicide across their lifespan based on biological, psychosocial, and developmental factors.

Nock et al.'s summaries of proposed approaches[19]
Social and Ecological Approaches: There exist theoretical models and empirical findings that suggest social and ecological influences such as peer (i.e., peer status and victimization, friendship and social support, peer influence), family (i.e., family communication and problem-solving, relationship quality, child maltreatment), and neighborhood contexts are influential.
Cognitive and Information Processing Approaches: Cognitive and information processing behaviors (i.e., hopelessness, perfectionism, burdensomeness, low belongingness, unbearability, problem-solving deficits, over-general memory, future thinking, attentional biases, implicit associations) interact with one another during suicidal crises.
Psychodynamics of Suicide: A psychoanalytic theory of suicide has grown to include assessment of affects, coping mechanisms, and relationships in the patient's internal and external world.
Cultural Factors: Increasingly, factors such as race/ethnicity, spirituality/religious affiliation, and sexual orientation are being researched as links to factors such as suicidal ideation, attempts, and completions.

Nock et al. have found evidence for a "strong interplay between each of these factors."[20] As a result, preventing suicide requires providing tailored solutions to at-risk individuals. Nock et al. proposed a person-centered approach that believes the success of all interventions depends on the extent to which each individual's fundamental human needs have been accommodated.[21] My need for connection and the support I received from my community was fundamental to helping me overcome my suicidal ideation.

The importance of taking a person-centered approach to help people struggling with suicide was reinforced during my conversation with Leanne Pooley when she said, "I think you have to be willing to listen rather than speak." Pooley is a filmmaker based in New Zealand. I reached out to her following the release of her film called *The Girl on the Bridge*, which follows a young woman named Jazz Thornton who struggled with suicide and is now a mental health activist working to provide individualized support for young people struggling with suicide.[22]

During the directing of this film, Pooley's brother suddenly took his life, causing her life and work to collide. Her initial response to his death "was similar to lots of people who lose somebody. I was angry with him; I felt it was a selfish decision he made." However, as part of her grieving process, and through the directing of her film, she began to understand the importance of creating empathy and seeing the world through the eyes of someone struggling with suicide. She noted she was "forever giving my brother advice" and people broadly try to "fix" those struggling with suicide. Instead, people should focus their efforts on supporting each person, "taking their hand," and walking with them as they take steps to help themselves in a way that maintains their autonomy.

A first step toward assisting someone is understanding how a person is feeling. This could be as simple as asking if a person is suicidal. Pooley remarked she never asked her brother if he was going to kill himself and laments, "People are afraid to ask outright, 'Are you feeling suicidal?'" There were many occasions where I wanted to tell someone I was struggling with suicidal ideation but didn't. Whether it was a sense of embarrassment, shame, or another emotion, something always seemed to get in the way of sharing how I was feeling with others. This only perpetuated my sense of isolation that persisted until ten months after my flight when I summoned the courage to tell someone. Reaching out to someone who seems to be struggling and offering to take them by the hand and act in a way that helps them manage a difficult emotional state can make a huge difference.

Statistics
According to a report by Centers for Disease Control and Prevention published in 2018: [23]
Suicide is the tenth leading cause of death in US. There were 1.4 million suicide attempts in the US, resulting in 48,344 deaths in the US. On average, this translates to 132 suicides per day, which means in the time it has taken for you to read this chapter, someone in the US has died by suicide. In the US, men died by suicide 3.56 times more often than women, and white males accounted for 69.67 percent of suicide deaths.
According to statistics from the American Foundation for Suicide Prevention:[24]
The age-adjusted suicide rate in 2018 was 14.2 per one hundred thousand individuals. The rate of suicide is highest in middle-aged white men. In 2018, firearms accounted for 51 percent of all suicide deaths. Ninety-three percent of adults surveyed feel suicide is preventable.
National Suicide Prevention Lifeline (twenty-four hours, English and Spanish). Are you in a crisis? Call 800-273-8255 or text TALK to 741741.

The American Association of Suicidology has provided a list of warning signs:[25]
When you recognize someone exhibiting these warning signs, it's okay to ask directly.
Acute Risks:
Threatening to hurt or kill him/herself or talking of wanting to hurt or kill him/herself. Looking for ways to kill him/herself by seeking access to firearms, available pills, or other means. Talking or writing about death, dying, or suicide, when these actions are out of the ordinary.
Additional Warning Signs:
Increased substance (alcohol or drug) use. No reason for living, no sense of purpose in life. Anxiety, agitation, unable to sleep or sleeping all of the time. Feeling trapped—like there's no way out. Hopelessness. Withdrawal from friends, family, and society. Rage, uncontrolled anger, or seeking revenge. Acting recklessly or engaging in risky activities, seemingly without thinking. Dramatic mood changes. Giving away prized possessions or seeking long-term care for pets.

CHAPTER 4

Starting Therapy

"I recommend you consider seeing a counselor," said Marissa.

We were sitting at a café table, watching people go about their days, listening to the drum of traffic and the occasional honk. A gust of wind blew the fallen leaves past our seats, and I proceeded to button up my coat. I stared at my empty coffee mug and pondered her comment. Little remained aside from some dregs and a bit of foam.

This wasn't the first time someone suggested I go to counseling, and it was something I had been mulling over for a few weeks following the end of my relationship and resignation from work. The weeks had not been easy; they were filled with repeated panic and anxiety attacks. I knew I was struggling to deal with my grief and needed help, but I was unsure of how best to proceed.

"I think you're right; seeking professional assistance to help me through this makes sense."

"Even an initial session here in London can be beneficial. I've always found my therapy sessions extremely helpful," she said.

Marissa was a very close family friend whom I had known since growing up in California. I reached out to her for guidance, as she was a marriage and family therapist. By pure coincidence, she happened to be in London as part of a longer trip through Europe and immediately extended her stay in London to help me.

"But I don't even know which therapist I should reach out to." The loud honk of a bus briefly shifted my attention. "I don't even know how to find a therapist."

She was about to take a sip of her coffee but paused, holding the mug in her hands. "I can definitely recommend a few therapists who I think would be good fits. They are all based in California, but you can try reaching out and scheduling an initial call with them. The important thing is to be gentle on yourself."

A few weeks later, I found myself sitting at my desk in my apartment in London. I had reached out to a therapist Marissa recommended, and we had agreed to have an introductory call. Only a few minutes remained until the start of our meeting. The beat of my heart quickened. The clock hit 8 p.m., and I clicked on the link to join the meeting.

That was the first time I connected with Sofia. After a brief introduction, I proceeded to share with her what had transpired in the previous few months—about the start-up, my relationship, and the prospect of having to move back to California.

"Wow, that sounds like a lot of goodbyes."

My brow furrowed and I squirmed in my seat. The sadness in her voice made me feel uncomfortable, as it briefly made me reckon with the pain I was dealing with.

"Yeah."

I began to feel a lump in my throat and looked away from the computer screen. I couldn't bring myself to engage in this discussion further, fearful that by doing so, the emotions bubbling up would spill out in the open.

Hoping to the change the topic, I asked her what the process of starting therapy entailed. She explained there would be an initial three-week trial period, she recommended meeting on a weekly basis, and I needed to fill out some intake forms. Importantly, she highlighted the fact that although our conversations would be confidential, she would have to report any mentions of self-harm or intent to harm others.

"Do you have any last questions for me?" asked Sofia.

"Yes, is there a particular type of therapy you like to use?"

"I do. I prefer a psychodynamic approach. I think talking about and exploring less conscious beliefs is important, as well as attempting to understand the emotions driving these beliefs." She paused. "I like to look into how former experiences and memories impact the current situation and use that to help deal with the process. Previously, I was a yoga teacher, so I like to see how things are doing in the body. Sometimes the thinking mind isn't that good at dealing with issues, and the body can give some good insight."

Wrapping up, I thanked her for her input, and we said our goodbyes.

* * *

Several tools are at your disposal to help you find a therapist. While I reached out to friends and family for recommendations, it is not the only way to do so. Other options include:

- PsychologyToday provides a directory of "clinical professionals, psychiatrists, and treatment centers who provide mental health services in the US and internationally."[26] As part of its databases, you can select for therapists based on insurance, specialty, location, mental illness, and more.
- GoodTherapy is an online directory that enables people to "find therapists and counselors, rehab and residential treatment centers, and mental health resources."[27]
- TherapyDen is an online search directory whose mission is to "make finding the right therapist or counselor as painless as possible."[28] With the aim of making therapy as inclusive as possible, individuals can filter for therapists based on language, faith, ADA accessibility, ethnicity, and sexual orientation.
- ZocDoc "offers a digital marketplace which connects patients and doctors. Patients can search ZocDoc's

marketplace to discover a wide selection of health care providers that are relevant."[29]

- National Alliance on Mental Illness (NAMI) is a grassroots mental health organization with a mission of providing "advocacy, education, support, and public awareness" to help all those affected by mental health issues.[30] In addition to offering education programs, the NAMI HelpLine is a toll-free line designed to offer "support and provide practical next steps" for a range of mental health related questions.
- 2-1-1 is a free telephone number in the US providing access to local community services.[31] Available in multiple languages, it provides information and referrals to "physical and mental health resources; housing, utility, food, and employment assistance; and suicide and crisis interventions."
- Employee Assistance Programs (EAP) are often offered through your job and can provide short-term counseling and referrals, amongst other services.
- Health plans typically provide listings of therapists covered by insurance, which can also be searched based on location and specialty.
- Your doctor should be aware of local mental health networks and can provide references.
- Therapists can offer a wealth of information of the local mental health network. You may call any therapist, explain your situation and what you are hoping to achieve with therapy, and ask them for a recommendation.

Once you have a list of candidate therapists, how do you know which one will be a good fit? There are a few things to keep in mind as part of your initial outreach, which can help guide your selection of a therapist.

The first thing to consider is the distinction between psychiatrists, psychologists, and therapists. They are all mental health professionals committed to helping individuals improve and maintain their mental health. However, psychiatrists, psychologists, and therapists all have various educational backgrounds, so they approach diagnosis and treatment of mental illness differently.

According to the American Psychiatric Association (APA), a psychiatrist is a medical doctor (MD or DO) who specializes in preventing, diagnosing, and treating mental illness. To become a psychiatrist, a person must complete four years of medical school, a one-year internship, and at least three years of specialization as a psychiatric resident. Psychiatrists are qualified to assess both the mental and physical aspects of psychological problems. Psychiatrists use a variety of treatments, including psychotherapy and medication, to help provide a picture of a patient's physical and mental state.[32]

The APA also explains a psychologist (PhD or PsyD) is trained to have the professional and clinical skills to help people learn to cope more effectively with life issues and mental health problems. On average, psychologists spend five years completing their doctoral degree and an additional two years of internships. Psychologists are qualified to help people cope with stressful situations, overcome addictions, manage their chronic illnesses, and can conduct assessments to help diagnose why a person thinks, feels, and behaves a certain way.[33]

The American Counseling Association states licensed professional counselors (LPC), licensed marriage and family therapists (LMFT), and licensed clinical social workers (LCSW) all are trained to work with individuals, families, and groups to treat mental, behavioral, and emotional problems. All have completed a two-year master's program and a one- to two-year internship. Therapists are also working toward becoming licensed and will provide care under the supervision of a licensed mental health specialist.[34]

To summarize, psychiatrists have broad medical training and will typically manage someone's mental health challenges with medication. Conversely, psychologists and masters-level therapists will commonly use psychotherapy or treatment methods that do not require medication. If you are unsure which form of treatment is best suited for you, you can try to reach out to your primary care provider for insight or to a practice that offers both, as it is common for all parties to collaborate and work together.

It's also important to note there are different types of psychotherapy. The APA segments the field of psychotherapy into four broad categories (psychoanalysis therapy, behavior therapy, cognitive therapy, and humanistic therapy) and defines each of them as follows:

In psychoanalysis therapy, you will develop a close partnership with your therapist with the aim of understanding the influence of your unconscious mind on your conscious behaviors, feelings, and thoughts. As part of this process, you will be encouraged to explore your past, your childhood, and stories surrounding your family of origin. As there is a lot to cover, a psychoanalytic approach is typically a long-term approach to therapy.[35]

In cognitive therapy, the therapy focuses on the influence of people's thoughts on their emotions and behaviors. Rather than focusing on a person's past experiences, cognitive therapy will center on the thoughts you are presently feeling and attempt to solve the problem behaviors you are facing by changing the underpinning thoughts.[36]

In humanistic therapy, this approach emphasizes the importance of helping each person be their true self and develop their maximum potential. Concern and respect for others are also important themes.[37]

Healthline.com elaborates in behavior therapy, you seek to identify and help change unhealthy behaviors.[38] Central to this approach is the notion all behaviors are learned and current problem behaviors can be changed.

It's important to realize the great majority of therapists do not conform to one approach. Rather, they incorporate different components from various branches of therapy to develop a unique treatment plan for each individual. The primary distinction is found between psychoanalysis and behavior therapy. Whereas psychoanalysis focuses on your past experiences and is a long-term form of therapy, cognitive therapy orients itself toward developing solutions to your present-day problems. Cognitive therapy also works on building your skills and is typically a shorter-term therapy. Which type of therapy is best suited for you depends on your goals, wants, and expectations for therapy. If you are starting out in therapy, I would encourage you to meet with therapists who use different approaches to gain a better insight of what works best for you.

* * *

Initially, I didn't have any idea about the different types of psychotherapy. I only asked Sofia that question in my initial call because my friends suggested I ask it. However, the phrase "psychodynamic approach" did not mean anything to me at the time. I also didn't have any inkling or understanding of the differences between licensed professionals. I relied entirely on Marissa's recommendations and didn't pause to consider the professional background of the person providing therapy—I also don't think it would have made much of a difference for me.

Of all the factors people recommend one should consider when starting therapy, I have found the most important one for me is often overlooked: whether a person is ready to begin therapy. I understood I was struggling with mental health challenges. However, the call with Sofia brought up several uncomfortable emotions to the surface I was not prepared for. I wasn't ready to engage with those emotions, and even though it would likely have been better for me to start therapy, I didn't. I decided instead to push the emotions aside, ignore them, and backpack around the Balkans for a couple of months. Only months later, when my mental health challenges reached a crisis point, did I follow up with Sofia and schedule an initial meeting with her.

CHAPTER 5

Internal Landscape

I hurried into the office and dropped my backpack and helmet at the far end of the couch. Turning to get some tea, I noticed the slight dampness of sweat on my back.

The aroma of mint wafted up from the mug. Outside, the silhouette of my bike was framed by the vibrant orange sunset. The call of a bird pierced through the rumble of the traffic. I sat down and lay may notebook across my lap.

"Where do you want to begin?" asked Sofia.

I brought my pen to my lips and took a moment to reflect on our previous session and the events of the past week.

"Yeah. We previously discussed a goal for me to develop a better understanding about how I respond to different situations. You mentioned this exploration can feel new and unsettling, and I was hoping to continue that discussion, as there have been a few moments in this past week that relate to that."

She nodded and flipped open her notepad.

The couch pillow slowly compressed as I leaned back. "I noticed once or twice this past week, I was feeling excited about something going well and found myself holding back from that feeling of excitement. It felt almost as if my excitement triggered some protective response. This is something I haven't felt before, something new, and I wanted to dig into that."

Sofia jotted down a few things and agreed that was a good place to start.

She paused to gather her thoughts. "One thing this could be is your body preventing an excitable state to lessen the distance of a possible fall from that state of excitement."

My eyebrows raised, and I quickly jotted down a few notes.

This could be an explanation for why I've been feeling this way!

She continued, "What's important is you create an open line of communication to that part of you. To be aware of that part and acknowledge it. One of the goals we have previously discussed, given the fact you have experienced some significant emotional wounds, is for you to try and develop a new internal landscape—to learn about who you are and how you respond to different situations. And, importantly, acknowledge doing so can be challenging. One analogy I like to use is that of a rough edge. As you explore your internal landscape, you are going to come across new rough edges. Initially, they will feel new and uncomfortable, but by bringing a sense of curiosity and awareness to each edge, it can soften and become less threatening."

A smile spread across my face. I visualized myself spelunking through a new, previously unexplored cave and slowly mapping the various passageways.

* * *

Why does therapy work?

It was a question that dogged me for many months, even after starting therapy. Everyone involved in mental health vouched for it, be it peers, friends, family, or other therapists. In my discussions, I routinely heard comments like "everyone should have a therapist" or "everyone should go to therapy." Intuitively, I agreed with them. Having gone to therapy for over three months at that point, I could personally attest to its benefits. But no one was able to give me a satisfactory answer to that question. At times, people mentioned releasing one's emotions could be cathartic, but I felt there was more to therapy than just voicing the emotions I felt within.

Posing this question to a friend, they recommended I read Dr. Irvin Yalom's book *The Gift of Therapy.* Yalom is an existential psychiatrist and professor of psychiatry who, through this book, imparts his wisdom of thirty-five years on how therapists can provide successful therapy. His approach to psychotherapy involved "removing obstacles blocking the patient's path."[39]

Yalom was strongly influenced by the work of Dr. Karen Horney. A German psychoanalyst who moved to the US late in life, she pioneered concepts including self-realization. In her work *Neurosis and Human Growth*, Horney proposes each individual has the propensity to develop as an "acorn into an oak tree" if nurtured in the appropriate environment.[40] Fundamental to this view involves the belief each individual has the potential for self-realization, which manifests itself through the development of "unique alive forces of their real selves: the clarity and depth of their own feelings, thoughts, wishes, interests; the ability to tap their own resources, the strength of their will power, the special capacities or gifts they may have; the faculty to express themselves, and to relate themselves to others with their spontaneous feelings. All this will in time enable them to find their set of values and their aims in life."[41]

Horney makes clear an individual will not automatically grow into an oak tree, as many "adverse influences" will stunt their development.[42] However, therapy can be helpful since it can remove these adverse influences impeding a patient's path. The challenge for the therapist is to offer a tailored solution that will best facilitate the patient's growth.

If the challenge for a therapist is to remove obstacles for the patient, then I would argue the patient's challenge is twofold; first, to acknowledge and recognize the obstacles barring the way to growth, and second, to demonstrate the desire to grow beyond those obstacles. I found neither of those challenges are easy to overcome, nor can they be done quickly, particularly when rooted in deep emotional traumas.

Unfortunately, most people in the US are opting for expediency when attempting to solve their problems. An article published by the American Psychological Association titled "Where Has All the Psychotherapy Gone?" noted "in 2008, 30 percent fewer patients received psychological interventions compared to in 1997."[43] This trend was fueled by an attempt by the managed behavioral-care industry to reduce costs associated with mental health and substance abuse benefits. While there were increasingly strict limitations on the benefits provided for mental health services, prescription drugs were not included in this effort to cut costs.

While 30 percent fewer patients received psychological interventions, "expenditures for psychotropic medications tripled."[44] Pharmaceutical companies also drove this trend, which "spent 4.2 billion dollars on direct-to-consumer advertising and a whopping 7.2 billion dollars on promoting to physicians."[45] Lori Gottlieb, in her book *Maybe You Should Talk to Someone*, remarks, "Of course, it's a lot easier—and quicker—to swallow a pill than to do the heavy lifting of looking inside yourself."[46] She goes on to acknowledge she is not opposed to the use of medication and is, in fact, a strong believer in the benefits these medications can offer. However, she poses the question as to whether "26 percent of the general population really needed psychotropic medications," particularly as today's patients' criticize psychotherapy for "not working fast enough."[47]

Initially, I also desired a quick-fix solution. My instinct was to ignore the obstacles and wish them away. In fact, one of the primary objectives I wrote in my notebook on my first session at therapy was to "get rid of my anxiety." I was dealing with a new depth of grief and emotions and believed the best course of action was to get rid of them. Alas, I soon realized that wasn't the correct approach. I could have continued trying to block out my obstacles, but that would only have served to keep me in a stunted state, unable to grow into the oak tree.

While it may be difficult to look under the hood or uncomfortable to come across a new rough edge, the reward for this effort is to be able to be more fully human. A striking example of the possibility for growth was made evident during my conversation with Yvette Kong, an Olympic swimmer from Hong Kong. From a very young age, she enjoyed being in the water and made it a goal of hers to qualify for the Olympics. She quickly became a swimming prodigy, breaking many of Hong Kong's swimming records by the age of sixteen and rising to rank twenty-first in the world. At the age of fifteen, she missed qualifying for the Beijing Olympics by one second.

Unfazed, she enrolled at UC Berkeley and joined the elite swimming team hoping to benefit from training with Olympic champions and international stars. Having never previously lived outside of Hong Kong, the transition to the US proved challenging. To add to the frustration, she missed qualifying for the 2012 Olympic Games by 0.1 seconds. Following an unsuccessful qualification attempt, "I wasn't feeling quite good. I really liked the water, but every day I felt a huge burden training and my body just felt heavy and wasn't performing well at all. I regressed further from not making the Olympics to not making the NCAAs—the college athletic championships—and I think I broke down."

Kong decided she needed to step away from swimming, as training depressed her. Initially, she felt things were improving, but soon thereafter began to experience sudden flashbacks of her time swimming. Describing that period, "I would start feeling like I wanted to break down, like I would want to cry." Acknowledging she had a problem was difficult, as she was afraid to talk about mental health because it would potentially "make me look weak." Only after summoning the courage to look herself in the mirror and acknowledge something was wrong was she able to address the problem she was facing. She ended up going to therapy to help parse apart her relationship with swimming.

She felt very confused about whether she still wanted to swim, so much so it felt like "a giant hairball, with so much stuff intertwined." Only after going layer by layer and untangling this mess was she able to recall certain traumas that occurred during her childhood. "I had a coach who yelled a lot and could be borderline verbally abusive. On the last day of qualifying for the Beijing Olympics, my coach left me, and I was all alone."

After months of therapy, she was able to untangle her hairball and realized, deep down at the core, she liked swimming. Motivated by this insight, she slowly went back to the pool, initially merely dipping her toes in the water. She noticed over the years, her pursuit of excellence had added layers of trauma to her time swimming, so instead, she then focused on "digging deep and finding that little girl again who just liked being in the water." After graduating, she wanted a change and opted to train at the University of Edinburgh with a goal of making the 2016 Olympics. She packed her bags, moved across the world, and began what became a "magical year for me where things finally got together." She changed everything about her mindset and training regimen, reduced her swim time by six seconds—from 1:13 to 1:07—and qualified for the Rio de Janeiro Olympics. Reflecting on her experience, "the first step for me was learning to be vulnerable and acknowledging vulnerability is a source of strength." Acknowledging her traumas and obstacles gave her an "inner peace and wellness that was really valuable for life and helped bring out the optimal and best self."

I have found the true gift of therapy for anyone willing to embark on that journey, which is the promise of developing into your fullest person. Like Kong, who only reached her fullest potential as a swimmer after addressing her traumas, I couldn't heal until I acknowledged my emotional wounds. My primary obstacle was forming a new relationship with my emotions. For the longest time, my instinct was to ignore and repress these new emotions; I tried blocking them out and pretending they weren't there. These efforts were mostly in vain, and I felt the more I pushed the emotions away, the more they pushed back. My efforts created a continual sense of fear and anxiety and kept me in a stunted state. Only after acknowledging my uncomfortable emotions and new rough edges—with Sofia's help and guidance—was I able to navigate these obstacles and approach them with a sense of curiosity and a desire for growth.

It's important to note just because our obstacles are removed doesn't mean it is easy to grow past them. Kong still had to commit a tremendous amount of effort, focus, and motivation to get back into the pool and train for the Olympic qualifications. Similarly, I worked with Sofia for over a year and placed a lot of effort going deep and exploring my internal landscape, any rough edges that arose, and incorporating the learnings and insights into my everyday life. Nevertheless, the rewards have entirely justified my hard work. I have been able to achieve an internal peace and clarity about what gives me meaning and fulfillment I hope will help me qualify for my own version of the Olympics.

PART 2

SURVIVAL

CHAPTER 1

Breathe

I hung up the phone.

This wasn't what I expected.

My abdomen clenched tight, and I found it difficult to breathe. I walked down the hallway to my bathroom to get a glass of water. The coolness of the black tile contrasted with the soft Saxony carpet I had been sitting on during the previous hour. I began filling my glass at the porcelain white washbasin and looked into the mirror. The dark circles under my eyes surprised me. My eyes were red and watery and fine lines began to appear across my face.

Three and a half years.

My legs began to wobble, so I put down my glass and leaned on the sink. The sound of muffled footsteps walking down the staircase took me away from my thoughts. It was still early in the morning, not yet eight. The sing-along pop songs of ABBA filled the flat, indicating it was Ricardo, my good friend and roommate of two years, heading down to the bathroom from his room upstairs for his morning shower.

Reaching the bathroom, he paused as he saw me.

"What's wrong?"

"My partner and I just broke up."

"Oooh, no. I'm sorry." He walked toward me, his arms out.

I rested my head on his shoulder and let him console me. I found the soft touch of his towel against my cheek comforting.

I thought we were going to spend the rest of our lives together.

We proceeded to the living room and sat down on the brown leather couch. Ricardo retracted the curtains, revealing the branches and green leaves of a common beach—our flat was one story up from ground level—and a grey, overcast sky. He spent most of the morning trying to cheer me up. Being with him provided a sense of peace. Eventually, he had to go to work, so we said our goodbyes. I was in no position to go to work that day.

The sound of the front door closing reverberated up the staircase. Staring up at the ceiling, it dawned on me I was all by myself. I didn't want to be alone, so I walked back to my room and tried calling my younger sister Didi. She didn't pick up—unsurprisingly, as it was five o'clock in the morning in Chicago. The bed creaked as I leaned back against the frame. A wave of sadness washed over me, and I found it difficult to breathe. Resting my head in my arms, hot tears streaked down my cheeks.

It hurts.

I gritted my teeth and wrung my hands as the sadness overwhelmed me.

Safety pins!

My eyes opened wide. Tears flowed uncontrollably, and my nose was runny. I stared at my wrists, scared.

The thought did not seem my own, but I knew it had come from within me. For fifteen minutes, I sat, anchored to the floor, and wrestled with this inner demon, scared of myself, scared of the moment, and in complete agony.

My phone lit up. A picture of Didi popped up on my screen. Miraculously, she had woken up early and was responding to my call. I quickly reached for the phone and answered.

"Shayne?"

I opened my mouth but felt a catch in my throat and couldn't speak.

"Shayne!"

I continued crying.

"It's going to be okay, just breathe. Breathe in, one, two, three, four." I heard her inhale. "And out, one, two, three, four."

I took a short, shallow breath.

"Breathe in, one, two, three, four. And out, one, two, three, four."

It took me a few cycles to register what she was saying. I focused on my breaths and tried to synchronize them with her counting.

"One, two, three, four."

I slowly inhaled. My heartbeat began to slow.

"One, two, three, four."

Exhaling, my chest relaxed. The warmth of the sunlight lent a sense of calm.

"One, two, three, four."

Air rushed in through my nostrils and my chest rose as my lungs filled to capacity.

"One, two, three, four."

My mouth opened slightly; air slowly seeped out. My belly gradually became smaller.

I opened my eyes. The emotion had ebbed, and I finally felt like I could speak.

* * *

At first glance, self-injury seems counterproductive. Why would someone want to purposefully cause themselves pain? How can there be any possible benefit to self-injuring? Dr. Janis Whitlock and Dr. Elizabeth Lloyd-Richardson explain in their book *Healing Self-Injury* the "physical pain of self-injury brings relief from unwanted thoughts and feelings."[48] By self-injuring, individuals hope to alter their emotional state through physical pain as a response to the feelings of significant emotions they are dealing with. In my case, the anguish I felt from the loss of my relationship was unbearable. It was an internal pain unlike anything I had previously felt, and my mind searched for a method to alleviate it. In that moment, the draw of injuring myself with safety pins seemed to outweigh the pain of the emotions roiling inside.

Healing Self-Injury goes on to share there has been a marked increase in rates of self-injury in the US over the last few decades. The population of individuals who self-injure also has expanded over this same period. Previously, individuals who self-injured had clear mental health challenges and a history of sexual abuse or other significant traumas. Now, however, most individuals who do self-injure represent various population groups that would otherwise be deemed healthy and without a history of trauma.

As our society becomes more aware of the prevalence of self-injury, efforts have been taken to determine whether there are factors in a person's life that contribute to this behavior. In his book *Treating Self-Injury*, Dr. Barent Walsh developed a bio-psycho-social model where he proposes self-injury is a phenomenon that relates to five general factors:[49]

- Environmental – Relating to family history (i.e., observing violence or substance abuse) or individual history (i.e., death of parent or caregiver, divorce, abuse)
- Biological – Disfunction of serotonin or other endorphins
- Cognitive – Interpretations of events being especially negative or pessimistic
- Affective – Susceptibility to frequent, intense, sustained emotions
- Behavioral – Understanding the actions that immediately precede, accompany, and follow acts of self-injury

Various reasons can lead a person to self-injury, underpinned by a complex set of unique circumstances. The challenge in helping a person overcome self-injury is understanding what unique set of factors contribute to their personal self-injury. Over the years of helping treat self-injury, Walsh has found nine "replacement skills" that can help individuals treat their self-injury.[50] Some of the skills include "mindful breathing skills, physical exercise, writing, artistic expression, playing, or listening to music."[51] Of note, Walsh shared "breathing skills are often the most important in learning to give up self-injury."[52]

But how exactly does breathing help to prevent self-injury? Journalist James Nestor recently published *Breath: The New Science of a Lost Art*, in which he explores the ways in which humans breathe and the manner in which breathing can influence our health. In an interview on National Public Radio, Nestor shares breathing can have a "profound effect on your mental state."[53] The reason for this relates to the influence breathing has on our nervous system. Namely, inhaling can trigger a response in our sympathetic nervous system—the system responsible for a fight or flight response and floods the body with stress hormones. Conversely, exhaling can trigger a response in our parasympathetic nervous system—the system that is active during rest and relaxation. He explains if someone were to put their hand over their heart and "take a very slow inhale, you're going to feel your heart speed up. As you exhale, you should feel your heart slow down. So, exhaling relaxes the body."[54]

When dealing with anxiety or stress, a common response is for someone to take quick, shallow breaths. Breathing so much actually has a deleterious impact on our bodies because with "each breath, we're stimulating our sympathetic side of the nervous system and constantly putting ourselves in a state of stress."[55] The antidote to this heightened sense of stress is to take deep breaths. While it sounds simple, breathing deeply "allows more air into the lungs and immediately switches the body into a relaxed state. When we control our breathing, we can influence so much of how our bodies operate, and that includes a practice for people with anxieties or depression."[56]

I can definitely attest to the power of breathing. Sitting alone in my room, I felt an intense amount of anxiety and stress. Being able to take deep, measured breaths allowed me to regain a sense of calm. Doing so helped me to exert some influence on the state of my body, and inhaling and exhaling slowly restored the balance between my sympathetic and parasympathetic nervous systems. In a moment of intense emotion, breathing offered a lifeline to help me manage the significant urge to self-injure.

It is important to note beyond helping me not self-injure in a moment of acute crisis, breathing also laid the foundation for me to better regulate a new set of intense emotions. To this day, I continually draw upon the lessons I learned about the benefits of breathing to help me provide a sense of calm if I am ever feeling sustained or intense emotions.

As part of my work with Sofia, I have learned a number of breathing exercises I continue to use to this day to help me reduce any anxiety or stress I may be feeling and regain a sense of balance. They include:
Box Breathing In this breathing exercise, the goal is to "draw" a box with your breath. On the first inhalation, you will visualize drawing one line of the box. Inhale slowly through your nose, hold your breath while counting to four, and then slowly exhale out. On your second inhalation, visualize drawing the second line of the box. Again, count to four after inhaling and slowly exhale. Continue with two more breathing cycles to draw the remaining two lines of a box.
Five Sensations Breathing Get settled by beginning with a several deep breaths. Try to slow your breathing. Notice your stomach expand and contract with each cycle. Continue your deep breaths throughout this exercise. Once you feel calmer and settled, begin by noticing five things you can see. Then, try to notice four different physical sensations you feel. Continue by identifying three different sounds you can hear. Then, two different smells. Lastly, try to notice one thing you taste.

Walsh also provides a number of breathing exercises he has used with his clients, which I have also found helpful in my life:
One to Ten to One Exhalation Breathing[57] When breathing in and out, focus on the sensation of breathing. I have found expanding your stomach when breathing in and contracting your stomach when breathing out helps me focus on breathing. After the first exhalation, say "one." Breathe in again and in the following exhalation, say "two." Repeat this until you reach "ten" and then continue counting down back to "one."

CHAPTER 2

Therapeutic Alliance

"Hi, how are you?"

I walked into Sofia's office, looking forward to our next session. I headed toward my usual spot on the far corner of the couch, placed my bike helmet on the ground, and took off my backpack. I heard the door close behind me and turned to see Sofia sitting down in her armchair.

She grabbed her notepad, and after a brief pause, she said, "I'm wondering how you are."

* * *

That moment acted as a microcosm of the learning curve I faced as I began to understand the nuances of the expected relationship formed between a therapist and client, or therapeutic alliance. It took me several weeks to grasp the therapeutic alliance is a unique relationship with a different set of rules.

One of the first things I noticed related to the notion of self-disclosure. While I, as a client, was expected to open up to my therapist and share very personal and intimate thoughts, emotions, and musings, she was not expected to disclose anything about her personal life. I initially found this jarring. Often, I was disclosing things to Sofia I had not even shared with family or close friends. Yet to this day, I know essentially nothing about her beyond the scope of our therapeutic alliance. To me, the most fitting description is that of a unidirectional flow of intimacy, with very particular boundaries set in place.

Dr. Irvin Yalom, an emeritus professor of psychiatry at Stanford University and existential psychiatrist, wrote *The Gift of Therapy*.[58] In it, he imparts his wisdom and knowledge gained while practicing psychiatry as a guidebook to the next generation of therapists and patients. When discussing the therapeutic alliance, he confirms it is expected clients entering therapy "trust fully, reveal all, hold nothing back, examine all nuances of their feelings to another."[59] Yalom stresses the need for the therapist to respond with "nonjudgmental acceptance" to their client and reinforces the notion clients benefit tremendously from the experience of being fully seen and understood.[60] In fact, he believes self-disclosure is an absolutely essential ingredient in psychotherapy: "No patient profits from therapy without self-revelation. It is one of those automatic occurrences in therapy of which we take note only in its absence. So much of what we do in therapy—providing a safe environment, establishing trust, exploring fantasies and dreams—serves the purpose of encouraging self-revelation."[61] Intuitively, it makes sense I was expected to open up and reveal the very personal challenges I was facing. Had I not done so, it would have been very difficult for me to address, overcome, and grow from those very same challenges.

Why the need for my therapist to hold back? Yalom explains from a purely practical and legal perspective, "Patients have confidentiality; therapists do not."[62] Anything I shared with Sofia (as long as there wasn't any threat of harm to myself or others) would remain confidential as part of our work together. The reverse did not hold true. At a deeper layer, though, Yalom explains, "One of the deepest fears therapists have about personal disclosure is there will be no end to it."[63] He has found therapists are concerned about the slippery slope that can be created from revealing their personal lives to their clients, and the clients will then demand further information about their therapist. Whether or not this is true—Yalom believes this is a "groundless fear"—many therapists tend toward minimal self-disclosure as part of the therapeutic alliance.[64]

The consequence of this imbalance in self-disclosure can lead to a power dynamic exacerbated by the fact a therapist has many clients while the client has only one therapist. Viewed from the patient's seat, Yalom explains clients tend to "idealize the therapist, yearn for dependency, and express gratitude toward a caring and attentive listener."[65] Nothing is inherently wrong with this imbalance in power. Quite the contrary, Yalom believes it is important therapists "loom large in the patient's mind" and the hour clients and therapists spend together each week is one of the most important hours for the client.[66] It was important for me to think about, reflect, and prepare for my sessions with Sofia, and to give them the attention they deserved, in order to make progress.

The imbalance in power can lead to unintended side effects. Toward the end of a session in therapy, as I stood up and was leaving the room, I had the sudden urge to blurt out, "I love you." I didn't. I was surprised and somewhat embarrassed this had sprung up, but also too preoccupied with the content of the discussion to consider it in that moment. However, Yalom shares the act of therapy, which involves "the act of revealing oneself fully to another and still be accepted," can be an act of intimacy.[67] And it is no wonder I momentarily felt those feelings of affection. It can be a common development for patients to develop feelings for their therapists. The important aspect is these feelings are never acted upon, as doing so can be very destructive for both the patient and the therapist.

Gradually, I became more comfortable with the differing expectations of self-disclosure that occur during therapy. I found imposing certain boundaries, while also encouraging my own self-disclosure, did allow for a continual improvement and growth from the mental health challenges I was facing.

* * *

One other area that took me some time to become accustomed to involved the practice of giving and receiving feedback during therapy. In my initial discussions, I always came prepared with an agenda for the meeting. At the time, it made sense. I was reeling from specific emotional wounds that occurred as a result of me returning to the US, and I wanted to focus our discussions on addressing them. Session by session, as we worked through these items, my list became progressively shorter. I became more and more concerned as the list shortened. I mused about what else there was to talk about and brought up my conundrum to a friend, whereupon they exclaimed, "That's when the magic happens!" Slightly taken aback by their response, I used their enthusiasm to head into my next meeting.

Twenty minutes into my session with Sofia, I ran out of things to say. Nothing on the page served as guidance for how to proceed. I nervously reached for my tea and took a sip to give myself some more time to think.

"I'm not sure what to say at this point."

"That's okay. When we have open-ended discussions, you can say things like, 'I'm not sure where to go now' or 'This pause seems a bit long for me.'"

This exchange was a formative moment, as I learned to navigate and build on our therapeutic alliance. Having this conversation helped me become more comfortable with not having an agenda for each meeting. I found being able to ask for guidance and input about how to proceed with the conversation invited Sofia into the discussion. The nature of our conversations became more of a back-and-forth dialogue that meandered throughout the hour. They became more open-ended, and I came to enjoy the unexpected twists and turns and comments that would arise in our sessions. I found Yalom's description of therapy quite fitting: "At its very core, the flow of therapy should be spontaneous, forever following unanticipated riverbeds."[68] While I didn't recognize this at the time, having open-ended discussions with Sofia invited her into the conversation and allowed for the both of us to leverage her inputs and insights. In doing so, we were able to further develop our therapeutic alliance, which helped me conduct a deeper self-exploration.

* * *

Having open-ended discussions also helped me become more comfortable with pauses in our conversations. I soon realized Sofia was perfectly comfortable with silence. Initially, I instinctively rushed to fill the silence that followed a pause. Over time, I became more comfortable with it. I learned to use the pauses as opportunities to ruminate on my thoughts. In many cases, our discussions were emotionally heavy and not easy to parse apart. Pausing and thinking, even for up to a minute, proved very helpful. Therapist Lori Gottlieb wrote, "If we create the space and put in the time, we stumble upon stories that are worth waiting for, the ones that define our lives...I knew there was tremendous payoff."[69]

Pausing and thinking also encouraged me to pay attention to my feelings in the exact moment of therapy. Yalom writes, "One of our major tasks in therapy is to pay attention to our immediate feelings—they represent precious data."[70] Sofia and I made it a habit to inquire about the here and now in each meeting; doing so provided a wealth of learning and understanding. If I was every feeling anxious, or angry, or sad, or was dealing with a particularly charged emotion, we would gravitate to that feeling. With Sofia's guidance, I became more comfortable being with those emotions and bringing curiosity to them in a place where I felt safe and secure. I discovered feelings actually corresponded to different sensations throughout my body. I would mention I felt a tightness in my chest, or sternum, or stomach, and we would take time to explore that further. This follows with Yalom's important axiom for therapy: "We learn best about ourselves and our behavior through personal participation and interaction combined with observation and analysis of that interaction."[71]

I learned to enjoy the process of self-exploration that took place every session with Sofia. I found there is something very unique about the therapeutic alliance. To sit across from someone and engage authentically with them. Gottlieb shares, "The therapy room seemed to be one of the only places left where two people sit in a room together for an uninterrupted fifty minutes. Despite its veil of professionalism, this weekly I-thou ritual is often one of the most human encounters that people experience."[72] It is very unique to be able to disclose very personal musings and thoughts with the knowledge I wouldn't be judged and to explore what may arise in a very personal way.

Yalom describes the therapy venture as an "exercise in self-exploration."[73] For me, it took time to become comfortable with opening up about very difficult and uncomfortable emotions, particularly as I had to do so in an environment where I wasn't sure of what was expected of me in terms of how to behave or act. The rules navigating acceptable social interactions between a therapist and a client are different than any other relationship I had encountered, be it familial, professional, or societal. Only as I became more comfortable with this particular set of rules and expectations and creating a space where I felt heard and accepted by Sofia was I able to gain the confidence to develop our therapeutic alliance, reveal myself more fully, be accepted, and together explore my feelings and thoughts.

CHAPTER 3

The Perils of "Be a Man"

"How was the flight?" asked Didi.

"It was fine, not too crowded. I just arrived at the hostel."

The square pattern of greens, greys, and blacks attracted my attention. The room had five bunk beds; their green bed frames matched the color on the floor. Looking out the narrow window, the sixteenth-century stone walls surrounding Dubrovnik's old town rose up in front of me. The Adriatic Sea, dark blue, stood in sharp contrast with the tree-covered mountains rising precipitously from its waters, culminating in gray barren peaks.

My bed was the bottom bunk in the bed tucked away in the far corner. My eyes adjusted as I stepped out of the light and walked toward the bed.

"The last week has been really difficult for me. There have been so many goodbyes." My chest tightened, and a pang of sadness suddenly emanated from my gut. "I said goodbye to my friends. I said goodbye to London."

I lay down and drew the bed curtain. Only the glow of my phone offered any light. "It feels like I've had to say goodbye to my way of life."

The tightness seemed to expand to my neck and throat, and I turned to face the wall. "I'm not sure if going on this trip is such a good idea. I've been experiencing lots of anxiety in the last week."

"Can you describe the anxiety?" she asked.

"Um, there seem to be two types." I paused. "One is a constant, steady anxiety. The other is a more sudden and intense attack." My brows furrowed and I took a quick, shallow breath.

"The attacks seem to happen without warning; one took place while at a jazz concert with my friends, another while going for a walk along the River Thames. The worst one happened when I was hungover after a night out."

Should I tell her?

My heartbeat quickened, and my hands felt cold.

"I…I want to share I've been dealing with the notion of self-harm. I'm a bit scared."

I held my breath as I awaited her response. I hadn't previously told anyone I had thought of injuring myself. Ever since the episode in my room in London three months ago, I had been haunted by dark thoughts of self-injury. Not in the sense I wanted to do it; rather, the notion of self-injury filled my mind. These demons loomed larger as my departure from London drew nearer. There were hours, afternoons, or days when I felt on the verge of crying. At the time, I just wanted to lie in bed and go to sleep. My inner turmoil reached a peak during the week up to my departure, so I decided I needed to tell someone. I couldn't keep it bottled up and longed for someone to tell me things were going to be okay.

"I want you to know I love you, and I think you're very strong for the way you've handled everything."

I smiled. Tears were running down my cheeks. A sense of relief pierced the tension in my chest and began to wash over me.

"Sometimes...," I noticed the catch in Didi's voice. "Sometimes, you can focus on the present moment as a way to diminish those thoughts. From what I've read about self-harm, sometimes the brain responds this way as a coping mechanism to deal with the emotions you're feeling."

I breathed deeply. The burden I had been carrying for the last few months seemed to have lessened ever so slightly.

"Thank you. Thank you for sharing that; I really appreciate it."

"Of course," she replied.

"I love you and I'll be sure to let you know how my trip is going over the next couple of days."

"Okay, love you too."

I hung up the phone and stared at the bed above me. The midday sun poured in as I drew back the curtain. The hills beckoned and I decided to go for a hike on the small peninsula just north of the old city. I ambled through the city streets, without any goal in mind, and proceeded to climb to the highest point—a radio tower—and enjoyed the view. The setting sun showered the barren peaks with reds and oranges. Enticed by the sea below, I headed toward the beach and went for a swim. The cold water invigorated me. I inhaled deeply as I came up for air and felt a new positive energy rush in and fill my body. Perhaps going on this trip was a good decision after all.

* * *

Prior to the summer of 2019, I would have been hard-pressed to remember a time when I cried. The summer of 2019 changed that; I routinely cried. I cried at home; I cried at work; I cried in front of my roommates; I cried while on calls with my parents and friends; I even cried in front of strangers and police officers. The intensity of my emotions overwhelmed me, and I needed to find an outlet for them. One of those outlets was to cry and release the pent-up anguish. While I didn't have any particular control over when I felt like crying, I learned to allow the tears to flow instead of push them away.

Another outlet involved sharing my difficulties with a number of friends. The heavy burden of my emotions was too much to bear and compelled me to share how I was feeling with others. I shared my difficulties even if doing so left me in a vulnerable position. What I found surprised me. Almost all my friends engaged deeply in these conversations and offered support in some way, shape, or form. Equally surprising, almost every single one of my friends whom I had opened up to, many of whom identified as male, shared they had dealt with similar struggles in their lives. One friend struggled with the death of a parent and flung himself into work as a response; another friend admitted to feeling stuck at work and unsure about how to proceed; another friend dealt with depression and suicidal ideation following a difficult breakup; and another friend said the "mind goes to dark places" following a significant injury, the end of a relationship, and a career transition all in a span of six months.

These conversations shocked me. Why didn't I know about my friends' struggles? Why hadn't these difficulties ever come up? I found these revelations particularly surprising as some of my friendships went back decades. I realized most of the time, our conversations focused on either the intellectual or quotidian and rarely broached the sphere of our emotions or how we were feeling. With this insight in mind, I began a personal experiment of sorts. I actively opened up with more and more people, in some instances friends or acquaintances I hadn't spoken to in months or years, to see how they would respond. Many did open up about their struggles, although I also heard a few respond they believed men shouldn't show emotions.

Why shouldn't men show emotions? I learned there are some significant cultural forces at play that encourage this behavior in boys at a very early age. Joe Ehrmann, a former NFL player and football coach, shared in the film *The Mask You Live In* that one of his earliest memories involves his father telling him to "be a man. Stop with the tears. Stop with the emotions. If you're going to be a man in this world, you better learn how to dominate, to control people and circumstances."[74]

I spoke with Professor Caroline Heldman, the Chair of Critical Theory and Social Justice at Occidental College, about masculinity in the US. In our discussion, she brought up the term "man box," which is the notion being a real man is "very clearly defined as being aggressive, violent, in control, and rational." She elaborates growing up and living within the confines of this very constricting definition of manhood "is damaging to boys and men because it sends the message they can't be emotional beings, even though human beings are inherently emotional beings." The consequence is boys, from a very early age, are encouraged to hide their emotions and not tell others when they are feeling hurt, afraid, sad, or generally most emotions. The one exception to this rule is anger. In fact, putting on a mask and "performing toughness, and acting like they are someone other than who they really are" is something widely encouraged in the US. Heldman elaborates not only are certain behaviors encouraged, but there is also a pervasive "social policing" that takes place through "popular culture, through parenting styles, and through educational styles that are incredibly damaging and insulting."

It's worth noting masculinity, like gender and femininity, is a social construct. Professor Lise Eliot of Rosalind Franklin

University explains, "Sex is a biological term; it refers to which chromosomes you have. Two xx is female, x and y is male. Gender is a social construct, these are expressions of femininity and masculinity, and both of these are spectrums, and they overlap."[75] It is believed men and women are fundamentally different creatures where, in fact, if fifty thousand girls and fifty thousand boys were given psychological tests, the resulting boy and girl bell curve responses would overlap by 90 percent.[76] Unfortunately, we tend to focus our attention on the non-overlapping traits, the 10 percent, as distinguishing factors between boys and girls. In this attempt at bifurcating what it means to be a man or a woman, Dr. Niobe Way, a psychologist and educator, shares, "We've made feminine all these things that include relationships, emotions, empathy. So, boys devalue the relational parts of themselves, their relational needs, their relational desires."[77]

When boys and men are inculcated with the belief expressing emotions is a sign of weakness and are pressured to never back down, to always be in control, and to use violence to solve problems, the results are deadly. Way shares, "Exactly at the age of fifteen, when we start to hear the emotional language disappear from boys' narratives, that's exactly the age when boys begin to have a rate of suicide five times greater than the rate of girls."[78] The difference becomes even starker in young men aged twenty to twenty-four, when they are seven times more likely to die from suicide than young women. This aggression can equally manifest itself through violence toward others. In the US, over thirty thousand people are killed annually by a gun, 90 percent of the homicide perpetrators are male, and almost half are under the age of twenty-five.[79] The danger in discouraging boys and men from speaking out about their emotions is exemplified by a story shared by Tommy, a member of San Quentin State Prison's Juvenile Lifers Program, in the documentary *The Mask You Live In*:

My father drank a lot. I was probably bullied the most by my dad. He ruled with intimidation and fear. I was always scared when Mom said, 'You're in trouble and I'm gonna tell your dad.' I knew I had an ass whipping coming and that meant he was going to hit me with whatever he had close to him, whether it was a fan cord he ripped out of the wall or his belt.

I was shy. I was quiet. I was always in my head. I just felt terribly alone.

The only culture where I felt like I belonged a little bit was the drug culture. I found it when I was twelve years old. I started smoking weed, at first because of peer pressure, but I soon liked it because I didn't have to feel the way I always felt, and I moved on to harder drugs.

My world changed when I picked up a gun. It became a whole lot more violent; people around me started dying. The guy I killed, we had conflict. I had been accepted in this drug culture. When he didn't pay me, I thought, 'My homeboys know if I don't do something to this guy, everybody's gonna take whatever I have, play me for a punk.' That's the story I was telling in my head. And I just felt all the fear and anxiety and everything else I had bottled up in me just burst, and I shot him six times.

And I ran.

I think that's the first time I ever felt like I had power. For so long, I felt so powerless in my life. That was a moment I finally stood up for myself.

But it came at such a huge price.

There is an urgent need to encourage and educate boys and men to step out of the tightly defined box of manhood to allow them to be their true and whole selves. Fortunately, there are many programs doing exactly that. One such organization is Ever Forward, a non-profit whose mission is to help all young men have the desire to be fully alive, loved, respected, held in high regard, and supported to help achieve their goals.[80] I spoke with Ashanti Branch, Ever Forward's founder and executive director, about his work. Originally from Oakland, California, he was raised by a single mother. He's a self-described "undercover math nerd" who is also an engineer and educator. Through his club, he hopes to provide young men spaces to "just talk about what they're going through in their lives in a healthy way." Branch explains the challenge he's facing is "everything turns into anger. Anger is a very respected emotion in my community. Unfortunately, fear, sadness, shame, and all other emotions are not seen as masculine and are not respected, so young men shy away from dealing with emotions in a healthy way." In many instances, many of the young men aren't even angry; they only express their emotions through anger.

To address this challenge, Branch works to give each young man the tools to add to their emotional language. When prompted to explain how he does this, he shares he was influenced by Professor Marc Brackett, a professor at Yale University and founding director of the Yale Center for Emotional Intelligence, who developed RULER. RULER is an approach to social and emotional learning that teaches emotional intelligence to people, and it stands for:[81]

- R – Recognizing emotions in oneself and others
- U – Understanding the causes and consequences of emotions
- L – Labeling emotions with a nuanced vocabulary
- E – Expressing emotions in accordance with cultural norms and social context
- R – Regulating emotions with helpful strategies

Branch teaches this model through experience with a goal of incorporating these insights into the young men's lives; his motto is, "If you can't name it, you can't tame it." He finds the key challenge involves the fact many of the young men either don't want to talk about their emotions or they find it difficult to name the emotions they are feeling, in part because they haven't "allowed other emotions, like sadness, in," as doing so can make them look weak. In response, he developed a workshop to help them "take off their mask." In each session, he asks all the participants to write their projected persona and emotions others see on the outside of the mask. On the inside, they are instructed to write the emotions they feel within themselves but don't share with others. Recalling the first time he tried this technique, he was blown away by the young men's responses. "After two months of working with them, that was the first time they opened up to each other." What he realized was "there was so much going on with each of them no one even knew." Spurred on by this success, he organized the Million Mask Movement to help young people take off their masks and be their true and full selves.

Throughout my childhood, I have no memory of my parents ever telling me to "be a man." I can certainly recount countless moments of them telling me to "grow up" and to "act my age," but their comments never had gendered connotations. As a child, I grew up in a household where we were encouraged to express our emotions, including those that made us sad.

I was also encouraged to try all kinds of activities. Sports, yes, but others as well including art, drawing, painting, ceramics, music, theater, and other forms of expression and play. This held true regardless of whether or not the activities were associated with boys or girls. I count myself incredibly thankful and grateful to have grown up in an environment where I didn't feel it was necessary to bottle up my emotions and to not feel shame to express my feelings. I am certain growing up in this environment helped me, while lying in my bed in the hostel, to open up with my sister, unbottle my emotions, and not keep them pent up with the prospect of more dire consequences.

CHAPTER 4

Economics of Therapy

One of the first things I noticed when reaching out to therapists were the high costs. Many of the therapists responded stating they charged one hundred to two hundred fifty dollars per fifty-minute session. Since I had returned to the US without having US-based insurance, I didn't have any mechanisms that could subsidize the cost of therapy. Thankfully, I was in the privileged position to be able to pay for these sessions without them creating a significant financial burden. While I was fortunate enough to be able to prioritize these mental health services, I wondered what impact, if any, the high cost of therapy did have on accessibility to mental health care.

I brought this up to Bridget Balajadia, a licensed clinical social worker (LCSW) and program manager at Catholic Charities Santa Clara. Balajadia previously explored setting up a private practice and had an intimate view into the costs associated for running one. From a therapist's perspective, she states "the ethical thing is to accept all patients regardless of ability to pay." This would imply she would have to bill for insurance coverage for individuals not capable of paying the full private pay costs out of pocket. Unfortunately, Medi-Cal, California's Medicaid assistance program serving low-income individuals, and Medicare, the national health insurance program covering individuals in the United States over the age of sixty-five, don't offer a lot. Medi-Cal takes a portion of the fees for providing mental health services, and what remains still has to cover the costs associated with running a practice and keeping the lights on. What remains "is basically pennies." A therapist must navigate additional hoops and paperwork when billing insurance. Medi-Cal only insures "certain types of treatment," which means therapists have to tailor their service to a client "because insurance tells me what is covered" regardless of whether or not the covered treatments suit the needs of the patient.

This leaves many therapists opting for private pay and attempting to work out an ethical approach to this route. A common solution involves the use of a sliding scale where the bulk of the clients are wealthier people who can pay the whole fee and a fraction of a therapist's clients pay a reduced fee. The problem is clients who can't afford private therapy end up being priced out of therapy because they are not able to find a good therapist for the amount they are able to pay. What results—according to a survey conducted by the National Alliance on Mental Illness (NAMI)—is "nearly half of the of the sixty million adults and children living with mental health conditions in the US go without any treatment."[82] This figure most likely undercounts the actual number of individuals living with a mental health condition and without access to treatment, particularly since the US's Health Resources and Services Administration has determined "124 million people in the US live in Mental Health

Care Health Professional Shortage Areas"—areas and population groups that have a dearth of necessary mental health care professionals.[83]

Offering private mental health care insurance could be a viable solution. However, Balajadia argues, "There's no coverage for seeing a therapist." Digging into health care policies, she rarely found health insurance that offered coverage for even basic therapeutic techniques. A survey conducted by NAMI confirms this view, as it found "34 percent of respondents with private insurance reported difficulties finding any mental health therapist who would accept their insurance."[84] This figure dwarfed the 13 percent of the same respondents who had difficulty finding other medical specialists and the 9 percent searching for primary care providers.[85] The NAMI report found the primary barriers for patients searching for mental health care in the US included "high rates of denials of care insurers, high out-of-pocket costs for mental health care, difficulties accessing psychiatric medications, and problems finding psychiatrists and other mental health providers in health insurance networks."[86] Balajadia summarizes wealthy clients can continue "paying for the exact treatment they need, want, and deserve while poor clients only get limited time bound services that may not even be medically indicated."

It is unfortunate how few people access or have access to mental health services because the World Health Organization (WHO) estimates investing "one dollar on mental health services can yield a return of four dollars."[87] Not providing these services is having significant adverse impacts; the WHO estimates continuing to neglect mental health results in losses of one trillion US dollars per year as a result of reduced economic productivity.[88] This then begs the question: Why isn't mental health coverage covered more by private insurance? I believe one contributing factor is we as a society do not value mental health in the same way we value physical health. Rarely do we view paying for mental health as an investment. If something was wrong, we tend to believe we should be able to work through it on our own, that paying someone to talk about one's problems is at best a waste of money and at worst a sign of weakness.

I imagine many more people would be willing to make the investment in their mental health if they had access to the best possible care. This includes reducing the out-of-pocket costs of going to therapy and providing resources to connect individuals to low-cost therapy and community resources; organizations such as Catholic Charities, NAMI, and the Substance Abuse and Mental Health Services Administration (SAMHSA) are doing just this. Closing loopholes in mental health insurance coverage is another option, which NAMI is working on diligently to help expand access and parity to mental health care coverage. One key policy enactment includes the passage of the Mental Health Parity and Addiction Equity Act in 2008, which barred health insurers from making mental health coverage more restrictive than insurance for physical ailments.[89]

From the start, I believed investing my time and resources into therapy was worthwhile. Even though going to therapy for over a year cost me upward of four thousand dollars and forced me to eat into my savings, I know definitively it was the correct decision. Had I not gone to therapy, I am certain I would not have addressed my emotional wounds in a healthy manner and would continue to be suffering from chronic anxiety, panic attacks, and suicidal ideation. My hope is we as individuals and as a society recognize the value of prioritizing mental health and take the steps to provide accessible, comprehensive, and affordable mental health care.

CHAPTER 5

Hope

Looking for a fun way to ring in the New Year, my cousins, Didi, and I decided to spend a few days together in Lake Tahoe, California. The idea was to rent a cabin in Kings Beach, a small town on the north shore of the lake. Everyone was excited to see The California Honeydrops, a blues band, at the Crystal Bay Casino on New Year's Eve. (To be honest, I had no idea who The California Honeydrops were, but I'd never miss out on an evening out with my sister and cousins.) The weekend was gearing up to be a relaxing, wholesome, "adult" trip—a far cry from the much more rambunctious, and often rowdy, trips to Tahoe that took place during our college years.

We left Berkeley early in the morning of the twenty-ninth and journeyed toward Tahoe, stopping only to ogle Ikeda's famous pies, a compulsory activity now ingrained in family tradition. Ikeda's is a restaurant and bakery that lies just off Highway 80, making it an easy pit stop on trips to and from Tahoe. It is a third-generation family-run business with a humble origin as a small fruit stand selling fresh, local produce. Choosing which pie you want is the most difficult decision. There are so many options—pecan, apple, marionberry, peach, razzleberry, chocolate truffle cream, and more. My typical order is raspberry, but I have found to overcome the difficulty of choosing just one, it is best to order as many as you can carry. Even now, the thought of those pies makes my mouth water.

We continued along and finally arrived at our cabin. We spent the days lounging around the living room, playing UNO with comically large cards and Monopoly—I will admit bankruptcies caused temporary ruptures in our friendships—enjoying the warmth of the fire as it snowed outside, and wandering outdoors for occasional jaunts through snow-covered alpine meadows.

While I enjoyed spending time with everyone, I couldn't shake a nagging sense of unease. It arose just before departing from Berkeley and lingered ever since. No amount of laughter could ease the discomfort I felt—a tightness that centered in my sternum and radiated outward.

This feeling persisted until New Year's Eve when, as a group, we agreed to go on a short hike, starting at the Brockway Summit Tahoe Trailhead and culminating at Picnic Rock. Picnic Rock sits on a hilly outcrop that affords fantastic views of the surrounding region. To the south, the view of Lake Tahoe spreads across the many peaks crowning its shores, with Freel and Monument Peaks, each standing over ten thousand feet. To the north, an uninterrupted view of snow-covered pine forests spanned the California-Nevada border.

It was a beautiful day. The sun was out, not a cloud in sight. The azure sky offered a beautiful contrast to the green needles and russet trunks. We hiked along a compressed snow path, slipping and sliding as we had not come prepared with appropriate footwear. The views were stunning. The stillness and quiet were a joy to revel in. But the feeling of unease continued to nag me and, while I was cognizant this was a beautiful moment, the happiness felt superficial, as if unable to penetrate my deeper core where my anxiety continued to smolder.

We reached Picnic Rock, savoring the moment and sitting in quiet contemplation.

"Seeing as it's New Year's, how do you all feel about taking a moment to share what we're grateful for from the past year and what we look forward to in the New Year?" asked Didi.

We all agreed and reflected on her question.

I took a seat on a nearby rock, digging my shoes a few inches into the recently fallen snow. Memories from 2019 flashed in my mind and a sadness arose from within. The ice on the rock began to melt and the cold moisture seeped through my pants.

Everyone took turns sharing their answers. With each response, the sadness in my chest continued to expand. I leaned forward, resting my head in my hands and staring at my shoes in the snow. The neon blue fabric contrasted with the crystalline white snow.

It was my turn. "This past year has been…This past year has been really difficult." Tears began to roll down my cheeks and onto my hands.

* * *

I knew why I was crying. Each September of the previous three years, I had set goals for myself. I tried to make them concrete and actionable, spanning all aspects of my life—professional, emotional, familial, physical, spiritual, etc. I had hoped they could provide a direction in my life, encourage me to continue growing and developing as a person, and give me something to look forward to in the upcoming year. Each year, as it ended, I would review my previous goals and reflect on whether I had achieved them. In the process, I also contemplated on what I had learned, noting which activities I had enjoyed and which I had found fulfilling. I found setting goals also lent a sense of agency to my life. Rather than passively watch life go by, I could be an active participant, influencing the direction and narrative of my own life.

Why September? Merely because I finished my master's program in September 2016 and that was when I started the practice. After three years of continued goal setting, September 2019 came and went, and I did not set for myself any goals. I didn't forget to do so. Instead, I purposefully put off the activity. I delayed doing this because I was fearful of what the future held. The trauma I experienced had created so much uncertainty it became very difficult to envision a positive outcome.

While I wouldn't have used the term then, I now think I was struggling with an immense feeling of hopelessness, which Nock et al. defines as having "negative expectations for the future."[90] Sitting on Picnic Rock, my future felt very uncertain and I frankly didn't have any expectations, let alone positive expectations, for the future. Such hopelessness also lent to the suicidal ideation I experienced following my return to California—hopelessness has been found to be a robust risk factor toward depression and suicidal ideation.[91][92] It was at that point my lack of orientation in life felt most prominent. An analogy I often share is it is akin to being a ship lost at sea, unmoored, and constantly at the mercy of the currents and the winds. I continued in that state for many weeks and months.

What I have since learned is if hopelessness is the ailment, then hope is the antidote. Hope can be a very powerful cure. In fact, it has been found hope can alter neurochemistry and improve our psychology and physiology.[93] But what is hope? And how can one become hopeful?

In his book, *The Anatomy of Hope*, Dr. Jerome Groopman—Chair at Harvard Medical School—defined hope as "the elevating feeling we experience when we see—in the mind's eye—a path to a better future. Hope acknowledges the significant obstacles and deep pitfalls along the path. True hope has no room for delusions. Hope gives us the courage to confront our circumstances and the capacity to surmount them."[94]

I wanted to learn more about the role of hope in mental health, so I reached out to Dr. Maria Sirois, a clinical psychologist by training but positive psychologist by choice. Positive psychology is the notion meaning can be created by focusing on positive aspects in one's life, as opposed to minimizing aspects that can bring us pain or hardship.[95] Sirois shared, "Hope looks and feels like the possibility of a better future." The challenge, however, is it must be a grounded hope. It must be rooted in a sense of realism, of "facing reality as it is," and being aware of the situation and challenges at hand. This notion of hope needing a dose of realism aligns well with Groopman's discussion hope doesn't "have room for delusions."[96] Interestingly, hope is often "triggered in dark moments." Sirois elaborated if life is going well, "you're in the flow," typically that person is not thinking about hope. Hope seems to arise when things go completely wrong and the only thing that can motivate is the possibility of a better tomorrow.

Sirois went on to explain hope for a better tomorrow is something that can be cultivated and developed. This can be done by focusing on the present moment and "taking positive action." Acknowledging our current life predicament is not good, or even bad; it is not an easy thing to do. I found accomplishing this step particularly difficult; my initial intent was to ignore or push away this reality rather than acknowledge it.

I was so intent on not facing my reality I delayed setting goals for months. My present situation was so uncertain I didn't even have a vague sense of what the upcoming year had in store. My future seemed shrouded, cloaked in an impenetrable fog. Acknowledging I couldn't see past that fog would make my present feel very unsettled. So, I avoided setting goals and kicked the metaphorical can down the road instead of contemplating the instability in my life. But our discussion, sitting atop Picnic Rock, forced me to confront this fear.

Only after this difficult step is taken can hope slowly build up, bit by bit, by "taking steps and actions toward a slightly better future," says Sirois. In this instance, "future" doesn't have to be a particularly expansive time scale. One can work toward building a slightly better afternoon or a better tomorrow. The important thing is to work on taking small steps to build toward that hope for the future.

Sirois experienced firsthand the power hope can have in improving someone's life. In a span of six months in 2010, her younger brother was diagnosed with stage four cancer and passed away, her marriage fell apart, and she had to deal with significant financial distress. This series of traumas left her feeling at a loss, in a world that didn't make sense to her, and in significant pain.

Even though she had, as a trained psychologist, "millions of positive psychology tools and practices" at her disposal, practicing them didn't help her. The "only thing that was helpful to me was remembering I could choose to live in honor of my brother." It was this choice that enabled her to not let his death "overwhelm her."

She was impressed by her brother's ability to say "yes to life," and so she began integrating some of those habits as a way to honor him. Doing so allowed her to say yes to life while also grieve her loss. Ultimately, this mindset and practice to "bring my brother's gifts forward" is what allowed her hope to grow and live for her.

* * *

Sitting at Picnic Rock, I was lucky enough to be surrounded by people whom I love and hold very dear and who supported me in this moment of need. Seeing me cry, they immediately walked over and consoled me.

"I know this year has been really difficult for you, but we are so proud of you for the way you've handled everything," said Didi.

Her words, and their hugs, helped. I gathered myself, said "thank you," and stood up.

As we retraced our steps down the mountain, a renewed sense of peace and clarity filled me up. This moment of reckoning felt very cathartic—as if a release. The angst that clung to my body and psyche dissipated—at least for the moment. I appreciated my surroundings with a renewed sense of excitement. Not only could I acknowledge the beauty around me, but I could also now feel the beauty and believed it to be beautiful. Walking through the woods on a gorgeous winter afternoon continued to feed my energy. Upon returning home, I opted for a slice of delicious raspberry pie and contemplated which goals I could set myself.

CHAPTER 6

Community-Based Care

"Food's ready!" called out Dad.

I dog-eared the page of my book and went inside for our Sunday family meal.

Mom, Dad, and I sat down at the table. My mouth watered as I looked at the feast before me—steaming rice and lentils, warm bread, and fresh bell peppers, cucumbers, and herbs recently harvested from our garden.

"How was your day?" asked Mom.

My arm hung in midair. "Today has been difficult. I miss my friends, and I don't know when I'll see them again."

"I know it's difficult, but try to take your time, try to stay positive," Mom said. "I found reverse culture shock can be the hardest. For me, returning from Peru after my yearlong exchange was more difficult than going to Peru because I wasn't expecting it."

I nodded and served myself a helping of steaming lentils, the evaporating water creating patterns on the plate. I found it comforting both Mom and Dad could empathize with what I was going through. Prior to living in Mexico as a family, both had participated in an exchange program in Peru the year after they graduated from college in the late 1980s. What struck Mom most upon returning to the US was seeing the stark disparity in wealth between both places.

It had only been a couple of weeks since I moved back from London and I was still adjusting to being in San Jose, California. While the culture shock wasn't as significant as what Mom described, there were still enough differences between London and California to provide a constant reminder I was no longer in the UK—driving instead of walking or taking public transit; going to the grocery store once a week instead of every couple of days; the different cuisines and restaurants; and signs indicating a house was available "to rent" instead of "to let."

"It's difficult to feel this way. I feel like my brain is broken." My body sank, and my stomach knotted up. I avoided making eye contact with both Mom and Dad and instead toyed with the lentils and rice with my spoon.

"What do you mean 'broken'?" Dad asked.

"I keep feeling this anxiety and just can't shake it."

Moments passed. I stared at our wooden table, still not making eye contact, wishing I could go curl up in bed. The tension in my stomach began to spread and my pulse quickened.

"I know we talked about the possibility of going to see a therapist. Do you think that's something you would want to do?" asked Dad.

I nodded.

"Okay, we can call Marissa and ask her for any recommendations," said Mom.

It occurred to me it would be worthwhile reaching out to Sofia again as my situation clearly was not improving. "Actually, I have reached out to Marissa, and she already provided some recommendations. I can follow up directly with the therapists and ask for an initial session this week."

"Okay, that sounds good," she said. She stood up, walked over, and gave me a hug.

My head rested on her shoulder. Excusing myself, I went to get my laptop to email Sofia.

The tightness in my stomach persisted the rest of the night. Memories of my time in London occupied my mind and my heart ached.

Lying in bed, Mom and Dad appeared in the doorway. "You're doing great. You've already set up a time to meet with the therapist. We know it's difficult, but you're doing the right things."

Their words pierced through the tightness in my stomach, which slowly disappeared. Feeling calmer, I walked over and hugged them, holding on tightly. Being physically supported by my parents reminded me of how important and lucky I was to have a community that could support and protect me during this challenging time. A sense of courage and certainty I could overcome my anxiety took hold as I headed back to bed.

"Good night."

* * *

I feel very fortunate to have had such a tremendous support system of friends and family who were responsive to my needs and so thankful I could rely on my parents' previous experience. I also recognize what a privilege it is to be able to count on a support system that never made me feel stigmatized or embarrassed for sharing what I was dealing with.

Unfortunately, of the estimated 792 million people living with a mental health condition around the world, few are able to access the critical care to help them manage and overcome their mental health challenges and traumas.[97] In many places, governments do not provide funding for these services; Human Rights Watch (HRW) estimates "countries spend less than 2 percent of their health budgets on mental health."[98] What results, according to the WHO's Mental Health Action Plan, is a significant "gap between the need for treatment and its provision all over the world."[99] Health systems around the world are routinely unprepared for the demand for mental health care, "between 35 to 85 percent of people with severe mental disorders receive no treatment."[100] In such environments, much of the responsibility for supporting individuals with mental health challenges falls on their family members. Faced with this challenge, many families "struggle to cope with the demands of caring for a relative with a psychosocial disability."[101] This struggle is compounded from a lack of understanding of the cause of many mental illnesses.

To improve access and quality of mental health care, organizations have begun focusing their effort on providing community-based health services to individuals dealing with mental illness. The WHO even listed "integration of mental health and social care services in community-based settings" as one of its top four objectives in its 2013–2020 action plan.[102] Community-based mental health care has been found to offer various benefits, including "greater accessibility and acceptability compared to health care facilities, greater clinical effectiveness through ongoing contact and use of trusted local providers, family involvement, and economic benefits."[103] In particular, the WHO recommends funding programs that include the "integration of mental health into general health care settings, and through maternal, sexual, reproductive, and child health, HIV/AIDS and chronic noncommunicable disease programs."[104] They go on to state encouraging these programs "would allow access to better and more cost-effective interventions for many people."[105]

I wondered what resources, if any, were available for people dealing with mental health challenges in my community. Looking for answers, I followed up with Bridget Balajadia. As program manager for the past twelve years at Catholic Charities Santa Clara, Balajadia had focused on helping anyone, regardless of faith tradition, receive access to the necessary resources to help address their lack of food, housing, health, education, or economic security. She had also developed a program to understand the extent to which childhood trauma, or Adverse Child Experiences (ACE), impacts rates of poverty in adulthood. Her thesis was providing access to mental health support and treatment to adults and children with significant levels of trauma would help alleviate poverty.

I asked Balajadia what steps could be taken so we as individuals, or as a community, could assist people dealing with mental health challenges. "The crux of my program is training people in the process I call accompaniment," she responded. "This notion came from my work overseas helping refugees. While in Morocco, I realized many of the people dealing with trauma had to stand up and fill the service gaps for themselves the government had largely failed to provide." She found the people living in her city had developed a clever way to access services that weren't provided to them by the government. "I lived in a large city, but it didn't have all of the necessary supplies. What would happen is on Thursday afternoons, guys would arrive in caravans of camels, and they would bring all of their stuff and wares to sell. They would descend on this one part of the city for five hours, and everybody in the community knew these guys were going to be there. It was a place where they could get their vegetables, their medicine, and their supplies for their house. At the end of the day, the guys would pack everything back up on their camels, and they'd leave and come back the next week. And it wasn't supported by the government, it didn't have a permit or anything, but everyone knew it happened. That was where the community knew, if they had a problem, they could go solve it at the market."

Inspired by this weekly gathering, Balajadia used the concepts of community support to develop her model of accompaniment. She explained accompaniment can take place in two different ways: personal accompaniment and community accompaniment.

Community accompaniment aims to develop relationships and build community for a group of people dealing with some level of trauma. Catholic Charities is working on developing their own community market model throughout parishes in Santa Clara. They invite agencies that provide social services outside the parishes and provide resources "beyond just a flyer." People can receive immediate access and support from a "doctor, substance abuse counselor, nurse, a hot meal, groceries, or an attorney, and it's open to anybody." The objective is the community can know and rely on a reliable resource within their community.

Personal accompaniment is the notion a person who "made it out of their trauma" can give back to those currently experiencing significant trauma. Someone who is traumatized can lean on this person, a person who can completely empathize with their experience, and walk them through the process of healing. Using this concept as a model, Balajadia is training "volunteers in complex trauma" so they can understand the connection between mind-body trauma and the role it plays in changing a person's behavior, outlook, or perspective. Volunteers and clients from the same neighborhoods are then paired up to provide support to clients over a period of three to nine months. Through a series of weekly sessions, the volunteers are able to provide individual support and also aid people in navigating the social service system. Critically, these weekly sessions also allow the clients to "express themselves fully, hear their own wisdom of what's coming up, be their own great leader, and have a sounding board to support and validate them."

Like the accompaniment model developed by Balajadia, community-based support significantly alleviated my struggle with mental health. Having this community provided me the resources and access to critical mental health services I required. I also relied on many friends and family who had previously gone to therapy and helped me navigate a period of uncertainty. Importantly, relying on a community and a group of individuals who had previously dealt with mental health challenges provided a sense of security and safety that helped me reach out for help, knowing I could rely on others if I ever stumbled.

CHAPTER 7

Parts

"Objective one: Get rid of anxiety."

My heart raced as I reviewed my notes. Sitting in the waiting room, I wondered if there was anything else I should have done to prepare for my first therapy session.

The ambient music allayed my nervousness only so much. A water filter stood by the doorway and a number of magazines rested on a coffee table in the center of the room.

Am I ready for this?

Sofia promptly walked out of her office as my watch struck 14:00.

We introduced ourselves and I walked into her office. A desk was tucked into a corner on my left and three chairs, all facing each other and positioned like a triangle, were toward my right. Sofia sat on the chair closest to the desk, and I opted for the chair opposite her, closest to the window.

I set my backpack and helmet on the floor, gingerly placed my tea on the table beside me, and sat down.

"Where should we start?" I asked.

"Why don't you share with me what brings you here today?"

I proceeded to share my story of leaving London and returning to the US.

"So here I am, back in San Jose. At this point, I'm just tired of all the stress and anxiety. I just want to get rid of it."

"Thank you for sharing."

I nodded and took a sip of tea, unsure of what would happen next.

Sofia continued to sit silently, and I glanced briefly at my notes.

"Objective one: Get rid of anxiety."

My heart beat faster.

"I did want to add, I've been struggling with the notion of self-harm, of self-injury."

"What kind?"

My brow furrowed; I didn't realize there were multiple types of self-injury.

Voicing my response was too much to bear. I slowly put out my left arm and proceeded to make a back-and-forth motion with my right hand over my left wrist.

I lowered my gaze. A sense of shame and embarrassment rose within me. "It feels like the concept of self-harm is haunting my thoughts. I feel like I can't really trust myself. It feels like a dark cloud that constantly follows me around."

Silence hung in the air.

"If you're okay with this, I would like to ask you to try something."

I nodded.

"What you can try is engaging with this cloud and thanking it for trying to protect you," she said.

I tilted my head and arched my eyebrow.

"Is this something you would like to try?" she asked.

"Well, I'm a bit nervous. I'm concerned about what might happen if I do engage the cloud or acknowledge it."

"You can thank the cloud and tell it you can really handle this by yourself, that you also have a support system to help get you through this tough period."

I hesitated. What she suggested felt very uncertain. The thought of engaging with this dark cloud scared me. What if the cloud took over?

It's okay; you can do this.

I closed my eyes. The room was completely still; I could only hear the sound of my breath.

I want to. I want to thank you for trying to protect me.

I just want to share with you that...that I have this under control, and you don't have to worry.

I really do have a tremendous support system. My parents, my sister, my friends, they're all looking after me. And I am also able to rely on myself.

I opened my eyes.

"How was that?"

I lifted my index finger to my mouth and looked up at the ceiling. "It was...it was new."

"I imagine. It's important to acknowledge this darkness, and to increase the parts within you that you can trust."

The clock in her room read 2:51. It was time to wrap up.

I jotted down my last few notes, put my notebook and pen in my backpack, and stood up.

"It was good you came in today."

A blue sky and the warmth of the sun welcomed me as I left the building. I biked home along the river path. I couldn't quite place it, but it felt like something had fundamentally changed within me. Somehow, engaging with this cloud shifted the equation. Unsure of exactly why, I sensed I could now trust myself, just a bit more.

* * *

This was one of the most impactful moments in my time going to therapy; it completely changed my perspective and attitude toward dealing with my impulse to self-injure. I never acted on this impulse, but it felt like I was constantly fighting against it. Prior to therapy, my initial instinct was to repress it and push it away. I wished to not have to deal with it. In our sessions, Sofia explained I had a protector part, and what I was feeling was a response to my emotional wounds and trauma. Her proposed approach, of engaging with my protective part, proved to be an opportunity for significant growth and learning. The goal was to engage with the protective part and not push it away. She recommended instead to say "thank you" and acknowledge it.

For many months, I didn't understand the concept of parts, and would occasionally bring this up to her. How could there be different parts within me? The implied multiplicity of having different parts made it sound like I didn't have a good handle of who I was, and I found this unnerving. The analogy Sofia used was, "Imagine you see a number of people in a car, and they take turns driving. Each part can be a passenger in a car, and throughout a drive, they each take turns driving the car." I was the car, and each passenger was one of the parts. It was a helpful visual, but it left me dissatisfied.

Wanting to learn more, I asked Sofia if there was a particular model she based her technique on. She shared, in fact, she was drawing from a model named Internal Family Systems (IFS). IFS was founded by Dr. Richard Schwartz in response to his clients' descriptions of various parts within themselves.[106]

I spoke to Cece Sykes, a psychotherapist and senior trainer for the IFS Institute. She first started seeing clients in the early 1980s and had worked with Schwartz for over twenty-five years. Sykes encouraged me to imagine the parts as "different emotional states." Each person still has a central way of the world; however, we can respond to circumstances in different manners based on the day. As an example, one day I could think I was doing really well at work, and on the other, think I was doing a really poor job.

Chris Burris, also a senior lead trainer at the IFS Institute who had been teaching IFS therapy for over twenty years, elaborates, "Our psyche is formed from how our brains evolutionarily developed. Somehow our psyches are shaped as having multiple states of awareness." As we live life, we tend to "repress our more vulnerable feelings of shame or inadequacy." The result is during moments of trauma, we tend to feel alone or isolated, which results in shame. Burris described the concept of holding "our most traumatic or vulnerable feelings at bay as our protective parts."

Of the IFS model, Sykes explains there are "three big categories of parts, two parts protect us, and one is the essence of our vulnerability." The part that is the essence of our vulnerability is called "exiles," which relates to the parts that have experienced trauma and can become isolated from our internal system in an effort to protect ourselves from feeling pain or fear.[107] The second part is called "managers." Sykes describes them as "our functioning parts. They can help us get jobs, take care of responsibilities, and take care of our relationships with family, partners, and others." In extreme instances, the managers can evolve to become very self-critical, judgmental, and perfectionistic. She describes this thought process as "if I work really, really hard, then I have value." The third part is called "firefighters." Firefighters react when exiles are activated in an effort to control and extinguish feelings; "they're trying to help us get away from the pain." The challenge is these parts can manifest themselves through "compulsive risk-taking habits such as drugs, alcohol, food restriction, gambling, or different kinds of sexual preoccupation." In extreme cases, these parts result in an individual having "suicidal or self-harming" thoughts, with a goal of extinguishing the pain currently being felt.

Sykes found through her work that many of her clients who underwent a life transition, felt lost, or lost a sense of who they were would tend to feel "shame, isolation, not attuned, and like no one gets us." Instead of engaging with these vulnerabilities and painful emotions, people "get very busy with manager stuff, or we get very busy with firefighter stuff." It became evident my "firefighter" part went into overdrive in response to the pain I was feeling. Rather than deal with it, my instinct was to push it away or even eliminate the pain.

The key challenge, and one Sofia helped me address, was to identify another way to deal with this pain. Sykes explains when I tried to repress my thoughts of self-harm, I was repressing "two things—repressing what's painful and repressing desires to comfort it." The result was a very stressful experience. Instead, we should realize these parts "have positive intentions," and we can work with these parts to deal with the pain—whether it's loss of identity, isolation, or abandonment—by building compassion to each part.

Burris shares the first step toward bringing compassion to our parts and ourselves is to bring a curiosity to the emotions we are feeling. This is not necessarily easy, as many people have learned to "muscle through or white-knuckle through things." Over time, we have developed habits that inhibit our ability to engage with our vulnerabilities. By being curious about all of our emotions, we can "start to care for and understand, even retrieve and remember," our vulnerabilities and exiles. In doing so, we are able to become more connected and authentic with ourselves and others.

Clients come to Sykes hoping to attain certain goals, which can vary from feeling less depressed, less anxious, or unhappy with a habit or tendency they have developed; "usually people have things they want to change about how they interact with themselves or the world." Through IFS therapy, Sykes encourages her clients to have self-compassion and a "clarity about ourselves, so we begin paying better attention to our actual feelings and perceptions." The result is individuals who can "have more control over what we do, what we say, and we have more choice over how we interact with the world and with other people."

The goal was to attempt to form an inner connectedness, or interconnectedness, between our parts, vulnerabilities, and essence in a way that is compassionate, helpful, and beneficial. The ultimate goal is to build relationships. By developing empathy to ourselves and to others, we can better handle emotional pains and disappointments that are common throughout life in a way that doesn't lead to shame, isolation, or something else. By engaging and acknowledging my firefighter part, I was able to begin creating a sense of empathy toward myself and become more resilient to the traumas I faced.

To this day, I continue to draw upon this practice of engaging my "managers" and "firefighters" directly. It has helped bring awareness to the various responses I have to moments of intense emotion, vulnerability, or self-criticism. Practicing this has allowed me to have compassion for different parts—and for myself—and be able to overcome traumas more easily.

CHAPTER 8

Día de Los Muertos

My phone rang as I walked through the door.

I had just returned home from a fun afternoon swim in the ocean. The salt still clung to my skin and my hair was dry.

"Hi, Mom!"

"Feliz Día de los Muertos! Happy Day of the Dead!" said Mom. "We just finished making our altar." It was Sunday, November 1, the first day of Día de los Muertos, a celebration traditionally celebrated in Mexico. Dad, Mom, Didi, and I had agreed to have a videocall to celebrate this occasion.

I put down my towel and refilled my water bottle. Didi joined the call as I made it to my bedroom.

"Look!" said Dad as he grabbed the laptop and walked out to the front yard. He showed us the decorations they had placed in the entryway.

Bouquets of cempasúchil—brightly colored yellow and orange marigold flowers—and candles framed the entryway. Papel picado—decorative, perforated paper—in the shape of skulls and skeletons, in all manner of reds, blues, pinks, and yellows, hung from the top of the door. The cempasúchil flowers and candles guide the path for the spirits to return to the altars and ofrendas—offerings.

Seeing the decorations immediately brought me back to the vibrant colors and rich aromas that filled the houses, streets, and cemeteries of Oaxaca, Mexico, during this festive period, a place where I had grown up and we had lived as a family for seven years.

Dad carried the laptop inside to show Didi and me their altar. I could see more bouquets of cempasúchil as well as individual flowers adorning the edge of the altar. Smoke rose from the burning copal—resin made from the copal tree—and wreathed its way up the altar; the incense was supposed to attract the spirits. There were many calaveras—skulls made of granulated sugar—with colorful patterns and decorations. A few loafs of Pan de Muerto—Bread of the Dead, a sweet bread typically flavored with anise and orange peel—a few shot glasses filled with mezcal, and even a bowl of freshly made mole negro—a delicious sauce typical of Oaxacan cuisine—were placed at the altar to feed and nourish the souls that arrived from their journey. Interspersed throughout these items were images, funeral invitations, and other mementos of friends, family, and loved ones who had passed away.

What is Día de los Muertos?
Día de los Muertos is a Mexican tradition that celebrates and honors the memory of those who have died. The celebration dates back to pre-Columbian times when people were wrapped and buried in a petate—straw bedroll—along with food to aid the person's spirit on its journey to Mictlán—the underworld in Aztec mythology. To assist in the journey, it was common for the deceased's family to organize a celebration. Día de los Muertos celebrates the transitory return of the spirits of the deceased to be with the family members of those who lived in the physical world. Through this tradition, it is believed someone's death isn't necessarily an absence, but a continued and evolving presence.[108]

During the seven years we lived in Oaxaca, we immersed ourselves in the Oaxacan culture, learned about this beautiful tradition, and began incorporating it into our lives. I had always appreciated Día de los Muertos, but it took a heightened meaning for me in 2020 as my grandfather, Papa, passed away. To honor his spirit and memory, and those of others, the four of us took turns telling stories. I recalled one of the last moments I shared with Papa before he passed.

Papa was looking out over the hills; oak trees dotted the landscape. The fertile San Juan Valley lay beyond with perfectly manicured blocks of green and purple lettuce designating different plots of agricultural land. The sun was setting and the dark reds and purples in the west gradually transitioned to the dark of night in the east. I could just begin to make out Orion's Belt.

I walked up and stood beside Papa.

"Look at the moon!" he said.

The full moon shone brightly in the sky. The occasional bat darted across. A cacophony of ribbits from frogs in the nearby pond filled the air.

I looked at Papa. He had a broad smile. The creases around his eyes were barely visible in the dim light.

"We've had a lot of good rain this season." He proceeded to speak at length about the new techniques he had been learning about in the field of holistic, regenerative land management; about the connection between healthy rangelands and sustainability; and about the role of soil as a carbon sink and its mitigation of climate change.

"Isn't that something!" he said.

Hearing him, stresses of the of the day melted off my shoulders. I looked out at the rangelands, rich in biodiversity with the many native grasses, and took a moment to recognize the beauty that was before me.

* * *

My grandfather—Richard Bernard Morris, or Papa, as we affectionately called him—passed away quietly in his sleep and surrounded by family on January 21, 2020. He was eighty-nine—"almost ninety," we said. I am privileged to have known him for so long and eternally grateful to have grown up with him as a role model. His wisdom and sage advice taught me the importance of leading a life of fulfillment and meaning, and his lessons have continued to help me navigate life's journeys. My lasting impression of him will be that of an unquenchable curiosity, a passion and excitement for life, and sunsets over the California hills.

His death was not sudden. His health declined over a number of years. He suffered from various maladies, namely leukemia. In the year preceding his death, there were many moments of concern, moments where we thought this could be "the moment" when his body succumbed to illness. There were enough moments an unexpected call from a family member or sudden exclamation mid-phone call evoked a sudden sense of anticipatory concern.

And the moments happened with an increasing frequency. There was one in the summer, then another in the fall, and once more during Thanksgiving. In January, Papa had weakened to such an extent my family decided to place him in hospice care.

All of Papa's eight children—my aunts, uncles, and mother—traveled to San Francisco to help care for him in his final days. We took care of Papa in turns, two at a time, staying in my grandparent's apartment and helping care for him and ensure he was as comfortable as possible. This continued, day and night, until the day he passed away.

Each of us came to terms with the prospect of Papa's death in our own way, either privately or as a group. We wrote letters, shared stories, reminisced of adventures gone by, or simply enjoyed each other's presence, sitting quietly and contemplating our bonds of friendship and family that had been strengthened by a shared love, joy, and gratitude for each other.

At the time, I found it curious many would read their letters or share their stories, even when he was sleeping. I wondered whether this act of closure meant more to the person expressing their love and affection. I shared this with Sofia and found her response intriguing. She said, "In death and saying good-bye, sometimes you can visualize relationships as being a third entity between two people to be nourished by both." Hearing this, I immediately visualized a floating ball of energy representing each relationship I had.

The concept of a third entity, or "analytic third," was proposed by Dr. Thomas Ogden, a psychoanalyst and writer. In his book *Subjects of Analysis*, he describes "the creation of a third subject is at the core of the psychoanalytic experience."[109] Ogden proposes the analytic third is created in the very first moment two people meet and is a "form of experience participated in" by both entities and is nourished through a deep connection made between one another.[110] While he first applied the term to the relationship between a therapist and client, its definition has since been expanded to encompass many other relationships and bonds.

As I continued to research the concept of an "analytic third," I noticed parallels between it and some of the customs celebrated in Día de los Muertos. Namely, they both invoked the notion of sustenance and nurturing—quite literally in the case of Día de los Muertos, as food and drink is left on the altar to nourish the spirits of our loved ones. By commemorating, reminiscing, and telling stories of those who passed away, we were also nurturing our relationships and this third entity. This ancient tradition seemed to perfectly understand the importance of nourishing and honoring the bonds formed with our loved ones.

I found Día de los Muertos also has a striking semblance to the notion of grief and dying. I came across the Kübler-Ross model, proposed by Dr. Elisabeth Kübler-Ross, a Swiss-American psychiatrist, who researched how imminent death affects individuals and their caregivers. In her book, *On Death and Dying*, she proposed individuals proceed through five stages of grief. They include:

- Denial and Isolation
- Anger
- Depression
- Acceptance
- Hope

It was initially believed individuals progressed through each stage linearly. Beginning with denial, then moving to anger, then to depression, acceptance, and finally hope. However, subsequent research determined the stages are instead more akin to "emotional states that occur in a variety of patterns."[111] I found Sheryl Sandberg and Adam Grant's description in their book, *Option B*, particularly evocative: "Grief and anger aren't extinguished like flames doused with water. They can flicker away one moment and burn hot the next."[112] The flames that flicker, wax, and wane do so differently for each person. Each person grieves differently and "each person's loss is different."[113]

Día de los Muertos acknowledges the uniqueness of grief. As we took turns, Mom, Dad, Didi, and I shared all manner of stories; some were happy, others sad, some proud or thoughtful. Throughout the call, the mood of the room rose and fell to match each of our states of grief. At one point, I asked Mom about her views on death, whereupon she responded, "The relationship does not end with death, but merely evolves."

While sad Papa passed, I was heartened by this image. The day he died, the whole family congregated at my grandparents' apartment and spent most of it grieving, praying, being in community, and reminiscing. Upon entering, I found it very difficult to speak for quite some time. All I could do was sit at the foot of Papa's bed and pray. I prayed for Papa, my grandmother, my mom, my aunts and uncles, anyone who had come to know and love Papa. I could not help but cry and grieve, for their loss as well as mine. At one point, everyone stood in a circle around Papa, held hands, and prayed. We prayed silently; at times, we voiced our prayers; we even sang in prayer.

Being connected, both physically and spiritually, and hearing our voices rise and fall in unison, I felt an incredible bond with my family. I understood then, deeply, even though this was a very difficult moment for each of us, our family bonds would help provide love, support, and strength in overcoming this difficult moment and help us lead lives that would honor Papa's spirit.

Later, my mom and I decided to head outside to catch some fresh air. We walked toward an empty bench and sat in quiet contemplation, enjoying the warmth of the sun. At one point, the wind picked up. I envisioned Papa's spirit in that wind, being carried by it, and traveling free and joyful across the bay. To this day, I find solace in this image and wish his spirit finds joy in the "next stage," and I have tried to channel his excitement and recognition of the beauty of this world whenever I feel down or anxious.

CHAPTER 9

Loneliness

I had just finished having a very pleasant Saturday morning hike with my friend Victor. We met in the morning at a trailhead overlooking Laguna Beach, California. Our hike took us along winding hills and down into a dry riverbed gulch. Our goal was to do a seven-mile loop, but we cut short the walk to summit back to our starting point as the midday sun heated up.

We followed this with lunch sitting under a terrace, enjoying the afternoon sun and a refreshing bottle of sparkling water. We spent most of the time catching up, as we hadn't seen each other since we both lived in London. Victor was one of only two people I knew since moving to San Diego, and I wasn't looking forward to the isolation that would come when we ended our day. On the drive back after saying our goodbyes, a sense of dread filled my heart.

I couldn't think of anyone else to be with.

* * *

Ever since I moved to London in 2015, I struggled with loneliness. In the last year or two of living there, I noticed I missed having a community. I had a number of friends and peer groups, but I craved something more, a sense of home and belonging. At the time, I thought part of it was living really far away from home in a different country. But some of these feelings of loneliness persisted after I moved back to California.

A 2018 study by the Kaiser Family Foundation found 22 percent of adults in the US and 23 percent of adults in the UK felt lonely. Many of the respondents reported they "feel they lack companionship, feel left out, or feel isolated from others, and many of them say their loneliness has had a negative impact on various aspects of their life."[114] Compounding this issue, two-thirds or more of respondents reported having "just a few or no relatives living nearby who they can rely on for support."[115]

Loneliness has become such a big issue in the US. Dr. Vivek Murthy, the US's nineteenth surgeon general, expressed the US was dealing with a loneliness epidemic. In his book *Together*, he notes he first noticed the detriment loneliness caused during his listening tour across the country. He saw "loneliness ran like a dark thread through many of the more obvious issues people brought to my attention, like addiction, violence, anxiety, and depression. The teachers and school administrators and many parents I encountered, for example, voiced a growing concern our children were becoming isolated—even, or perhaps especially, those who spent much of their time in front of their digital devices and on social media. Loneliness also was magnifying the pain for families whose loved ones were struggling with addiction to opioids."[116] In Murthy's view, loneliness was inextricably linked to other health problems. "In some cases, loneliness was driving health problems. In others, it was a consequence of the illness and hardships people were experiencing."[117]

Loneliness is not the same as being alone or isolated. Instead, loneliness is the subjective feeling you're lacking the social connections you need. It can feel like being stranded, abandoned, or cut off from the people with whom you belong—even if you're surrounded by other people. What's missing when you're lonely is the feeling of closeness, trust, and the affection of genuine friends, loved ones, and community.[118] Murthy goes on to identify three particular "dimensions" of loneliness:[119]

- Intimate or emotional loneliness is the longing for a close confidant or intimate partner, someone with whom you share a deep mutual bond of affection and trust.
- Relational or social loneliness is the yearning for quality friendships and social companionship and support.
- Collective loneliness is the hunger for a network or community of people who share your sense of purpose and interests.

I experienced all three types of loneliness throughout my transition from London to San Diego. The end of my long-term relationship and the loss of a close confidant and intimate partner left a void in my intimate and emotional loneliness. I also experienced collective loneliness in London.

I count myself fortunate I have many quality friendships and have benefited from their tremendous support. Staying with my parents and being in the Bay Area, a place where I grew up and developed a strong community of friends and family, definitely helped diminish my sense of loneliness. Most of my transition coincided during the COVID-19 pandemic, which exacerbated every dimension of loneliness. While shelter-in-place orders and limits on gatherings were critical measures to diminish the spread of this virus, they also created roadblocks for me as I strove to connect with strangers, friends, and family.

If loneliness is an epidemic, then Murthy argues connection is the cure. Through his work, both as a doctor and surgeon general, he found "togetherness raises optimism and creativity. When people feel they belong to one another, their lives are stronger, richer, and more joyful."[120] He strongly believes building a more connected world can have far-reaching benefits to various aspects of our society, including other public health challenges we face such as addiction, violence, disengagement among workers and students, and political polarization.[121] Murthy concludes, "Human connection is also a universal condition. We are hardwired for connection."[122]

How can we cultivate connection? I spoke with Kalina Silverman, the creator and founder of Big Talk. Big Talk is a communication approach that facilitates meaningful connections in life—with family, friends, coworkers, strangers, and even oneself—through the process of skipping small talk to ask more open-ended and thought-provoking questions.[123]

Her epiphany for starting this communication practice occurred when she was enrolled in college as a freshman. At the time, "[she] really struggled and felt really lonely, and [she] didn't know what was going on." In her first couple of years, she really tried to "sweep all of that under a rug," until one day, when she spoke to a fellow classmate whom she "thought was fun and confident, and then we opened up to each other about how much we struggled freshman year. So much so we both contacted the school counselor. That was a moment for me to realize everyone's going through this, just no one talks about it. And why don't we talk about it?" She remembers feeling so ashamed of asking for help and seeking counselling or therapy she hid in a corner when making the phone call.

While Silverman studied journalism in college, she "decided to create a social experiment video project where I walked up to strangers and skipped the small talk" with a goal of talking about things that really mattered in life. In a TEDx Talk she gave, Silverman explains she attempted to have "deeper, meaningful conversations" by asking strangers what they would do if they "found out [they] were going to die tomorrow?"[124],[125] Tellingly, most of the responses of those who participated in the unprompted Big Talk related to a striving for connection. Their answers included:[126]

- "Call a lot of my friends."
- "I'd probably text all my friends."

- "I would take a road trip to go see someone today. I would tell them I love them."
- "Be with my family."
- "Get on an airplane to go be with my son."

It's curious when prompted with such a deep question, most individuals gravitated toward connection. I imagine confronting our own life and death clarifies what we really find important, and that connection, whether its intimate, relational, or collective, is a critical component to who we are as humans.

As I contemplated Silverman's question, I realized my response also fit into the framework of connection. If I found out I would die tomorrow, I would immediately fly home and be with my family. I would want to share my last moments with them, reminisce about shared adventures and happy memories, enjoy one last meal together, go for a walk at sunset, thank them for all their support, reassure them I've lived a full life and would be with them in spirit, and take the opportunity to say "I love you" one last time.

It is unlikely in this last day, even if I tried, I would be able to reach out and connect with all of my friends and family. While the prospect of this saddens me, I can rest assured knowing I have taken time to express my appreciation to friends and family. I developed this practice of being proactive in maintaining my friendships while living abroad in London. I tried compensating for the distance by being more diligent about keeping contact with them. This manifested itself in all sorts of ways, whether it was sending postcards, scheduling regular videocalls, sending texts, or coordinating in-person visits. I have also taken to writing letters; I wrote a number of letters of appreciation to friends when leaving London, I wrote thank-you letters to those who supported me finding a new job, and I try my best to send notes of appreciation for birthdays and special occasions.

When prompted how someone could engage in Big Talk, Silverman shared, "You really have to be vulnerable and comfortable with it and it'll naturally evolve the more you practice. It's kind of a skill. But then there are actual tools you can use to have these kinds of conversations and connect with people, whether that's something like a meetup group, or a card game, or an app. You have to make an effort."

Engaging in Big Talk entails a different type of conversation. It's not merely making an effort and having continual conversations with people; the content of the conversations matters as well.

Although Big Talk doesn't happen all the time, people are particularly responsive when it does take place. It has offered a tremendous opportunity for creating common ground and fostering connection because at its core, it necessitates a sharing of one's own life story. When engaging in deep conversation and sharing the highs and lows of their life, we can strike to the core of our "universal human experience and create connection."[127] As I have become more comfortable engaging in meaningful conversations with a wide range of people, I have also developed a few prompts that can kickstart these conversations. A few of them include:

- What is something you are most proud of that has happened in the past year?
- What is something you are hopeful for?
- What are you grateful for?

Since these questions are thought-provoking, it is best to be patient when having these conversations, particularly if it's the first time you are having them with someone.

As I wrapped up my conversation with Silverman, she reflected on her experiences using Big Talk. "It's just crazy how this simple idea is so universally resonant. And so needed for a lot of people." She has found "so many people have been struggling with feelings of disconnection or loneliness or lack of empathy." Practicing having more meaningful conversations has helped me diminish the sense of loneliness I felt and nurture stronger connections with others.

PART 3

GROWTH

CHAPTER 1

Finding Meaning

I woke up as the first rays of light hit my room; the flannel blankets maintained a cocoon of warmth around me. The sparrows called to each other as they took their morning baths in the fountain outside. I stretched, taking effort to stay under the covers and avoid the chill of the early morning. The tightness in my chest remained from the previous day.

The anxiety that accompanied it, ever since my bout of suicidal ideation on the flight, hadn't gone away either. While I had successfully pulled myself back from the brink and preferred life to death, I was now dogged by a primary question. What is the purpose of life?

I had asked myself this many times before. However, this question, and the implications of its answer, took on a new importance following my difficulties with suicidal ideation. With the stakes higher, I found myself needing a more compelling answer. It wasn't as easy to pass off any existential angst that had arisen in previous moments of introspection now that I had gone through such a threatening moment to my existence.

I gritted my teeth and clenched my blanket. The answer to this question continued to elude me.

The bed squeaked under my weight. The carpet felt soft underfoot as I walked to the middle of the room to begin my morning stretches. Commencing, the tightness in my hamstrings flared slightly.

Maybe I've been asking the wrong question.

I sat on the floor. The muscles in the back of my legs slowly awakened.

Rather than asking—what is the meaning of life? Maybe the question I should be asking is—how can I learn the meaning of life?

My eyes opened wide. Reframing this question brought me back to some of the calculus classes I took in high school.

This could be a good approach. Just because I didn't know the answer to a mathematical problem or equation didn't mean the answer didn't exist.

A smile spread across my face. My lungs expanded with a deep inhalation and the tension in my chest melted away as my lungs contracted.

I found this breakthrough very empowering, as it brought a sense of agency to my search for the meaning of life. The pressure of needing to have an immediate answer was supplanted by the notion I could now take steps to find this answer. Rather than being weighed down with a sense of dread for not knowing, I now recognized this search would be a process of discovery. Being oriented toward a new direction alleviated my discomfort of not having an answer and helped me take steps along this path.

I mulled over this question for many days and weeks thereafter. My initial instinct was to look to my friends and family for guidance. I made it a habit to ask them about their life stories, hoping to glean any pearls of wisdom about how they found meaning. While I did not know it at the time, I seemed to have been following the advice of German American developmental psychologist Dr. Charlotte Bühler when she said, "All we can do is study the lives of people who seem to have found their answers to the questions of what ultimately human life is about against those who have not."[128]

The New Year came and went, and I continued focusing my energies on this one central question. Coincidentally, a friend and I had planned an overnight backpacking trip in Henry W. Coe State Park, lying in the eastern hills of the Santa Clara Valley in California. Neither of us had backpacked before, but we rented our gear and set off on a sixteen-mile loop through the park. It was absolutely fantastic. Our route took us along lofty ridges, across steep canyons, and along creeks. We walked through chaparral and oak groves and saw all manner of fauna. At one point, walking south along a ridge on the eastern side of the park, we even saw the snowcapped Sierra, Nevada mountains hundreds of miles to the east.

Early on during the first day of hiking, we trudged along an incline. Sweat beaded down my neck and the pack weighed down on my hips. A trail of dust followed us. The constant pitter-patter of our feet and poles was occasionally interrupted by the high-pitched call of a hawk riding the thermals far above us.

After thirty minutes of an uphill climb, we saw the ridgeline. I looked up and was greeted by a field of grasses rustling in the wind, glistening and golden under the midday sun. Off in the distance, I saw an oak tree. The tree was dead; its branches were bereft of leaves and its phloem—the part of the tree below the surface—laid bare as its bark had fallen off. I paused to take a sip of water and continued staring at the oak tree.

It occurred to me, for that tree, life meant growing, flourishing, passing on its progeny, and eventually dying. This same cycle could be said for all other plants and trees, with the obvious difference being each grows according to its own rhythm. Each plant and tree had the same objective of flourishing as best as it could and in its own way.

Questions occupied my mind.

Does this cycle apply to humans? What can I do to grow and flourish as this oak tree has done?

Grasshoppers chirped in the grasses around me.

How can I live my fullest self?

I recounted my epiphany to Sofia during our discussion focused on finding meaning. She suggested I read Viktor

Frankl's *Man's Search for Meaning.* Frankl was an Austrian psychotherapist who was cast into the Nazi concentration and extermination camps, and his work recounts his time in the concentration camps, including Auschwitz. The focus of the book is "less about his travails, what he suffered and lost, than it is about the sources of his strength to survive."[129] Following his time in the concentration camps, Frankl proceeded to develop his own theory called logotherapy. Logotherapy focuses on "the meaning of human existence as well as on man's search for such a meaning"[130] and builds on his belief that "man's search for meaning is the primary motivation in his life."[131]

Frankl explains the "meaning of life differs from man to man, and from moment to moment."[132] In his work, he uses the analogy of asking a chess master what the best chess move entails.

"'Tell me, what is the best move in the world?' There simply is no such thing as the best or even a good move apart from a particular situation in a game and particular personality of one's opponent."[133]

The implication is, to find meaning in life, each person is ultimately responsible for determining the right answer for themselves, based on the tasks, circumstances, and challenges life presents each individual.

I was instantly engrossed and read *Man's Search for Meaning* from cover to cover in a matter of days. I put it down and then read it all over again. I felt as if I was beginning to put the pieces of a puzzle together, which offered a roadmap to the answer to my one central question. Instead of having to determine the purpose and meaning of my whole life, my responsibility was pared down to determining meaning in my life in this one particular moment. Reading this work lent a sense of relief as identifying what brought me meaning in one point in life seemed like a much more manageable problem to try and tackle.

What brings me meaning? I reflected much on this question. One morning, while at my parent's house in San Jose, I walked to the backyard and sat down in the hammock chair. It was tied to a large branch of our avocado tree and croaked under my weight as it rocked back and forth. The blank page of my journal lay before me.

I considered all I had learned and read in the previous months and tried to parse apart the sources of meaning and fulfillment in my life. Passages from Frankl's works sprung up in my mind, along with those of Dr. James Hollis, a renowned Jungian psychoanalyst who expressed meaning is "inherent to us" and can be represented by "finding something truly worthy of investing our energies."[134]

A hummingbird darted from flower to flower, the bright pink coloring shining resplendently in the sun.

What is worthy of my energies?

I brought the pen to the page and after some time, wrote down:

- Community

- Making a positive human and environmental impact
- Learning

I valued all three of these aspects and felt leaning on them could help provide a direction to my life. Devoting my efforts to these three tenets could also act as a compass toward meaning. I thought back on my moment walking past the oak tree and smiled. An enthusiasm to learn and discover grew within me. It now seemed clear. There wasn't one particular answer to—what is the meaning of life? Rather, it varied from person to person and even from moment to moment in my own life. All I had to do was bring a constant curiosity, examination, and reflection to what brought me meaning and realize it could change with time.

CHAPTER 2

Learning to Comfort

I sat in the waiting room, looking forward to my upcoming session with Sofia. The room was square with seats lining three sides of the room. On the far side, various brochures and pamphlets provided information and resources about depression and anxiety or espoused the benefits of yoga and meditation. Another man sat across from me, although we didn't acknowledge each other.

At the top of the hour, clients started arriving and leaving. The door swung open, and Sofia appeared. I stood up and walked to her office, pausing briefly to make myself tea.

Sunlight shone through the windows and onto the far end of the brown couch—my usual seat during my sessions with Sofia. My backpack slung on my shoulder and the aroma of lemongrass filled the room. I sat down, placed a pillow on my lap, and took out my notepad and pen.

There was only one thing written on the page.

"My grandfather passed away this weekend."

"I'm sorry." Sofia's inner brow raised, and the edges of her lips lowered.

I had previously mentioned to Sofia my grandfather's health had been declining for some time. I explained to her what had taken place and how he had passed away surrounded by his family.

"One of the most heart-wrenching moments was watching my grandmother grieve. I can't imagine what it must be like to lose a partner of sixty years. I mean, I've found it difficult processing the end of a partnership of three years." I paused and looked outside the window, reflecting on the difficult emotions I had experienced following the end of my relationship.

The tea had cooled somewhat. The citrus tasted rich and zesty. "I know I can't entirely empathize with what she's dealing with, but I do want to be able to be there for her. Do you have any suggestions? I'm just not sure how I can best support her."

Sofia took a few notes. She stared pensively at the wall behind me. "Well, I'm wondering how you would like to be comforted if you were in that situation?"

I considered her question. "I would want her to know I'm here for her, and I would want to help her in any way she thinks is best."

* * *

One area of growth that occurred after going to therapy for a few months involved learning how to comfort others. This was very unexpected, but it stemmed from the fact I personally required so much comfort during my difficult moments. By learning about what best worked for me, I was able to translate that into helping others. This insight really took form after speaking with Sofia about comforting my grandmother.

I shared many years back, as an undergraduate student at UC Berkeley, my friend and housemate was suffering from high levels of anxiety. He routinely had anxiety and panic attacks. They happened when were in class together, or when we'd go out to eat. I tried helping him as best as I could, but I don't think I did a very good job. I wasn't ever sure of what to do or say.

Through therapy, I have since learned working to listen and understand what the person in need of comfort desires is sufficient. This notion is best summarized by Sheryl Sandberg and Adam Grant in their book *Option B*:

"There's no one way to grieve and there's no one way to comfort. What helps one person won't help another, and even what helps one day might not help the next. Growing up, I was taught to follow the Golden Rule: Treat others as you want to be treated. But when someone is suffering, instead of following the *Golden Rule*, we need to follow the *Platinum Rule*: Treat others as they want to be treated. Take a cue from the person in distress and respond with understanding—or better yet, action."[135]

Through my research on the topic of comfort, I learned about Jen Marr's work teaching people to be better at comforting others. She strongly believes people can learn and develop their ability to comfort and has been using evidenced-based processes to teach children and adults the lessons she has learned. I spoke with her, wanting to learn more about comfort and explore if my experience in therapy was similar to the work she was doing.

In 2012, she made a profound discovery and realized so many people were hurting and so few people knew how to help. Her role in forming the first Lutheran Church Charities K-9 Comfort Dog team in Connecticut led her to be an integral part of Sandy Hook Elementary School's recovery from the tragic mass shooting. Every day for five years following the tragedy, she would visit Sandy Hook Elementary and work in crisis response with comfort dogs. She has since founded Inspiring Comfort, a pioneering organization that believes "comfort is a teachable skill" and uses evidence-based programs to "equip people with the skills to comfort others to help them cultivate care and connection."[136] She also authored the book *Paws to Comfort*, "an everyday guide to learning how you can help mend our disconnected world."[137]

I asked her if any one particular moment led her to this realization. "My a-ha moment occurred while sitting with a group of students at a school. There had been a tragedy and two students had died over the course of the weekend in separate accidents, and I was with a group of boys who were best friends with the brother of one of the students who had just died." In this particular case, she was there with comfort dogs, listening and offering support. She noticed none of the students, each with a phone in their hands, had actually reached out to their friend. Suddenly compelled to speak up, she interrupted them and said, "You know, just text. Just say you're here and you care, and you'll always be here."

That moment was a revelation for her, as she realized how much we as a society had lost our way. The students didn't abstain from reaching out because they didn't care. Rather, they didn't reach out because they didn't know how to, or they felt awkward reaching out. Having helped other groups of people who were dealing with tragedy or feeling alienated from not having heard from their friends, it suddenly made sense to her why so many people felt lonely. The question then became, what now? What more needs to be done?

It became clear to Marr comforting required two key aspects: action and repetition. She uses the analogy of filling a jar with marbles: "We can consider everybody being a jar in need of filling. When someone needs comfort, you can put one marble in the jar." Marr took this to heart and her work epitomized action. She showed up to Sandy Hook Elementary day after day for five years, repeatedly adding marbles and showing people she cared. By continually showing she cared, she was able to develop relationships and trust with the students and faculty.

Learning about comfort helped me appreciate my friends and family who comforted me during my grieving process. For me, grieving was not a one-off event, it didn't occur once and then never again. It was a continual process, sometimes ebbing and sometimes flowing, but always present in some manner; it was also not possible to merely ignore the grief and behave as if nothing had happened. As my grief evolved over time, so, too, did my need for comfort. At times, I needed to go for a walk with a friend, other times to just sit and chat, other times a phone call would suffice.

Learning to comfort has also been one of the most important insights I gained while navigating my mental health crisis. Being able to help my friends and family as they go through their own difficult times has been empowering. I have worked diligently to try and incorporate the lessons learned in therapy as well as through my conversations with Marr and others. Primarily, these insights have helped me be more comfortable engaging in conversations with others when they are sad or grieving. While not necessarily easy, I feel like I am equipped to engage in these emotionally charged discussions instead of glossing over them. Being able to draw on my own personal experiences of grieving and receiving comfort has also helped me empathize with someone who needs comfort. In instances where I don't quite know how to respond, I've learned that saying "I don't know what to say," or asking them "How can I best support you?" can still be very helpful. I have also taken Marr's mantra of "repetition" to heart and made it a habit to check in and comfort those who are going through difficult moments, acknowledging their needs for comfort can change over time.

I have also very much incorporated "action" into my attempts to comfort others. I have tried to go beyond words to show I was there for someone. This can be as simple as offering to give someone a hug, arranging for their favorite meal to be delivered to them for dinner, or flying across the country for the weekend to be with them. Comforting others does take a lot of effort and energy, particularly when discussing such emotionally charged topics, but I have found the friends I hold most dear are the ones who reached out and comforted me, or I had comforted them. Offering and receiving comfort enables individuals to help and support each other during their own difficult moments and offers an opportunity for a deeper connection.

Marr offers a number of prompts anyone can use to offer comfort. These questions can be used more than once, with different friends and in various settings. They can be key for you to act, again and again, when comforting someone.[138]
1. Do you need a hug or someone to talk to?
2. When you are ready to talk, I'll be here for you. Always, no matter what.
3. I'm bringing you lunch today. Do you still love minestrone soup?
4. Do you want to tell me about it?
5. I'm so sorry for what you're dealing with, do you need a hug or a friend?
6. I don't know what to say, but I can promise I'm a good listener.
7. Do you have time for a walk today?
8. My shoulder is here right now. Cry, scream, say whatever you need to say. I'm just here to listen.
9. I'm going to pop over to do your dishes and just hang out with you. What time is good?
10. No matter how bad things are, I'm here. Please tell me what you need.
11. I'm at the store and have grabbed some milk and chocolate mint ice cream for you, what else do you need?
12. I haven't heard from you in a while, tell me what's going on.

Marr offers a number of prompts anyone can use to offer comfort. These questions can be used more than once, with different friends and in various settings. They can be key for you to act, again and again, when comforting someone.[138]
13. What day this week would be the best for me to bring you dinner?
14. Hey, hi. What's up? It's been a while since I've seen or heard from you. You okay?
15. Let's go over here and get some hot tea or coffee and rest for a few minutes.
16. Can we talk? Whatever is going on, I've got your back.
17. Can I come over and just be with you? We can play a game or watch a movie or just chat if you're up for it.
18. I have no idea how you're feeling right now, but I really care and I'm here.
19. Do you have anyone to plow your driveway and shovel your sidewalk and porch?
20. I love you. I'm here.
21. What would help you today?
22. How is this week going for you?
23. Do you need to sit down and rest for a bit?
24. I'm free today at twelve and am going to pop over. If you are not up for seeing me, I understand, but I'll be there with a vanilla latte.
25. You are not alone. I am here and I care.

CHAPTER 3

Play

My heart pounded. I rested my hands on my knees and tried catching my breath, a task made all the more difficult at altitude. A layer of dust caked my ankles and legs.

I stood up and inhaled slowly, bringing my arms above my head. With each breath, my lungs filled to capacity with the crisp, mountainous air.

I looked back at what appeared to be a five-hundred-meter drop. My gaze followed the not-so-sturdy rope that had helped me climb up the last twenty-five meters of the escarpment. Beads of sweat rolled down my neck.

I walked up the last few steps toward the summit, which consisted of a boulder with a small red circle painted on its top. Below the red dot read, "Bobotov Kuk 2523 M"—the tallest mountain in Montenegro.

A rectangular metal box, covered in stickers and chained to the rock, lay to the right. I opened it and found a book. Its pages were filled with names and countries from all over the world, and they rustled as a gust of wind passed. I placed the book back in the box and surveyed the vast expanse in front of me. I was standing at the top of Bobotov Kuk, a large limestone massif that towered over the surrounding Dinaric Alps in Montenegro's Durmitor National Park.

I walked toward the edge of the summit and sat down. My hydration pack pressed tightly against my back. The water was fresh and cold. As my legs dangled over the one-hundred-meter drop, I reveled in the moment. Steep fields of scree extended below me, small pieces of the mountain that were slowly eroding over eons. On the climb up, I had sunk down to my ankles and at times felt I was doing a better job of sliding backward than forward. Beyond the scree lay a boulder field. It had been such fun to navigate the technical stretch, clambering over rocks and trying to determine the best path through the field.

The wind picked up and a cloud covered the peak, shrouding it in secrecy, dimming the light, and lending an ethereal feel. Everything was grey. I shivered and riffled through my pack to find my jacket.

My stomach grumbled. I snacked on some burek, a baked pastry filled with a savory cheese that was common in the Balkan region, and took a few last sips of water.

The cloud passed and suddenly revealed a dazzling array of colors. A patchwork of light and dark greens dotted the valleys before me; grasses, which attempted to grow on any bit of land that wasn't too steep. In flatter regions, pockets of shrubs were able to take root. At lower elevations, the green shrubs transitioned to vibrant oranges and yellows of the fall foliage. The sun warmed my back.

Suddenly, the wind died down. The rush of the wind was replaced by absolute silence. Not one sound; complete solitude. I closed my eyes and tried engraving as much detail of the view before me in my memory. My lips curved upward into a smile. Pure bliss.

My watch beeped as it hit the three-hour mark—three hours since the start of my run from the mountain town of Žabljak, passing the Crno Jezero (Black Lake), over one thousand meters below and fourteen kilometers away. I quickly finished my burek, wiping the residual grease on my shorts, and stood up. I shaded my eyes with my hand and noticed the sun had just passed its peak. The views were stunning, but I did not want to get stuck in the mountains past sunset. And I couldn't wait to run the downhill section.

* * *

I got into trail running in the spring of 2019. I found being in the mountains to be so invigorating. I enjoyed exploring some of the most beautiful mountain regions in the world, savoring the quiet and solitude while also pushing myself both physically and mentally. Trail running quickly became one of the most fun activities.

Trail running also offered a reprieve for me while struggling with mental health. As I packed up my things in London and prepared to leave the UK, I decided I wanted to take some time off and backpack throughout the Balkans. Without much planning, I boarded a one-way flight to Croatia and crisscrossed the region, always on the lookout for mountains and possible trail runs. Day after day, I spent five, six, even eight or nine hours running in the mountains, taking breaks only to bus from one country to the next. While my struggles with mental health didn't vanish on this trip, trail running and being in the mountains did offer a temporary respite.

While researching different fields of psychiatry for this book, I came across the work of Dr. Stuart Brown. Brown has a background in psychiatry and has researched the evolution of human and animal play.[139] Brown did not start out as a play researcher. He in fact started out investigating a much more somber area—researching the lives of murderers. Through his work, he identified a common theme: the adverse impact of lack of play in childhood. His clinical research into the causes and prevention of violence showed him authentic play is a "state of being that can be accessed and used by everyone, and play is as important to humans as vitamins or sleep."[140]

Brown defines play as being "done for its own sake, it's voluntary, it's pleasurable, it's non-repetitive, it produces a sense of wellbeing, it's flavored by culture, it's altered by temperament, it's a fundamental survivor drive that comes out of our deepest center of our brain and fuels action and activity."[141] In addition to bringing pleasure and meaning, a key aspect of play, or a play state, is it "takes one out of the sense of time."[142]

Brown argues the importance of play is fundamental to who we are as humans and is deeply intertwined with our biological processes. He writes play "has evolved over eons in many animal species to promote survival. It shapes the brain and makes animals smarter and more adaptable. In higher animals, it fosters empathy and makes possible complex social groups. For us, play lies at the core of creativity and innovation."[143] Many of his studies have demonstrated play, and even the anticipation of play, decreases anxiety and increases pleasure through the release of dopamine—the reward hormone.[144]

Brown offers a cautionary tale if one does not play, there are consequences. Bluntly, he states, "The opposite of play is not work, it's depression."[145] Thankfully, his research has illuminated certain areas to help individuals identify and nurture play in their life. He recommends each one of us "look at our own play history and background, what is it that evokes joy and a sense of pleasure?"[146] He argues we can identify what we each call play by focusing on which activities we spend time on without a purpose, do something we don't want to end, participate in something where we lose track of time, or lose our sense of self-consciousness. Fundamentally, identifying and incorporating play into our lives is a key factor that leads not only to happiness, but to "being a fulfilled human being."[147]

Considering my play history, trail running ticked all of the boxes of play. I enjoyed it, I lost track of time doing it, I never wanted it to end (only my sore legs wanted it to end), and I didn't care what others thought when I trail ran.

In the winter of 2020, I spoke to Michelle Myers, a friend and marriage and family therapist, about the benefits of playing to my mental health. I had found many of these activities, particularly running, diminished my anxiety. On many occasions, I felt running helped me process my emotions in a physical manner. They also served as a physical check-in to better understand how my body was feeling. Myers commended me on continuing my running, and she stressed the importance of "incorporating other components to help digest the therapy; it's difficult to go deep in therapy without doing so."

The importance of incorporating play into our lives, and its ability to provide meaning and fulfillment, while also mitigating possible mental health challenges was reinforced through my conversation with Jeff Sparr. Sparr is a self-taught artist and cofounder of PeaceLove, "an organization that uses expressive arts, a fun way to be able to help people find peace of mind." Sparr himself was diagnosed with obsessive-compulsive disorder (OCD) as a collegiate tennis player. It was a very challenging time for Sparr; "I did not know what was going on, I basically thought I was losing my mind and didn't have any resources or anybody to talk to." He struggled to find access to mental health services and instead "sucked it up, and then got worse." For over thirty years since his diagnosis, he has dealt with a debilitating illness that impacts him every day. Despite this, he considers himself "one of the lucky ones," as his diagnosis has helped lead him to receive help through medication, exposure therapy, and benefited from the support of a loving family. His venture into art and painting was sudden; "someone mentioned to me painting might be good for me, and I was coming home from work one day and I stopped at an art supply store and never stopped."

Painting made a profound and lasting impression on him. In a keynote speech he gave at the YMCA175 conference in 2019, he explains, "It was like I had found a superpower. It gave me a sense of control not only OCD, but all mental illnesses can rob you of. It gave me a way to express what I couldn't find the words to say. It provided me a vulnerable space, a safe space, where I could share my art and my story."[148]

He went on to explain he decided to share his story following a moment that changed his life. He had just raised sixteen thousand dollars in an art showing and thought, *I paint, it makes me feel better, maybe it will help somebody else.*[149] Two weeks later, he walked into a psychiatric children's hospital, which he also happened to be a member of the board and prior patient; "walking through the hospital, I had a bag over my shoulder, paints, and brushes. I walk to the unit, and there are eight- to twelve-year-old children battling all kinds of mental health challenges." Having three young kids of his own at the time, "it hit really hard, and I panicked." He realized he didn't have any qualifications, he wasn't a doctor nor an art therapist, "all I wanted to do was help." He then did the only thing he felt qualified to do—he shared his story. He also shared his art, his process, how he made it, and how he used it to find peace of mind. The children's responses surprised him; "I was surprised they were interested, and more, how much these kids understood. They got what I was talking about." At last, he passed out the paints and brushes. He proceeded to tear up a piece of paper and, throwing the pieces into the air, proclaimed, "There are no rules! There are just two things; I want you to have fun and I want you to make mistakes." The children "started painting on the canvasses, they started painting on the tables, they painted on each other, they painted on me." At the end of the class, the children wanted to share; they proudly held their paintings up and "shared what gave them peace of mind as best they could, and in many cases their own struggle, and the other children applauded."[150]

That was his first experience in sharing his story and trying to help others use fun and creativity to relate to their emotions. Spurred on by his love of art, he went on to create PeaceLove with the intention of creating awareness around mental health and allowing for creative expressions and play to provide peace of mind. To date, PeaceLove has held workshops throughout the US and world, and has impacted more than sixty-five thousand lives.[151]

Throughout the entire time I went to therapy, I enjoyed many forms of play. I journaled, meditated, read, drew, and more. While I did not necessarily recognize each activity as play, I knew doing so made me feel better and I worked diligently to try and do at least one or two activities each day. I noticed these activities also helped me process and absorb the lessons I had during my discussions with Sofia. They helped me consider and process the feelings or emotions that surfaced in different ways. I do believe playing was a key component in helping provide joy and meaning at a time when I was struggling with anxiety and hopelessness, and gave me the strength and motivation to continue making an effort one day at a time. To this day, I prioritize play and proactively immerse myself in moments that bring enjoyment.

CHAPTER 4

Telling My Story Impacted My Story

The clock in the upper righthand corner of my laptop ticked over to 17:43.

A wave of apprehension began to arise within me. Not quite to the level of a panic attack, but still perceptible. My 18:00 call with Sofia was fast approaching. I was nervous about this call because I had decided now, at last, was the moment I would share something with her I hadn't shared with anyone. My heartbeat quickened and my palms started to sweat. The chair creaked as I tilted my weight backward.

I went for a walk and got some fresh air. It was a warm day. The sun was setting over the Pacific Ocean. The horizon line melted between the ocean and the sky, and the blues slowly transitioned into hues of red. A few clouds dotted the sky.

I walked along my normal neighborhood loop. Moving and getting fresh air did help, but I was still nervous. I tried to time my walk to return home just before my call. Arriving, I glanced at my watch, 17:56. Four more minutes.

I filled up my glass with water, went to my room, and logged into the video calling app. The spinning wheel on the screen continued for a bit longer than usual. Sofia appeared moments later.

"How are you?" She smiled and waved and took a moment to check her microphone and audio.

I breathed slowly and reviewed my notes.

"I wanted to share something with you. I probably should have told you before, but...," I said.

She looked on expectantly.

"I've been..."

My palms were sweating, and I took a sip of water.

"I've been dealing with suicidal ideation."

It was the first moment I had actually said the word "suicide" aloud.

I proceeded to explain it started in December of 2019. At the time, the notion of suicide was always at the front of my mind. I didn't necessarily have any intention to die by suicide, but the thought of suicide was ever-present inside me, and it would pop up in all manner of circumstances.

"People would ask me, 'Do you have any plans for the weekend?' and my first instinct was to blurt out 'to kill myself,' even though I never said this. This would happen with friends and family, at work, in passing conversation. And it was really scary. My response for the last ten months has been to push back against this instinct, but the harder I push, the harder it pushes back. It almost feels like a spring."

"Well, I'm so glad you brought this up," she responded. "I know this can be scary, and acknowledging this can be scary. I think it's important for you to realize you have been able to handle this adversity and also have a web of connectedness and support, you have parts of you that are reacting in a constructive way." She paused. "It seems like that there is a push and pull between your logical side on the one hand, and your impulsive side on the other. Am I getting that right?"

"Yes, I think that's correct. I think I have this fear of the underlying impulsiveness. I wish I would be able to run away from the emotion, but that doesn't seem to be possible."

Sofia paused for a moment. "I'm thinking of the different parts of the brain. It could be the primal part has been stuck on a solution while the logical one, the one that has evolved, knows this impulsiveness is not the correct solution."

She continued, "It's okay to engage with this fear when things are okay. Dealing with this fear now, when it's less charged, is better as you can create a different relation to that impulse and emotion."

We spent much of the hour discussing this internal push and pull I was feeling and exploring how I could best address this impulsiveness during moments when it wasn't so charged.

Toward the end, I said, "I do want to share this with Mom and Dad because I think they deserve to know this about me. I wanted to share this with you first, almost as practice, so it's not as charged when I have this conversation with them."

A week later, I decided it was time to tell Mom and Dad. I was nervous because I wasn't entirely sure how they would respond, but I knew with certainty telling them was the correct course of action.

I could hear the low rumble of the traffic off in the distance as I called Mom with bated breath. The sun had set at that point and the stars had come out. I paced back and forth in the front yard. The dew on the grasses wetted my feet.

I continued waiting for Mom to pick up the phone.

"Hi, Shayne! We were just having dinner and about to sit down and watch a movie." She smiled widely as she walked from the kitchen to the living room and sat down on the couch in her usual spot. The chatter of the TV could be heard in the background.

I kept pacing back and forth on the lawn. A neighbor walked by with a dog.

"I have something to share. It's a bit heavy."

Her smile faded and she focused her gaze on me. She furrowed her brow, and a look of concern crossed her face. She walked over to sit next to Dad, who was reading at the time. He muted the TV, and both were now paying attention.

"This is hard." I took a deep breath. A single tear ran down my cheek.

"I want you to know I've been having suicidal ideations."

I proceeded to explain all I had been struggling with since December 2019. I shared I had already told Sofia and I wanted to share this with them now, as I felt it was important they know. I also explained what suicidal ideation was and the role hopelessness had on my emotional state then.

Silence hung in the air.

Dad, looking over his reading glasses, finally asked, "Well, how are you feeling now?"

"Honestly, I feel a lot better now that I've been able to share this with you. I feel like a weight has been removed from my shoulders."

Gently, he proceeded to ask a number of questions about how I was feeling. He asked me if I was still dealing with these ideations. He asked if I was taking care of myself now, if I was eating well, exercising, and sleeping enough.

"Is there anything you need from us right now?" he asked.

"I would have to think about it, but I don't think so."

"Well, if there's anything you do need, don't hesitate to ask. Know we're here for you and love you," said Dad.

"Absolutely!" said Mom.

"I think I am okay right now. Sharing this with you has already been a big help."

"Okay, well, let us know. We love you."

"Love you too."

* * *

Opening up to Sofia and my parents about my suicidal ideation represented a culmination of personal effort to be more vulnerable. Experiencing suicidal ideation was the scariest moment I experienced throughout my emotional traumas. These thoughts and emotions were also the moments I tried to ignore and repress the most. I was so scared by these thoughts I didn't even want to acknowledge the word "suicide." In fact, I didn't even write the word in my journal. My approach was to not acknowledge it, hoping doing so would mean the thoughts didn't exist.

That sense of fear was what prevented me from sharing this with others, which perpetuated a sense of isolation. Being alone with my anxiety and suicidal ideation was tremendously difficult. I wanted to break through this isolation and share my struggles with others, but opening up and being vulnerable wasn't easy. Over time, my desire to forge a connection with others about my challenges outweighed the fear of being vulnerable.

This balance between connection and vulnerability is something Dr. Brené Brown, a research professor at the University of Houston, identified in her research on vulnerability. In her TEDx Talk, she shares, "The ability to feel connected, it's why we're here. It's neurologically how we're wired."[152] What she found in her research is "in order for connection to happen, we have to allow ourselves to be seen, really seen. The thing that underpinned this was excruciating vulnerability."[153] I craved this connection, which was what compelled me to begin being vulnerable about my experience. Gradually, I started sharing tidbits of my challenges with loved ones and close friends. I found sharing my story, and being vulnerable, lent a sense of power.

I reached out to Kate Milliken, a video producer by trade who was diagnosed with multiple sclerosis (MS). I asked her about her experience documenting her story through video and sharing it and her vulnerabilities so openly. She could vividly remember the moment she was diagnosed; she received a "very drastic phone call from a neurologist who said, 'I've seen your MRI. You have MS; you have to go to the hospital right now. Don't even pack. You could be paralyzed.'" At the time, she was thirty-five, single, and felt "like [her] life was fucking over." She was able to find an osteopath who put her on a supplemental regimen that helped her feel better. Throughout this, "I documented positive moments where I felt things were going to be okay. I documented really scary moments. I have a video of me crying hysterically on the telephone because I feel so bad." She compiled thirty-two mini films into a fifty-minute video, which she shared online, and received a huge response with eighty thousand unique visitors, 65 percent of whom watched the video in its entirety. Motivated by this success, she founded MyCounterpane, a platform for patients and caregivers dealing with MS to tell their story based on how they feel. The goal is to encourage each person to share their stories and receive the emotional support they need to feel better.[154]

When I asked her if she had any insights from this experience, she responded, "What I discovered, in retrospect, is when you put your moments out there and you're courageous enough to document them, they hold so much power," particularly the moments that "showcase the power of adversity."

Dan McAdams, a professor of narrative psychology at the Northwestern University, has studied the impact of life stories. In his book *The Redemptive Self*, he argues, "People create stories to make sense of their lives."[155] In my process of making sense of my life, I was able to look back and view the events of my life in a new light and explore what influence, if any, they had on the direction of my future story. Engaging in this process allowed me to identify the growth I had achieved and helped create a sense of agency for my own narrative identity. Or, as McAdams writes, endeavoring to understand one's life as a grand narrative "provides our lives with some semblance of purpose, unity, and meaning. Our stories provide justification and motivation for the lives we have chosen to lead."[156] In a twist of fate, my motivation to honestly be seen by others helped me honestly see myself.

When I shared my challenges of suicidal ideation with my parents, I immediately noticed a powerful transition in my body and headspace. The impulse I had been bottling up for ten months suddenly disappeared. The process of telling them how I felt was as if I had suddenly let go of the spring I had been pushing back for months. I felt the tension and negative energy dissipate out of me. It was as if I had found the magic key to unlock the spring, and I no longer needed to push back. There was an evident step change and improvement in my mental health after that moment of vulnerability. The notion of suicide evaporated and the frequency with which it arose significantly decreased to the point where it was no longer a challenge for me.

Why was this moment so powerful? I think sharing my experience with suicidal ideation was the climax in my journey of opening up, being vulnerable, and being seen. It was the moment when I laid out all of the challenges and difficulties I had experienced. I was completely open and honest, and following that, there wasn't anything else to hide. In that moment, I was able to share my true self with Mom and Dad, people I love and appreciate, and they accepted me. Equally important—and this is something I recognized only months later—sharing this moment also allowed me to see myself for who I was. I was able to acknowledge my challenges and difficulties and come to terms with them. It was the ultimate moment of coming to terms with my emotional traumas and acknowledging all of the wounds and difficulties that had resulted from them.

Curiously, a key driver to telling Sofia, Mom, and Dad about my struggles was the fact that I was writing this book. I knew

I wanted to tell my story through this book in an authentic and honest manner. This motivation forced me to reflect and evaluate what my story consisted of. Doing so forced me to acknowledge all aspects of my challenges, including my struggles with suicidal ideation. While I didn't understand this at the time, it was one of the biggest gifts this book provided me. Milliken explained, "When people share their moments of a journey, like illness or other issues, they start coming to terms with it, they start accepting it."

Reflecting on my experiences gave me a different perspective and gave me the space to look back on all of my emotional traumas in a new light. Not merely as someone reeling from the traumas, but as someone who has experienced them and is now trying to find meaning from it all. Writing this book allowed me to come to terms with my story, my lows and difficulties in their entirety. And through that process, I was able to better understand my own story.

CHAPTER 5

Growth from Suffering

"I've been reflecting about this for the last few months," I said.

It was April 2020, and I had been meeting with Sofia for over four months.

"When we first started, my primary goal was to be able to manage the critical situation I was facing. But now, I think I am in a better place. I don't feel as if I'm in a crisis or need to immediately address certain emotions or thoughts."

"I think that's true," said Sofia. "You have a lot of agency and have used your time well."

She paused. "You have also managed to integrate some of those experiences and have more awareness of some of the emotions you've had that were previously in the shadows."

"I have tried to be deliberate in acting on what we discuss," I said. "The question I now have is, was there any learning or meaning to the experiences I had?"

My fingers tapped on the desk as I wondered how else to frame this question.

"Hmm, was there any purpose for what happened? There were many difficult things, a lot of suffering. And to what end?"

Verbalizing what I was thinking helped make clear the point I was trying to make. "Yeah, why was there suffering? And should I just accept suffering happens, or should I try to find some learning from this experience?"

I stopped and stared past the laptop screen, considering whether I wanted to say anything else. Satisfied, I turned my gaze toward Sofia.

She jotted down a few notes and looked up when she finished. "What you can try doing is change the relationship you have with suffering. A lot of people get stuck on suffering on a global scale. One analogy I learned early on in my training is this: Picture a tree. As it grows, sometimes there are dry years, sometimes there's just the right amount of rain, and sometimes there are years with many storms. Each season, it continues to grow. And with each difficult season, it begins to have its own gnarls, fallen branches, and imperfections. What's important is you grow to love the tree as it is and accept the suffering, which causes the imperfections and is part of the tree."

My eyes crinkled and the corners of my mouth curved upward. I enjoyed this metaphor of a tree of life and recalled afternoons spent climbing oaks trees in the California hills. I agreed a tree, even with its many gnarls, was still beautiful.

Perhaps, by extension, my own life can be beautiful, even with its imperfections.

Our fifty-minute session came and went, and it was time to say goodbye. I logged off from our videocall, jotted down some last musings and discussion points, and wondered what I could do to facilitate my process of acceptance.

* * *

After reading *Man's Search for Meaning*, I was surprised one of its key tenets of logotherapy—Frankl's concept an individual's primary motivation is to find meaning in life—argues a person can find meaning in the face of suffering. Frankl writes witnessing a person turn tragedy into triumph in the face of suffering "is to bear witness to the uniquely human potential at its best."[157] Reading this, I wondered if my experience dealing with so much suffering represented a prime opportunity to find new meaning. In one of my sessions with Sofia, I asked her if she was aware of any body of research that dealt with meaning gained from suffering. She replied, in fact, there was such a body of research titled post-traumatic growth (PTG).

PTG, as a term, was first coined in the early 1990s by Dr. Richard Tedeschi and Dr. Lawrence Calhoun. The concept of PTG, however, dates back millennia, and suffering as a lesson is depicted in various religions including the Judeo-Christian tradition, Islam, and Buddhism.[158]

In their book *The Posttraumatic Growth Workbook*, Dr. Tedeschi and Dr. Calhoun documented the stories of survivors of all manners of trauma—combat, rape, cancer, natural disaster, and more. Their findings formed the basis for PTG, which purports "personal transformation can occur in the aftermath of trauma."[159] What they found is survivors of trauma experienced growth in five broad categories. Some individuals experienced growth with one of these factors; others identified growth in all five areas.

- Improved relation to others
- New possibilities in life
- Newfound personal strength
- Spiritual change
- Appreciation for life

What struck me about PTG was the notion the actual trauma a person experienced had no direct influence on growth. This was because people exhibited growth not during trauma, but instead in the aftermath of trauma. Equally striking was the fact trauma is subjective; what one person might find traumatic may not be for another person. I struggled with the notion of trauma as a relative concept until I read Frankl's analogy of suffering to a gas.

"If a certain quantity of gas is pumped into an empty chamber, it will fill the chamber completely evenly, no matter how big the chamber. Thus, suffering completely fills the human soul and conscious mind, no matter whether the suffering is great or little. Therefore the 'size' of human suffering is absolutely relative."[160]

PTG identified a typical progression individuals take in their road to growth. Dr. Tedeschi noted when someone is reeling from a trauma that has challenged their core beliefs, they can only focus on survival. The consequence is very little growth can occur during the initial experience of trauma. Recalling my experience, I can agree with this sentiment. During the weeks and months that followed my departure from London and eventual return to California, I was focused exclusively on survival. Most of my effort was trained on repressing any impulses for self-injury and suicidal ideation. At a time when every moment felt like an internal battle with my psyche, growth felt incomprehensible.

PTG purports once the phase of survival has passed, ever so slowly, the process of healing can begin. In an interview with the American Psychological Association, Dr. Tedeschi elaborates commencing this healing can only occur if people "face up to the trauma rather than avoid it."[161] Facing up to my trauma was something I found very difficult and, in fact, actively avoided. The emotions I felt were too overwhelming, scary, and foreign. Rather than acknowledge them, I did my best to avoid them.

Such a response appears to be common. Dr. Tedeschi and Dr. Calhoun found many survivors of trauma who were able to grow benefited from having an "expert companion."[162] I couldn't agree more. It was only with the help of my expert companion, Sofia, I was able to face up to and acknowledge my trauma and begin facing my inner demons.

Only when a survivor of trauma faces up to their emotions, instead of numbing or avoiding them, are they able to explore the meaning of their trauma and experience growth. The trick, it seems, involved a person's ability to "figure out how to face distress and also have momentary breaks"[163] from their trauma.

This was no easy task. It took me months to even understand how I could simultaneously face my trauma and take a break from it. Only after Sofia shared her story about each person learning to love their tree of life did I begin to understand the concept of a duality of emotions. I realized my tree could include both gnarls and broken branches as well as beautiful blossoms and colorful flowers. My tree could consist of both trauma and beauty at the same time, and both have equal weight to make up the tree in its entirety.

In this light, I was able to change my relationship with suffering and break through what apparently was a contradiction to face my trauma and take a break from it.

It was only once I started writing this book I was able to witness firsthand the capacity for humans to grow from their trauma. In October 2020, I met Omar Alshogre. At the time, he was living in Stockholm, Sweden, and looking forward to starting university in the beginning of 2021. During his childhood, Alshogre experienced a level of trauma I could not even begin to imagine.

He grew up in Syria and was a teenager as the Syrian civil war consumed his country. At the age of seventeen, he was imprisoned by the Syrian regime and sent to a detention center. During his three years in this center, the guards tortured him on a daily basis. He was routinely beaten, hanged from the ceiling, starved, burnt, had his fingernails pulled out, and more. Speaking of his time there, the predominant feeling of his time while in prison was fear; "it was a hard place, a place I wouldn't be able to survive, I was afraid of torture, I was afraid of pain, I was afraid of the people around me, I was afraid of dying of thirst. I was afraid."

Alshogre calls his time in the Syrian regime's prisons as the University of Whispers. This is due to the fact "you're not allowed to speak" in the prison, only whisper, because the guards would torture anyone they heard speaking. Nevertheless, the prisoners gradually began whispering to each other and helping each other deal with their situations. A doctor taught him how to treat his wounds, a psychologist helped him use his last moments to enjoy prison, and a lawyer spoke of how to build a dictator-free prison. Ultimately, others helped him learn "how to survive prison." That being said, he never thought he would get out, not when he was carrying out dozens of bodies a day to the isolation room and not when survival was a constant fight every single day. Fortunately, he was able to escape. His family managed to have him smuggled out of prison, whereupon he made his way through Turkey to Sweden.

When prompted about how he viewed his time in prison, he quickly responded, "It gave me a lot; I can't hide that. Those three years in prison changed my life, saved my life." I pressed him on how such a trauma could save his life. He elaborated prison "gave me the opportunity to be where I am today. To speak at the US senate, be a public speaker, have a family in Sweden, speak at Brown University about switching trauma into a driving force, and work to create value for the Syrian people and change what they are going through."

Feeling inspired following my conversation with Alshogre, I set aside time to reflect on whether I had grown in response to my traumas. Like the duality of being with trauma and taking a break from it, my answer would have a similar duality. On the one hand, I do believe I put in a lot of effort to invite the uncomfortable emotions that accompanied my traumas and am certain I have many more tools at my disposal to "face up" to moments of grief. I also can identify with a number of areas of growth named by Dr. Tedeschi—namely, a newfound personal strength and uncovering new possibilities in life. On the other hand, I am still dealing with the lingering effects of trauma and believe I am still recovering from this process.

Despite this, I am confident about my response to growth, which Dr. Tedeschi mentioned involves the importance of sharing the "lessons learned" beyond those who experienced suffering.[164] I continue to have a strong desire and conviction to share my experiences and learnings to a wider community. I have found imparting the learnings and wisdom I have gained from my trauma adds a sense of meaning to the suffering I experienced, a belief, at a minimum, sharing my experiences can help reduce suffering in others.

CHAPTER 6

Wrapping up Therapy

"I've been reflecting on this past year of therapy—of where we started, what we've covered, and where we are today. I think I have learned a lot in the last year, and it's a credit to you and your help. I'm really thankful for everything you have done to help me face and overcome my challenges." I broke off to collect my thoughts.

Sofia remained silent and smiled.

"I think I've gotten to the point where I know I will have challenges and bumps in the road, but I now think I have the tools to deal with them and feel confident I can handle them." A catch in my throat prevented me from continuing.

"I think we might be at the stage where we can start wrapping up our work together," I said.

The corners of my lips pulled sideways. I wasn't sure how Sofia would respond and was worried sharing this would disappoint her.

"I think you're in a much better place as well, and I think now is a good time to think about finishing our work together," she said.

I exhaled and leaned back against my chair.

"I will add I think now is a better time to wrap up our work than the previous time you asked to do so. At the time, I felt there were still some unfinished things and knew your move to San Diego would be a challenge, so I pushed back. But I do agree you are now in a good spot."

"I just want to reiterate my thanks to you for all the help and support you've provided; it's been absolutely critical," I said.

"And I want to say it has been an honor to work with you, and I have enjoyed it as well."

Sofia explained, when finishing working with a client, she typically recommends reviewing the material and discussions covered as a way to consolidate the learnings. "Where would you like to start?"

"Hmm." The stars had started to come out and framed the palm trees' silhouettes outside my window.

I leafed through the pages of my notes.

Acknowledge the darkness

Even though I'm hurt, I can handle this

Grieving goes in waves

My eyebrows raised; it felt crazy it had been almost a year since my first session.

"Maybe we can start from the beginning and focus on the initial issues that brought me here," I said.

"Okay, let's do that. I would ask one thing. If you're okay with this, pause after saying or thinking about something. Just sit with it and see whatever comes up. Is that something you want to do?"

My head bobbed up and down. The palm fronds rustled in the wind and the hum of distant traffic could be heard. The rug felt soft against my feet.

I closed my eyes and breathed deeply. In and out. Memories from my relationship, the start-up, and moving back to the US popped up.

My solar plexus tightened; a sadness arose in the pit of my stomach.

Connect with emotions, be curious about the feeling

The sadness persisted. I didn't shy away from it. Instead, I continued feeling sad.

More memories popped in my head.

Protector mechanism

Develop internal landscape

Grow to love the tree you are

The tightness in my chest melted away, and the corners of my lips rose. I began to feel a sense of pride.

My stomach grazed my desk as I inhaled deeply.

Running, journaling, art, friends

Be gentle with myself

I opened my eyes and looked at Sofia. A smile spread across my face.

I recounted what I had experienced: "This exercise really exemplified my growth in the past year. I am taking such a different approach to my emotions than when I first started therapy. At the time, I was perpetually having anxiety and my response was to wish it away. I wanted the absence of these emotions because I thought that was the best approach. Fast forward a year, I no longer want to avoid a bad feeling. Instead, I am now comfortable allowing the uncomfortable emotion to persist, and I believe I have the tools to sit with them without them overwhelming me."

Sofia's eyes twinkled. "I'm so glad you shared that. It's important to bring a curiosity to these emotions. To not judge them but instead be curious about how you're feeling and lean into the emotions. To see what happens in that moment and be with the emotion."

"As I continued playing through my year, reaching my time in San Diego, I felt a growing sense of pride. I now have a job; I'm getting settled in San Diego and working to create community."

"Yes, you have come a long way."

"At the beginning, I was obviously dealing with some very dark impulses. Thankfully, the frequency of these impulses has dropped dramatically, and the intensity of each moment has diminished as well. Every once in a while, there will be some anxiety and the waves will come, but I also feel like I have worked this muscle, so to speak, where I can now handle these difficult moments," I said.

Sofia nodded. "I just want to share it's important to have compassion for the various parts of yourself. It takes an effort to heal but it will take you to a better place. I think it's courageous to explore the impulses you've had, because it can be burdensome but it's really important."

We continued going over the past year for the rest of our session and continued into the following one. She asked me a number of questions about my experience.

Wrapping up, Sofia asked, "My last question: Is there anything you're worried about?"

I brought my hand to my mouth and pondered her question. "No, I don't think so. One of the reasons I felt comfortable with wrapping up is I now think I have the tools to handle any challenges that may arise in my present situation."

"Okay. One last thing: You shouldn't worry about losing any particular gains. If and when something difficult happens, sometime in the future, I want to highlight it's important to be gentle on yourself and not beat yourself up. And remember if something difficult does happen, you can bring curiosity to it, say, 'Oh, there it is.' And be curious about each new rough edge as you keep exploring and getting to know yourself."

I smirked and nodded. I could definitely envision being in a stressful situation or a difficult moment and being critical of myself and appreciated Sofia's reminder. As I dutifully wrote down some notes, I pondered if there was anything else I was worried about.

"I have found our weekly meetings have offered a very unique and safe space for introspection and self-disclosure. One possible concern could be how I maintain this practice and cultivate this reflection outside of therapy."

"There are a few things you can try, like peer support groups, podcasts. You can also always go back to therapy," she said.

I noticed the time on the computer, 17:47. Sofia appeared to have noticed this as well.

"Is there any last thing you want to bring up?"

I shook my head. "Only that I want to thank you for all of your guidance and help over the past year. You have been absolutely key in helping me get to where I am right now. So, thank you."

And with that, we said our goodbyes and logged off for the last time. I felt a chapter closing, and with that, a twinge of sadness. Sofia and I had developed a very close working relationship over the past twelve months. She had helped me through some of the most difficult moments in my life, and suddenly we weren't going to see each other again. I remembered her sharing by law, she isn't allowed to reach out to me. She can only respond if I ever reach out to her.

It was likely our communication was going to end, and it saddened me. However, I tried to hold the sadness in the context I was proud of myself for the lows I had come from and the growth I had exhibited by going to therapy. I acknowledged it took a lot of effort to investigate deeply many of the uncomfortable emotions I had and was proud of doing so.

I took a deep breath, took a sip of water, and decided this was a good opportunity to go for a walk, get some fresh air, and reflect on my last therapy session.

CHAPTER 7

A Bank of Positive Memories

I stopped pedaling and glided along the bike path.

The "13" on the upcoming mile marker indicated I had reached the halfway point of my bike ride. The ocean roared toward my right. The waves crashed, large and tempestuous. A sudden surge of wind retrained my focus back to my bike ride. Gradually, I angled the bike to the side and slowed to a stop.

The bike frame pressed down on my shoulder as I walked down the trail to the beach. The dune was covered in green succulents and dotted with purple flowers. The wind howled as it rushed onshore. I felt the cold and humidity seep through my jacket; the salty air filled my nostrils.

I had woken up early to go for a bike ride along Ocean Beach in San Francisco, California, with the hopes of getting back home prior to the arrival of the oncoming storm. The large waves and choppy water served as a warning to any would-be surfers and swimmers. The dense mist limited visibility; I could barely make out the Marin Headlands, although I did notice there wasn't anyone else on the beach.

I left my bike on the ground, took off my socks and shoes, and took a few steps toward the water. My feet sank into the undisturbed sand. The coarse grains rubbed against my toes.

I closed my eyes, took a deep breath in, and exhaled.

After a few repetitions, I raised my arms over my head, held my breath, and slowly lowered my arms as I exhaled.

What do I see? Snowy plovers, their brown and white feathers flittering in the wind, rushing toward the receding water; a breaking wave; the foam and the spray; the ocean stretching as far as the eye could see; and the clouds, grey and dreary.

I breathed in, and out.

What do I feel? The force of the wind; the sweat on my brow; the weight of my jacket on my shoulders; and the cold sand on the soles of my feet.

I breathed in, and out.

What do I hear? The roar of the wind; the sound of a wave crashing; and the call of a seagull flying past.

I breathed in, and out.

What do I smell? Salt and the crispness of the air.

I breathed in, and out.

What do I taste? Mint, a remnant from brushing my teeth earlier.

My chest rose slowly as I breathed in the fresh air through my nose. Barely opening my mouth, I allowed the air to leave and felt my stomach compress.

* * *

Sofia first introduced this technique to me, calling it the 5–4–3–2–1 technique. She shared it initially as a way for me to cope with anxiety attacks or stressful situations. She posited focusing and being present to all five senses engaged different parts of the brain and could help provide a sense of calm. I appreciated her input and did my best to practice this technique if the need ever arose.

At some point—I'm not entirely sure when—I began to practice this technique with something else in mind. My intent was to try and use this practice to engage all five senses and help me retain and remember moments of joy, serenity, or happiness. This was likely in response to finding it so difficult to think of any positive moments when dealing with suicidal ideation on my flight. Over time, I continued using the 5–4–3–2–1 technique to create a bank of positive memories and moments I could draw upon if ever I was in a bad headspace.

Curious about whether this exercise had any other impact on me, I reached out to Brenda Stockdale, director of behavioral medicine, or mind-body medicine, at various cancer centers throughout the US. For over twenty years, she has worked with patients dealing with a range of autoimmune challenges in the field of psychoimmunology. Her journey began when she experienced firsthand the power of mind-body medicine when she was able to use many of the practices to fully recover from her lupus diagnosis.

One practice, in particular, that contributed to her healing was the use of what she called "micromoments." She describes the micromoments as "moments of immediacy, where you shift your focus for just a few seconds." A micromoment can be anything from looking at the sunset, a bite of food, or an aroma. Through her research, she has found being present to the moment, even for very short amounts of time, can cause significant "changes in your physiology, including changes in heartrate variability. We can also see changes in the brain through functional magnetic resonance imaging (MRI) scans, and there can be mood changes through the release of gamma-aminobutyric acid (GABA)—an amino acid that acts as a neurotransmitter in the brain—that can have a calming effect."

I asked her whether my 5-4-3-2-1 technique was at all related to these micromoments. Pleasantly, she agreed it was entirely relevant. She explained my exercise had two-fold benefits; in addition to the immediate benefits of being fully present to the moment, there are also added benefits to remembering and recalling these moments. "The limbic system—a structure in the brain that deals with emotions and memory—doesn't distinguish between reality and imagination. If you recall water running, it stimulates the auditory cortex; if you imagine looking at the ocean, it stimulates the visual cortex; if you imagine touching a smooth rock or sand, it stimulates the sensory cortex; and each stimulates the limbic system." So, engaging our senses in these moments is an "incredibly powerful way of altering our mood, body, and physiology."

I found this insight fascinating. My conversation with Stockdale increased my curiosity about the connection between the mind and the body. I wondered if the relationship between the two had anything to do with my difficulties in recalling positive memories. Spurred on by this interest, I came across Dr. Rick Hanson's work on positive brain change. Hanson is a psychologist and senior fellow at the Greater Good Science Center at UC Berkeley who has investigated how people can turn everyday experiences into a powerful sense of lasting wellbeing.[165]

In order to understand how a longer lasting sense of wellbeing can be achieved, Hanson found it is important to understand the notion of negativity bias. He and his colleagues found our brains have evolved to learn "faster from pain than from pleasure."[166] From an evolutionary perspective, this makes sense, as it was a way in which our ancestors stayed alive. Hanson explains for millennia, our ancestors "needed to get some carrots, food, and so forth, but they really needed to avoid those sticks, because if you fail to get a carrot today, you'll have a chance to get one tomorrow. But if you fail to avoid that stick today, that predator, no more carrots forever."[167] The challenge we now face is our brains are still designed to look for, and overfocus on, bad news or negative moments, yet very few of us now live in such harsh conditions. The implication is it is harder for us to "learn from our beneficial experiences and turn them into lasting neural structure. Most positive experiences wash right through your brain like water through a sieve while negative ones get caught every time."[168] Fortunately, Hanson has found our brains are capable of "positive neuroplasticity, or our brain's capacity to reorganize itself in response to various sensory experiences."[169]

Positive neuroplasticity is only made possible because of one of the most complex objects in the universe: our brains. While physically the brain consists of approximately three pounds of soft, gooshy, tofu-like tissue, it has about 1.1 trillion cells and approximately one hundred billion neurons. Neurons are designed to transmit information to other cells and each average about five thousand connections. All the neurons end up creating a vast network that can transmit information incredibly quickly—anywhere between five to fifty times per second.[170] Every single aspect of mental activity, whether it's our thoughts, feelings, joys, sorrows, or basic bodily functions that keep us alive, requires neural activity. Taken together, all the information stored in our individual nervous systems comprises each person's mind. Fascinatingly, repeated patterns of mental activity require repeated patterns of brain activity, and repeated patters of brain activity can change the neural structure and function of our brains.[171] Hanson summarizes this behavior as "neurons that fire together, wire together."[172]

It is our brain's capacity to reorganize itself in response to various sensory experiences Hanson refers to when he discusses positive neuroplasticity.[173] By deliberately stimulating our brains, we can actually "turn passing positive experiences into a lasting psychological resource hardwired in our own nervous system."[174] Hanson developed a process, appropriately titled HEAL, that can help turn passing experiences into lasting inner strength. As an acronym, HEAL stands for:

- H – Have a positive experience
- E – Enrich it
- A – Absorb it
- L – Link the positive experience to negative material in order to soothe and even replace it

The HEAL process isn't particularly arduous; it only requires a few seconds to take in a positive moment, but Hanson found those who participated in this process experienced improved resilience, positive emotions, compassion, gratitude, and reduced anxiety and depression.

In the spring of 2020, I brought up to Sofia that, while I felt things were improving, I was fearful of relapsing and once more dealing with dark thoughts, namely that I would suddenly return to the headspace of self-harm, anxiety, and suicidal ideation. I was fearful all of the work I was putting into my healing process would just crumble away and return me back to square one, almost like a bad joke. Sofia responded many things can be done to prevent a relapse. We mentioned a number of different activities we had reviewed that worked then and could continue to work to this day, including exercise, meditation, therapy, art, creating connections and finding community, and more.

I acknowledged these activities were helping me, but I was also keenly aware employing all of these tools and habits required effort. It wasn't always easy; there were definitely days when I was less motivated to exercise, breathe, or draw, but I typically tried to practice one or more of these activities every day. There were also times when I found some of these practices weren't very helpful or useful. Other days, I changed my habits and decided to do something entirely new. There were also many days when I needed help and received help to get me over the hump.

One of the key insights I've had throughout my journey of recovery is making this effort, day in and day out, is actually much easier than not making any effort and letting life just happen. It is entirely feasible I would still be having anxiety attacks, thoughts of suicide, or impulses to self-harm if I had continued attempting to repress and ignore my uncomfortable emotions. Instead, I put in a lot of effort to recognize my emotional wounds, label them—both negative and positive—and tried to work through them through therapy. I also incorporated other habits in my life to help me digest the learnings.

While I did not know it standing at Ocean Beach, trying to be present to the moment and enjoy a beautiful morning at the ocean, that exercise was part of a larger effort that contributed to my growth in building lasting change. Each micromoment has acted as a building block to create a new and different life. I have recovered from the traumas I experienced through small daily activities that changed my behavior, my mood, and even my brain and physiology to add up to where I now feel like I am thriving. That is not to say things are no longer difficult, but I now have a bank of positive habits that have led to lasting change and can help me deal with any new difficulties that may arise.

Acknowledgments

To say "it takes a village" to write this book would be an understatement. I have received so much help and encouragement from people from all over the world, and for that, I am incredibly grateful.

To Mom, Dad, and Didi, thank you so much for your love throughout my mental health crisis. Your support, guidance, and encouragement are what helped me get to where I am today.

Sofia, thank you very much for our year of therapy. It is your instruction and guidance that helped me overcome some of the most challenging demons and learn about myself throughout it all.

Thank you to Ricardo Amores, Mathilde Fajardy, Raph Zufferey, and Erik Hanko for providing a shoulder to lean on as I transitioned away from London. And a big thank you to Britt Abrahamson, Pauli Mazzarino, Juan Mendoza, Ben Rounds, Taehoon Ahn, and Navtej Singh for making the effort and being there for me in the good times and the bad.

Thank you, Katie Morris, Julie Morris, and Cat Bordhi. Your instruction as I dipped my toes into the writing process was invaluable.

In learning about different fields of mental health, Anna Kramarz and Michelle Myers's insights proved incredibly helpful.

While researching aspects of this book, I had the great fortune of meeting and speaking with an inspiring group of people, all doing exciting work in the field of mental health. Thank you, Andy Breunig, Ashanti Branch, Brenda Stockdale, Bridget Balajadia, Caroline Heldman, Cece Sykes, Chris Burris, Connie Gersick, Jeff Sparr, Jen Marr, Kalina Silverman, Kate Milliken, Leanne Pooley, Maria Sirois, Melissa Grady, Omar Alshogre, and Yvette Kong.

A big thank-you to the team at New Degree Press, especially Eric Koester, Brian Bies, Judy Rosen, Mackenzie Joyce, and Colin Lyon. I can confidently state this book would still not be published if it weren't for your dedication, time, patience, and instruction in helping me get from idea to book.

Lastly, a special thank-you to everyone who supported me in my pre-sale book campaign: Alykhan Jivraj, Jim & Mags Petkiewicz, Peggy Bryan, Barbara Lynn, Valerie Sarma, Britt Abrahamson, Taehoon Ahn, Sarah Morris, Eric Koester, Sureya Melkonian, Janice Cassidy, Kathleen Flibbert, Janine Bajus, Venkataraman Srinivasan, Otto Hentz, Sourojeet Chakraborty, Phil Nemecek, Carlotta Leung, Olivia Cordova, Anne Morris, Teddy Morris-Knower, Nancy Bolan, Joseph Michon, Shahid Mallick, Nancy Morris, Satej Soman, Jeffrey von Arx, Michelle Nacouzi, Chet & Tricia Petkiewicz, Ben

Reeve, Elias Jimenez, Jacob Morris-Knower, Joe & Julie Morris, Patrick Sullivan, Jack Morris, Katie Kuszmar, Jeff Cassidy, Max Bates, John Allen, Stacy Dever Levy, Jordan Schlitzer, Stephen Pope, Bob Malone, Barbara Pope, Kent Abrahamson, Mary Ann Wilmarth, Celine Woznica, Birgitta Ericsson, Monica Rising, Bonnie Cassidy, Paul Francis, Jan Hamby, Andy Hsia-Coron, Kathleen Jackson, Yuri Woo, Mark Potter, Katie Morris & Josh Hoffman, Mathilde Fajardy, Pat Ward, Hannah Lyons-Galante, Dennis Moorman, Janine Fitzgerald, Erik Hanko, Steven O'Connell, Elisa Sipols, Mary Weissert, Caroline Morris, Conor Carroll, Kathryn Seib Vargas, Chad Nobel, Joanna Thurmann, Jacob Cohen, Daniel Miles, Isaiah Lyons-Galante, Amy Morris, Catherine Mitsuoka, Will Juri, Chris Cassidy, Julien Renard, Didi Boring, John Ezaki, Arvind Srinivasan, Rich Morris, Phil Rhein, Kim Yaged, Ben Rounds, Navtej Singh, Michelle Myers, Robert Doerner, Vincent Zaballa, Mark Portillo, Anna Kramarz, Amanda You, Gayla Jamison, Didi Petkiewicz, Corryne Deliberto, Molly Morris, John Paton, Mary Ellen Galante, and Tom & Gloria Henry.

Appendix

PT 1, CH 1: DISEQUILIBRIUM

Eldridge, Niles, and Stephen J Gould. "Punctuated equilibria: an alternative to phyletic gradualism." In *Models in Paleobiology*, edited by TJM Freeman, 82 – 115. San Francisco: Cooper & Co, 1972.

Gersick, Connie J. G. "Revolutionary Change Theories: A Multi-level Exploration of the Punctuated Equilibrium Paradigm." *The Academy of Management Review* 16, no. 1 (January 1991): 10-36. https://doi:10.2307/258605.

PT 1, CH 2: HISTORY OF MENTAL HEALTH

American Psychological Association. "Americans becoming more open about mental health." Accessed January, 26 2021. https://www.apa.org/news/press/releases/2019/05/mental-health-survey.

Etymonline. "Origin and meaning of mental by Online Etymology Dictionary." Accessed January 26, 2021.

https://www.etymonline.com/word/mental.

Farreras, Ingrid. "History of Mental Illness." Accessed 26 January 2021. https://nobaproject.com/modules/history-of-mental-illness.

Human Rights Watch. "Living In Chains." Accessed January 26, 2021. https://www.hrw.org/report/2020/10/06/living-chains/shackling-people-psychosocial-disabilities-worldwide#.

Lesage, A. D., Morissette, R., Fortier, L., Reinharz, D., and Contandriopoulos, A. P. "Downsizing psychiatric hospitals: needs for care and services of current and discharged long-stay inpatients." *Canadian journal of psychiatry. Revue canadienne de psychiatrie*, 45, no. 6, (August 2000): 526–532. https://doi.org/10.1177/070674370004500602

World Health Organization. "Gender And Women's Mental Health." Accessed January 27, 2021. https://www.who.int/mental_health/resources/gender/en/.

World Health Organization. "Mental health: strengthening our response." Accessed January 26, 2021. https://www.who.int/news-room/fact-sheets/detail/mental-health-strengthening-our-response.

PT 1, CH 3: SUICIDAL IDEATION

American Association of Suicidology. "Warning Signs." Accessed June 14, 2021. https://suicidology.org/resources/warning-signs/.

American Foundation for Suicide Prevention. "Suicide Statistics". Accessed June 14, 2021. https://afsp.org/suicide-statistics/.

Bagley, Christopher. "Suicidal Behaviour And Suicidal Ideation In Adolescents: A Problem For Counsellors In Education." *British Journal Of Guidance & Counselling* 3, no. 2 (October 1975): 190-208. doi:10.1080/03069887508260420.

Centers for Disease Control and Prevention. "Suicide Rates Rising Across The U.S., CDC Online Newsroom, CDC." 2021. Accessed June 14, 2021. https://www.cdc.gov/media/releases/2018/p0607-suicide-prevention.html.

Joiner, Thomas. *Why People Die By Suicide*. Cambridge, Massachusetts: Harvard University Press, 2007.

Nock, Matthew K, ed. *The Oxford Handbook of Suicide and Self-Injury*. Oxford: Oxford Univ. Press, 2014.

Pooley, Leanne. *The Girl on The Bridge* (Augusto Entertainment & Bloom Pictures, 2020). Video, 91:00 at 24 fps. https://www.thegirlonthebridgefilm.com/.

Walsh, Barent. *Treating Self-Injury*. New York: The Guilford Press, 2012.

PT 1, CH 4: STARTING THERAPY

211. "Homepage." Accessed January 16, 2021. https://www.211.org/.

American Counseling Association. "Who are Licensed Professional Counselors?" Accessed January 16, 2021. https://www.counseling.org/PublicPolicy/WhoAreLPCs.pdf.

American Psychological Association. "Different Approaches To Psychotherapy." Accessed January 16, 2021. https://www.apa.org/topics/therapy/psychotherapy-approaches.

American Psychological Association. "What Do Practicing Psychologists Do?" Accessed January 16, 2021. https://www.apa.org/topics/about-psychologists.

Goodtherapy. "Goodtherapy - Find The Right Therapist." Accessed January 16, 2021. https://www.goodtherapy.org/.

Healthline. "Behavioral Therapy: Definition, Types, And Effectiveness." Accessed January 16, 2021. https://www.healthline.com/health/behavioral-therapy.

National Alliance on Mental Illness. "Home." Accessed January 16, 2021. https://www.nami.org/Home.

Psychiatry. "What Is Psychiatry?" Accessed January 16, 2021. https://www.psychiatry.org/patients-families/what-is-psychiatry-menu.

Psychology Today. "Psychology Today: Health, Help, Happiness + Find A Therapist." Accessed January 16, 2021. https://www.psychologytoday.com/us.

Therapyden. "Find Local Therapists, Psychologists And Counselors." Accessed January 16, 2021. https://www.therapyden.com/.

Zocdoc. "Find a Doctor." Accessed January 16, 2021. https://www.zocdoc.com/.

PT 1, CH 5: INTERNAL LANDSCAPE

American Psychological Association. "Where Has All The Psychotherapy Gone?" Accessed January 16, 2021. https://www.apa.org/monitor/2010/11/perspectives.

Gottlieb, Lori. *Maybe You Should Talk To Someone: a therapist, her therapist, and our lives revealed.* Boston: Houghton Mifflin, 2019.

Horney, Karen. *Neurosis And Human Growth.* New York: Norton, 1991.

Yalom, Irvin. *The Gift Of Therapy.* New York City: HarperCollins e-Books. 2014.

PT 2, CH 1: BREATHE

Gross, Terry. "How The 'Lost Art' Of Breathing Can Impact Sleep And Resilience with James Nestor." May 27, 2020. In *Fresh Air,* Produced by Fresh Air. Podcast, MP3 audio, 36:16. https://www.npr.org/sections/health-shots/2020/05/27/862963172/how-the-lost-art-of-breathing-can-impact-sleep-and-resilience

Walsh, Barent. *Treating Self-Injury.* New York: The Guilford Press, 2012.

Whitlock, Janis, and Elizabeth Lloyd-Richardson. *Healing Self-Injury.* New York: Oxford University Press, Incorporated, 2019.

PT 2, CH 2: THERAPEUTIC ALLIANCE

Gottlieb, Lori. *Maybe You Should Talk To Someone: a therapist, her therapist, and our lives revealed.* Boston: Houghton Mifflin, 2019.

Yalom, Irvin. "Irvin D. Yalom, MD." Accessed December 26, 2020. https://www.yalom.co

Yalom, Irvin. *The Gift Of Therapy.* New York City: HarperCollins e-Books. 2014.

PT 2, CH 3: THE PERILS OF "BE A MAN"

Ever Forward. "Ever Forward." Accessed January 9, 2021. https://everforwardclub.org/#overview

Ruler Approach. "What is RULER? – RULER Approach." Accessed January 9, 2021. https://www.rulerapproach.org/about/what-is-ruler/.

Siebel Newsom, Jennifer. *The Mask You Live In* (The Representation Company, 2015). Video, 1:37:00 at 24 fps. https://therep-project.org/the-mask-you-live-in-watch-from-home/

PT 2, CH 4: ECONOMICS OF THERAPY

Centers for Medicare & Medicaid Services. "The Mental Health Parity And Addiction Equity Act (MHPAEA) – CMS." 2021. Accessed January 9, 2021. https://www.cms.gov/CCIIO/Programs-and-Initiatives/Other-Insurance-Protections/mhpaea_factsheet.

Health Resources & Services Administration. "Shortage Areas." Accessed January 9, 2021. https://data.hrsa.gov/topics/health-workforce/shortage-areas.

National Alliance on Mental Illness. "The Doctor Is Out." Accessed January 9, 2021. https://www.nami.org/Support-Education/Publications-Reports/Public-Policy-Reports/The-Doctor-is-Out/DoctorIsOut.

World Health Organization. "Investing In Treatment For Depression And Anxiety Leads To Fourfold Return." Accessed January 9, 2021. https://www.who.int/news/item/13-04-2016-investing-in-treatment-for-depression-and-anxiety-leads-to-fourfold-return.

World Health Organization. "Mental Health In The Workplace." Accessed January 9, 2021. https://www.who.int/teams/mental-health-and-substance-use/mental-health-in-the-workplace.

PT 2, CH 5: HOPE

Groopman, Jerome. *The Anatomy Of Hope.* New York: Random House. 2005.

Nock, Matthew K, ed. *The Oxford Handbook of Suicide and Self-Injury.* Oxford: Oxford Univ. Press, 2014.

Sandberg, Sheryl, and Adam Grant. *Option B: Facing Adversity, Building Resilience, And Finding Joy.* New York: Knopf, 2017.

Sirois, Maria. "Maria Sirois – About." Accessed December 12, 2020. http://mariasirois.com/about.

PT 2, CH 6: COMMUNITY-BASED CARE

Human Rights Watch. "Living In Chains." Accessed November 11, 2020. https://www.hrw.org/report/2020/10/06/living-chains/shackling-people-psychosocial-disabilities-worldwide.

Kohrt, B. A. Asher, L. Bhardwaj, A. Fazel, M., Jordans, M. Mutamba, B. B. Nadkarni, A. Pedersen, G. A. Singla, D. R. and Patel, V. "The Role of Communities in Mental Health Care in Low- and Middle-Income Countries: A Meta-Review of Components and Competencies." *International journal of environmental research and public health*, 15, no. 6 (June 2018): 1279. https://doi.org/10.3390/ijerph15061279

World Health Organization. "Mental Health Action Plan 2013 – 2020." Accessed May 23, 2021. .https://www.who.int/publications/i/item/9789241506021.

PT 2, CH 7: PARTS

Internal Family Systems. "The Internal Family Systems Model Outline - IFS Institute." Accessed February 6, 2021. https://ifs-institute.com/resources/articles/internal-family-systems-model-outline.

Schwartz, Richard C. "Richard C. Schwartz, Ph.D. - The Founder Of Internal Family Systems | IFS Institute." Accessed February 6, 2021. Hhttps://ifs-institute.com/about-us/Richard-c-schwartz-phd.

PT 2, CH 8: DÍA DE LOS MUERTOS (DAY OF THE DEAD)

Instituto Nacional para el Federalismo y el Desarrollo Municipal. "Día De Muertos, Tradición Mexicana Que Trasciende En El Tiempo." Accessed May 31, 2021. https://www.gob.mx/inafed/es/articulos/dia-de-muertos-tradicion-mexicana-que-trasciende-en-el-tiempo?idiom=es.

Kübler-Ross, Elisabeth, and Ira Byock. *On Death & Dying.* New York: Scribner, 1969.

Ogden, Thomas. *Subjects of Analysis.* New York: Routledge, 2019.

Sandberg, Sheryl, and Adam Grant. *Option B: Facing Adversity, Building Resilience, And Finding Joy.* New York: Knopf, 2017.

PT 2, CH 9: LONELINESS

Big Talk. "Landing." Accessed June 6, 2021. https://www.makebigtalk.com/.

Kaiser Family Foundation. "Loneliness And Social Isolation In The United States, The United Kingdom, And Japan: An International Survey – Introduction." Accessed January 28, 2021. https://www.kff.org/report-section/loneliness-and-social-isolation-in-the-united-states-the-united-kingdom-and-japan-an-international-survey-introduction/.

Murthy, Vivek. *Together: The Healing Power of Human Connection in a Sometimes Lonely World.* New York: Harper Wave, 2020.

Silverman, Kalina. "How to Skip The Small Talk And Connect With Anyone." Filmed February 15, 2016, in Westminster

College. TEDx Talks. (19:41) https://www.youtube.com/watch?v=WDbxqM4Oy1Y.

PT 3, CH 1: FINDING MEANING

Buhler, Charlotte. "Basic theoretical concepts of humanistic psychology." *American Psychologist* 26, no. 4 (June 1971): 378 386. https://doi.org/10.1037/h0032049

Frankl, Viktor E, Ilse Lasch, Harold S Kushner, and William J Wnislade. *Man's Search For Meaning.* Boston: Beacon Press, 2015.

Gottlieb, Maja. "Discovering & Living Your Purpose With James Hollis PhD (Podcast) EP33." January 1, 2018. In *Integrate Yourself* EP33, Produced by Maja Gottlieb. Podcast, MP3 audio, 1:01:15 https://www.youtube.com/watch?v=eEB-EBwihg4&list=PLfMEgAElB1ITM901loN7JqsrTgtg7ihkN&index=17&t=1804s.

PT 3, CH 2: LEARNING TO COMFORT

Inspiring Comfort. "25 Things You Can Say & Do For People Struggling." Accessed November 23, 2020. https://www.inspiringcomfort.com/blog/25-things-people-want-to-hear-when-they-are-struggling.

Inspiring Comfort. "The Skill Of Human Care And Connection | Inspiring Comfort." Accessed November 23, 2020. https://www.inspiringcomfort.com/.

Option B. "Option B: Build Resilience In The Face Of Adversity." Accessed November 23, 2020. https://optionb.org/.

Paws to Comfort. "Paws To Comfort." Accessed November 23, 2020. https://www.pawstocomfort.com/.

PT 3, CH 3: PLAY

Brown, Stuart. "Play is more than just fun." Filmed March 1, 2008 in Monterey, CA. TED video, 26:21. https://www.ted.com/talks/stuart_brown_play_is_more_than_just_fun?language=en#t-780462.

Brown, Stuart. "Stuart Brown, MD - National Institute For Play." Accessed February 13, 2021. http://www.nifplay.org/dt_team/stuart-brown-md/.

Brown, Stuart, and Christopher Vaughan. *Play: How it Shapes the Brain, Opens the Imagination, and Invigorates the Soul.* New York: Avery, 2014.

PeaceLove. "About – Peacelove." Accessed February 13, 2021. https://peacelove.org/about/.

Sparr, Jeffrey. "YMCA175 Keynote Speech." Filmed September 20, 2019 in London, UK. Video, 17:43.

https://www.youtube.com/watch?v=_pmeuEYznqQ.

Taking Charge of Your Health. "The Practice Of Play With Dr. Stuart Brown." May 23, 2011. In *Taking Charge of Your Health*, Produced by University of Minnesota Center for Spirituality and Healing. Podcast, MP3 audio. 7:39. https://www.takingcharge.csh.umn.edu/practice-play-dr-stuart-brown.

PT 3, CH 4: TELLING MY STORY IMPACTED MY STORY

Brown, Brene. "The Power of Vulnerability." Filmed October 6, 2010 in Houston. TED video, 20:03. https://www.ted.com/talks/brene_brown_the_power_of_vulnerability/transcript?language=en.

McAdams, Dan P. *The Redemptive Self.* Oxford: Oxford University Press, 2007.

Milliken, Kate. "Mycounterpane Blog - Healing Through The Story Of You." Accessed January 12, 2021. https://blog.mycounterpane.com/.

PT 3, CH 5: GROWTH FROM SUFFERING

Frankl, Viktor E, Ilse Lasch, Harold S Kushner, and William J Wnislade. *Man's Search For Meaning.* Boston: Beacon Press, 2015.

Speaking of Psychology. "Transformation After Trauma With Richard Tedeschi, PhD." December 18, 2019. In *Speaking of Psychology*, Produced by American Psychological Association. Podcast, MP3 audio, 51:26. https://www.youtube.com/watch?v=gUtudXE99-U.

Tedeschi, Richard G, and Bret A Moore. *The Posttraumatic Growth Workbook: Coming Through Trauma Wiser, Stronger, And More Resilient.* Oakland: New Harbinger Publications, 2016.

PT 3, CH 6: WRAPPING UP THERAPY

PT 3, CH 7: A BANK OF POSITIVE MEMORIES

Hanson, Rick. "Getting Started - Dr. Rick Hanson." Accessed January 24, 2021. https://www.rickhanson.net/get-started/.

Hanson, Rick. "The Science of Positive Brain Change." Video, 3:16. https://www.rickhanson.net/the-science-of-positive-brain-change/.

Hanson, Rick. "The Science Of Positive Brain Change - Dr. Rick Hanson." Accessed January 24, 2021. https://www.rickhanson.net/the-science-of-positive-brain-change/.

Hanson, Rick. "When Good Is Stronger Than Bad." Accessed January 24, 2021. https://www.rickhanson.net/online-courses/tgc-public-summary/.

Voss, Patrice, Maryse E. Thomas, J. Miguel Cisneros-Franco, and Étienne de Villers-Sidani. 2017. "Dynamic Brains And The Changing Rules Of Neuroplasticity: Implications For Learning And Recovery". *Frontiers In Psychology* 8, no. 8 (October 2017): doi:10.3389/fpsyg.2017.01657.

Endnotes

1 Niles Eldredge and Stephen Jay Gould, "Punctuated equilibria: an alternative to phyletic gradualism," in *Models in Paleobiology*, ed. TJM Freeman. (San Francisco: Cooper & Co, 1972): 82-115.

2 Connie J. G. Gersick, "Revolutionary Change Theories: A Multilevel Exploration of the Punctuated Equilibrium Paradigm," *The Academy of Management Review* 16, no. 1 (January 1991): 10-36.

3 "Mental health: strengthening our response," World Health Organization, accessed January 26, 2021.

4 "Origin and meaning of mental by Online Etymology Dictionary," Etymonline, accessed January 26, 2021.

5 "History of Mental Illness," Ingrid Farreras, accessed January 26, 2021.

6 Ibid.

7 Ibid.

8 A.D. Lesage, R. Morissette, L. Fortier, D. Reinharz, and A.P. Contandriopoulos, "Downsizing psychiatric hospitals: needs for care and services of current and discharged long-stay inpatients," *Canadian journal of psychiatry. Revue Canadienne de psychiatrie* 45, no. 6, (August 2000): 526-532.

9 "Americans becoming more open about mental health," American Psychological Association, accessed January 26, 2021.

10 "Living in Chains," Human Rights Watch, accessed January 26, 2021.

11 "Gender And Women's Health," World Health Organization, accessed January 27, 2021.

12 Matthew K. Nock, ed., *The Oxford Handbook of Suicide and Self-Injury* (Oxford: Oxford Univ. Press, 2014), 11.

13 Ibid, 8.

14 Christopher Bagley, "Suicidal Behaviour And Suicidal Ideation in Adolescents: A Problem for Counsellors in Education," *British Journal of Guidance & Counselling* 3, no. 2 (October 1975): 190-208.

15 Matthew K. Nock, ed., *The Oxford Handbook of Suicide and Self-Injury* (Oxford: Oxford Univ. Press, 2014), 19.

16 Thomas Joiner, *Why People Die by Suicide* (Cambridge, Massachusetts: Harvard University Press, 2007), 120.

17 Barent Walsh, *Treating Self-Injury* (New York: The Guilford Press, 2012), 22.

18 Thomas Joiner, *Why People Die by Suicide* (Cambridge, Massachusetts: Harvard University Press, 2007), 120.

19 Matthew K. Nock, ed., The Oxford Handbook of Suicide and Self-Injury (Oxford: Oxford Univ. Press, 2014), 155.

20 Ibid,184.

21 Ibid, 206.

22 Leanne Pooley, *The Girl on the Bridge* (Augusto Entertainment & Bloom Pictures, 2020), video, 91:00 at 24 fps.

23 "Suicide Rates Rising Across the U.S., CDC Online Newsroom, CDC," Centers for Disease Control and Prevention, accessed June 13, 2021.

24 "Suicide Statistics," American Foundation for Suicide Prevention, accessed June 14, 2021.

25 "Warning Signs," American Association of Suicidology, accessed June 14, 2021.

26 "Psychology Today: Health, Help, Happiness + Find A Therapist," Psychology Today, accessed January 16, 2021.

27 "Goodtherapy – Find the Right Therapist." Goodtherapy, accessed January 16, 2021.

28 "Find Local Therapists, Psychologists and Counselors," Therapyden, accessed January 16, 2021.

29 "Find a Doctor," Zocdoc, accessed January 16, 2021,

30 "Home," National Alliance on Mental Illness, accessed January 16, 2021.

31 "Homepage," 211, accessed January 16, 2021.

32 "What is Psychiatry?," Psychiatry, accessed January 16, 2021.

33 "What Do Practicing Psychologists Do?," American Psychological Association, accessed January 16, 2021.

34 "Who are Licensed Professional Counselors?," American Counseling Association, accessed January 16, 2021.

35 "Different Approaches to Psychotherapy," American Psychological Association, accessed January 16, 2021.

36 Ibid.

37 Ibid.

38 "Behavioral Therapy: Definition, Types, And Effectiveness," Healthline, accessed January 16, 2021.

39 Irvin Yalom, *The Gift of Therapy* (New York City: HarperCollins e-Books, 2014), 1.

40 Karen Horney, *Neurosis and Human Growth* (New York: Norton, 1991), 17.

41 Ibid.

42 Ibid, 18.

43 "Where Has All The Psychotherapy Gone?," American Psychological Association, accessed January 16, 2021.

44 Ibid.

45 Ibid.

46 Lori Gottlieb, *Maybe You Should Talk to Someone: a therapist, her therapist, and our lives revealed* (Boston: Houghton Mifflin, 2019), 266.

47 Ibid, 257.

48 Janis Whitlock and Elizabeth Lloyd-Richardson, *Healing Self-Injury* (New York: Oxford University Press, 2019), 94.

49 Barent Walsh, *Treating Self-Injury* (New York: The Guilford Press, 2012), 71.

50 Ibid, 149.

51 Ibid.

52 Ibid, 151.

53 "How the Lost Art of Breathing Can Impact Sleep and Resilience with James Nestor," interview by Terry Gross, May 27, 2020, in *Fresh Air*, produced by *Fresh Air*, podcast, MP3 audio, 36:16.

54 Ibid.

55 Ibid.

56 Ibid.

57 Barent Walsh, *Treating Self-Injury* (New York: The Guilford Press, 2012), 356

58 "Irvin D. Yalom, MD.," Irvin Yalom, accessed December 26, 2020.

59 Irvin Yalom, *The Gift of Therapy* (New York City: HarperCollins e-Books, 2014), 85.

60 Ibid..

61 Ibid, 109.

62 Ibid, 94.

63 Ibid.

64 Ibid.

65 Ibid, 40.

66 Ibid, 44.

67 Ibid, 11.

68 Ibid, 34.

69 Lori Gottlieb, *Maybe You Should Talk to Someone: a therapist, her therapist, and our lives revealed* (Boston: Houghton Mifflin, 2019), 260.

70 Irvin Yalom, *The Gift of Therapy* (New York City: HarperCollins e-Books, 2014), 65.

71 Ibid, 63.

72 Lori Gottlieb, *Maybe You Should Talk to Someone: a therapist, her therapist, and our lives revealed* (Boston: Houghton Mifflin, 2019), 260.

73 Irvin Yalom, *The Gift of Therapy* (New York City: HarperCollins e-Books, 2014), 162.

74 Jennifer Siebel Newsom, *The Mask You Live In* (The Representation Company 2015), video, 1:37:00 at 24 fps.

75 Ibid.

76 Ibid.

77 Ibid.

78 Ibid.

79 Ibid.

80 "Ever Forward," Ever Forward, accessed January 9, 2021.

81 "What is RULER? – RULER Approach," Ruler Approach, accessed January 9, 2021.

82 "The Doctor Is Out," National Alliance on Mental Illness, accessed January 9, 2021.

83 "Shortage Areas," Health Resources & Services Administration, accessed January 9, 2021

84 "The Doctor Is Out," National Alliance on Mental Illness, accessed January 9, 2021.

85 Ibid.

86 Ibid.

87 "Investing in Treatment for Depression and Anxiety Leads To Fourfold Return," World Health Organization, accessed January 9, 2021.

88 "Mental Health in The Workplace," World Health Organization, accessed January 9, 2021.

89 "The Mental Health Parity and Addiction Equity Act (MHPAEA) – CMS," Centers for Medicare & Medicaid Services, accessed January 9, 2021.

90 Matthew K. Nock, ed., *The Oxford Handbook of Suicide and Self-Injury* (Oxford: Oxford Univ. Press, 2014), 236.

91 Sheryl Sandberg and Adam Grant, *Option B: Facing Adversity, Building Resilience, And Finding Joy* (New York: Knopf, 2017), 127.

92 Matthew K. Nock, ed., *The Oxford Handbook of Suicide and Self-Injury* (Oxford: Oxford Univ. Press, 2014), 236.

93 Jerome Groopman, *The Anatomy of Hope* (New York: Random House, 2005), xiv.

94 Ibid.

95 "Maria Sirois – About," Maria Sirois, accessed December 12, 2020.

96 Jerome Groopman, *The Anatomy of Hope* (New York: Random House, 2005), xiv.

97 "Living In Chains," Human Rights Watch, accessed November 11, 2020.

98 Ibid.

99 "Mental Health Action Plan 2013 – 2020," World Health Organization, accessed May 23, 2021.

100 Ibid.

101 "Living in Chains," Human Rights Watch, accessed November 11, 2020.

102 "Mental Health Action Plan 2013 – 2020," World Health Organization, accessed May 23, 2021.

103 B.A. Kohrt, L. Asher, A. Bhardwaj, M. Fazel, M. Jordans, B.B. Mutamba, A. Nadkarni, G.A. Pedersen, D.R. Singla, and V. Patel, "The Role of Communities in Mental Health Care in Low- and Middle-Income Countries: A Meta-Review of Components and Competencies," *International journal of environmental research and public health* 15, no. 6 (June 2018): 1279.

104 "Mental Health Action Plan 2013 – 2020," World Health Organization, accessed May 23, 2021.

105 Ibid.

106 "Richard C. Schwartz, PhD – The Founder of Internal Family Systems – IFS Institute," Richard Schwartz, accessed February 6, 2021.

107 "The Internal Family Systems Model Outline – IFS Institute," Internal Family Systems, accessed February 6, 2021.

108 "Día De Muertos, Tradición Mexicana Que Trasciende En El Tiempo," Instituto Nacional para el Federalismo y el Desarrollo Municipal, accessed May 31, 2021.

109 Thomas Ogden, *Subjects of Analysis* (New York: Routledge, 2019), 2.

110 Ibid, 5.

111 Elisabeth Kübler-Ross and Ira Byock, *On Death & Dying* (New York: Scribner, 1969), xiv.

112 Sheryl Sandberg and Adam Grant, *Option B: Facing Adversity, Building Resilience, And Finding Joy* (New York: Knopf, 2017), 75.

113 Ibid, 279.

114 "Loneliness and Social Isolation in The United States, The United Kingdom, And Japan: An International Survey – Introduction," Kaiser Family Foundation, accessed January 28, 2021.

115 Ibid.

116 Vivek Murthy, *Together: The Healing Power of Human Connection in a Sometimes Lonely World* (New York: Harper Wave, 2020), xv.

117 Ibid, xvi.

118 Ibid, 8.

119 Ibid.

120 Ibid, xvi.

121 Ibid, xix.

122 Ibid.

123 "Landing," Big Talk, accessed June 6, 2021.

124 "How to Skip the Small Talk and Connect with Anyone," Kalina Silverman, filmed February 15, 2016 in Westminster College, on TEDx Talks, 19:41.

125 Ibid.

126 Ibid.

127 Ibid.

128 Charlotte Bühler, "Basic theoretical concepts of humanistic psychology," *American Psychologist* 26, no.4 (June 1971): 378-386.

129 Viktor E. Frankl, Ilse Lasch, Harold S. Kushner, and William J. Winslade, *Man's Search for Meaning* (Boston: Beacon Press, 2015), ix.

130 Ibid, 98.

131 Ibid, 99.

132 Ibid, 107.

133 Ibid, 108.

134 "Discovering & Living Your Purpose with James Hollis PhD (Podcast) EP33," interview by Maja Gottlieb, January 1, 2018, in *Integrate Yourself* EP33, produced by Maja Gottlieb, podcast, MP3 audio, 1:01:15.

135 "Option B: Build Resilience in The Face of Adversity," Option B, accessed November 23, 2020.

136 "The Skill of Human Care and Connection – Inspiring Comfort," Inspiring Comfort, accessed November 23, 2020.

137 "Paws to Comfort," Paws to Comfort, accessed November 23, 2020.

138 "25 Things You Can Say & Do for People Struggling," Inspiring Comfort, accessed November 23, 2020.

139 "Stuart Brown, MD – National Institute for Play," Stuart Brown, accessed February 13, 2021.

140 Ibid.

141 "The Practice of Play with Dr. Stuart Brown," interview by Taking Charge of Your Health, May 23, 2011, in *Taking Charge of Your Health*, Produced by University of Minnesota Center for Spirituality and Healing, podcast, MP3 audio, 7:39.

142 Ibid.

143 Stuart Brown and Christopher Vaughan, *Play: How it Shapes the Brain, Opens the Imagination, and Invigorates the Soul* (New York: Avery, 2014), 5.

144 "The Practice of Play with Dr. Stuart Brown," interview by Taking Charge of Your Health, May 23, 2011, in *Taking Charge of Your Health*, Produced by University of Minnesota Center for Spirituality and Healing, podcast, MP3 audio, 7:39.

145 "Play is more than just fun," Stuart Brown, filmed March 1, 2008 in Monterey, CA, on TEDx Talk, 26:21.

146 "The Practice of Play with Dr. Stuart Brown," interview by Taking Charge of Your Health, May 23, 2011, in *Taking Charge of Your Health*, Produced by University of Minnesota Center for Spirituality and Healing, podcast, MP3 audio, 7:39.

147 Stuart Brown and Christopher Vaughan, *Play: How it Shapes the Brain, Opens the Imagination, and Invigorates the Soul* (New York: Avery, 2014), 9.

148 "YMCA175 Keynote Speech," Jeffrey Sparr, filmed September 20, 2019 in London, UK, Video, 17:43.

149 Ibid.

150 Ibid.

151 "About – Peacelove," PeaceLove, accessed February 13, 2021.

152 "The Power of Vulnerability," Brené Brown, filmed October 6, 2010 in Houston, on TEDx Talks, 20:03.

153 Ibid.

154 "Mycounterpane Blog – Healing Through the Story of You," Kate Milliken, accessed January 12, 2021.

155 Dan P. McAdams, *The Redemptive Self* (Oxford: Oxford University Press, 2007), xx.

156 Dan P. McAdams, *The Redemptive Self* (Oxford: Oxford University Press, 2007), xii.

157 Viktor E. Frankl, Ilse Lasch, Harold S Kushner, and William J Winslade, *Man's Search for Meaning* (Boston: Beacon Press, 2015), 112.

158 Richard G. Tedeschi and Bret A. Moore, *The Posttraumatic Growth Workbook: Coming Through Trauma Wiser, Stronger, And More Resilient* (Oakland: New Harbinger Publications, 2016), 4.

159 Ibid.

160 Viktor E. Frankl, Ilse Lasch, Harold S. Kushner, and William J. Winslade, *Man's Search for Meaning* (Boston: Beacon Press, 2015), 44.

161 "Transformation After Trauma with Richard Tedeschi, PhD," recorded December 18, 2019, in *Speaking of Psychology*, produced by American Psychological Association, podcast, MP3 Audio, 51:26.

162 Ibid.

163 Ibid.

164 "Transformation After Trauma with Richard Tedeschi, PhD," recorded December 18, 2019, in *Speaking of Psychology*, produced by American Psychological Association, podcast, MP3 Audio, 51:26.

165 "Getting Started – Dr. Rick Hanson," Rick Hanson, accessed January 24, 2021.

166 "When Good Is Stronger Than Bad," Rick Hanson, accessed January 24, 2021.

167 "The Science of Positive Brain Change," Rick Hanson, video, 3:16.

168 Ibid.

169 Patrice Voss, Maryse E. Thomas, J. Miguel Cisneros-Franco, and Étienne de Villers-Sidani. "Dynamic Brains and The Changing Rules of Neuroplasticity: Implications for Learning and Recovery." *Frontiers In Psychology* 8, no. 8 (October 2017): 1675.

170 "The Science of Positive Brain Change – Dr. Rick Hanson," Rick Hanson, accessed January 24, 2021.

171 "The Science of Positive Brain Change – Dr. Rick Hanson," Rick Hanson, accessed January 24, 2021.

172 Ibid.

173 Patrice Voss, Maryse E. Thomas, J. Miguel Cisneros-Franco, and Étienne de Villers-Sidani. "Dynamic Brains and The Changing Rules of Neuroplasticity: Implications for Learning and Recovery." *Frontiers In Psychology* 8, no. 8 (October 2017): 1675.

174 "The Science of Positive Brain Change," Rick Hanson, video, 3:16.